CRAZY
TOWN

ROBYN DOOLITTLE
CRAZY TOWN
THE ROB FORD STORY

VIKING

VIKING

an imprint of Penguin Canada Books Inc., a Penguin Random House Company

Published by the Penguin Group
Penguin Canada Books Inc.
90 Eglinton Avenue East, Suite 700, Toronto, Ontario, Canada M4P 2Y3

Penguin Group (USA) Inc., 375 Hudson Street, New York, New York 10014, U.S.A.
Penguin Books Ltd, 80 Strand, London WC2R 0RL, England
Penguin Ireland, 25 St Stephen's Green, Dublin 2, Ireland (a division of Penguin Books Ltd)
Penguin Group (Australia), 707 Collins Street, Melbourne, Victoria 3008, Australia
(a division of Pearson Australia Group Pty Ltd)
Penguin Books India Pvt Ltd, 11 Community Centre, Panchsheel Park, New Delhi – 110 017, India
Penguin Group (NZ), 67 Apollo Drive, Rosedale, Auckland 0632, New Zealand
(a division of Pearson New Zealand Ltd)
Penguin Books (South Africa) (Pty) Ltd, 24 Sturdee Avenue, Rosebank,
Johannesburg 2196, South Africa

Penguin Books Ltd, Registered Offices: 80 Strand, London WC2R 0RL, England

First published 2014

1 2 3 4 5 6 7 8 9 10 (RRD)

Copyright © Robyn Doolittle, 2014

Manufactured in the U.S.A.

LIBRARY AND ARCHIVES CANADA CATALOGUING IN PUBLICATION

Doolittle, Robyn, author
Crazy town : the Rob Ford story / Robyn Doolittle.

Includes index.
ISBN 978-0-670-06811-1 (bound)

1. Ford, Rob, 1969–. 2. Mayors—Ontario—Toronto—Biography.
3. Political corruption—Ontario—Toronto. 4. Toronto (Ont.)—Politics
and government—21st century. I. Title.

FC3097.26.F67D66 2014   971.3'54105092   C2013-907940-8

eBook ISBN 978-0-14-319134-6

Visit the Penguin Canada website at **www.penguin.ca**

Special and corporate bulk purchase rates available; please see
www.penguin.ca/corporatesales or call 1-800-810-3104, ext. 2477.

For my parents

Rob Ford died on March 22, 2016, 18 months after being diagnosed with a rare form of cancer.

CONTENTS

TIMELINE

1956

September 1   Doug Ford Sr. and Diane Campbell are married.

1962

Doug Ford Sr. and Ted Herriott start Deco Adhesive Products.

1969

May 28   Robert Bruce Ford is born at Humber Memorial Hospital in Etobicoke.

1983/1984

Rob Ford is a first-year student at Scarlett Heights Collegiate Institute. This is also his brother Doug Ford Jr.'s graduating year.

1995

June 8   Doug Ford Sr. is elected in Etobicoke-Humber as a Progressive Conservative MPP in the Ontario government under Premier Mike Harris.

1997

November 10   Rob Ford runs for Toronto City Council in Ward 3
Kingsway Humber. He finishes fourth with 9,366
votes.

1998

January 1   The "megacity" is born. Seven municipal governments amalgamate to form the new City of Toronto.

July 25   Kathy Ford's boyfriend, Michael Kiklas, dies after
being gunned down by Kathy's estranged husband,
Ennio Stirpe.

1999

February 15   Rob Ford is charged with drunk driving and possession of marijuana in Miami, Florida. (The drug
charge would later be dropped.)

May   Doug Ford Sr. finishes his term as an MPP.

2000

August 12   Rob Ford marries Renata Brejniak at All Saints
Roman Catholic Church in Etobicoke.

November 13   Rob Ford is elected to Toronto City Council in
Ward 2 Etobicoke North with 5,750 votes.

2001

              Rob Ford is told he is no longer welcome to coach
football at Newtonbrook Secondary School in North
York after a heated altercation with a player.

August   Rookie councillor Rob Ford makes headlines after
it is revealed that he spent just ten dollars of his
office budget after six months in office. By contrast,
Giorgio Mammoliti, the biggest spender on council,
spent $43,150.

2002

March 6	Councillor Rob Ford allegedly calls Councillor Giorgio Mammoliti a "Gino boy."

2003

November 10	Rob Ford is re-elected in Ward 2 with 79 percent of the vote.

2005

	Rob and Renata Ford have a daughter, Stephanie.
March 31	Kathy Ford is accidentally shot in the head at her parents' home by her boyfriend, Scott MacIntyre.
July 19	Councillor Rob Ford calls Councillor Gloria Lindsay Luby a "waste of skin." She calls him a "jerk."

2006

April 15	Security removes Rob Ford from a Toronto Maple Leafs NHL game after he drunkenly berates a couple in the crowd. When news of the incident breaks, Ford initially lies and says he wasn't at the game. He later admits to having been there and apologizes.
June 28	During a council debate on grants for AIDS programs, Rob Ford says, "If you're not doing needles and you're not gay, you won't get AIDS, probably."
September 22	Doug Ford Sr. dies of cancer at the age of seventy-three.
November 13	Rob Ford is re-elected in Ward 2 with 66 percent of the vote.

2007

March 7	Rob Ford tells council that cycling in a bike lane is like swimming with sharks. "Roads are built for buses, cars, and trucks. Not for people on bikes. And,

you know, my heart bleeds for them when I hear someone gets killed, but it's their own fault at the end of the day."

2008

	Rob and Renata Ford have their second child, a son named Douglas.
March 5	Rob Ford controversially suggests that "Oriental" people are "slowly taking over" because they work so hard. "Those Oriental people work like dogs," he says.
March 26	Rob Ford is arrested and charged with domestic assault and threatening death against his wife, Renata. The charges are later dropped due to inconsistencies in Renata Ford's testimony.

2010

March 25	Rob Ford declares his candidacy for mayor.
June 17	News breaks that Rob Ford offered to help a man named Dieter Doneit-Henderson "score" OxyContin on the street. Doneit-Henderson secretly recorded their phone conversation.
August 18	The *Toronto Sun* reports that Rob Ford was charged with marijuana possession in Florida a decade earlier. The drunk driving charge comes out. Ford apologizes for his mistakes and his poll numbers go up.
August 25	City council orders Rob Ford to repay $3,150 he solicited from lobbyists for his private football foundation.
October 25	Rob Ford is elected mayor with 383,501 votes, or 47 percent of the total cast.
December 7	Hockey personality Don Cherry criticizes "pinkos" in a speech at Rob Ford's inauguration ceremony.

2011

May 13	Toronto's audit committee votes to review Rob Ford's campaign expenses.
October 24	The mayor calls 911 after a comedian from CBC's *This Hour Has 22 Minutes* shows up in his driveway.
December 30	The *Toronto Star* reveals police have been called to the mayor's home for a handful of domestic incidents in recent months.

2012

January 11	Kathy Ford's estranged boyfriend, Scott MacIntyre, is arrested after walking into the mayor's home, demanding Rob Ford pay back money MacIntyre says he is owed, and then threatening to kill him.
January 17	City council revolts against the mayor's budget cuts in a 23–21 vote.
February 7	Mayor Rob Ford speaks, and then votes, on a motion to overturn the order requiring him to pay back $3,150 in football donations.
March 12	Lawyer Clayton Ruby announces he is filing a conflict-of-interest lawsuit against the mayor because of the February 7 vote. Ruby argues that Rob Ford broke the law when he spoke to, and then voted on, an item at council where he stood to benefit financially.
March 17	On St. Patrick's Day, Rob Ford spends the night partying with friends, first at City Hall and then at a downtown bar called the Bier Markt. A waiter at the Bier Markt thinks he might have seen the mayor snort cocaine in a private room. A member of Ford's staff later tells police he thought he saw Ford take an OxyContin pill.
May 2	Rob Ford confronts *Toronto Star* reporter Daniel Dale in a public park behind his home.

November 26   A judge concludes that Rob Ford did violate the Municipal Conflict of Interest Act. He orders Ford out of office.

2013

January 25   Rob Ford wins his conflict-of-interest appeal on a technicality. He remains as mayor.

February 23   The mayor shows up at a military ball impaired. He is asked to leave by a member of the organizing committee.

March 7   Former mayoral candidate Sarah Thomson accuses the mayor of groping her at an event.

March 26   The *Toronto Star* reports that the mayor's staff want him to seek treatment for an alcohol issue. The paper reveals that Ford had been asked to leave the military ball after showing up "intoxicated." The mayor calls the paper "pathological liars."

May 16   The *Toronto Star* and Gawker reveal that Mayor Rob Ford has been filmed smoking what looks like crack cocaine. A drug dealer tried to sell the footage to both outlets for one hundred thousand dollars. Both publications reveal a photo of Ford standing in front of a yellow-brick house alongside three young men, one of whom had recently been shot dead. (The house would later be revealed as 15 Windsor Road, a suspected crack den.)

May 24   After eight days, the mayor makes an official first statement about the video story: "I do not use crack cocaine, nor am I an addict of crack cocaine." Rob Ford blames the *Star* for going after him.

May 25   *The Globe and Mail* publishes a story that alleges Councillor Doug Ford Jr. was a hash dealer in high school. The mayor's brother denies this.

June 1   An Ipsos Reid poll shows that half of Toronto residents don't believe the video story.

June 13   Police across Ontario launch a series of pre-dawn raids as part of Project Traveller, a massive investigation into drug and gun smuggling. The dealer who tried to sell the *Star* and Gawker the video is arrested, as are the two surviving men pictured alongside Ford in the infamous 15 Windsor Road photo.

August 16   The *Star* reports that Alexander "Sandro" Lisi, a friend of, and occasional driver for, the mayor, is under police investigation for trying to obtain the video.

October 1   Sandro Lisi is arrested and charged with drug offences, including trafficking marijuana. His arrest is part of a covert police investigation dubbed Project Brazen 2, a probe aimed at the mayor's activities.

October 31   On the day that hundreds of pages of search warrant documents connected to Project Brazen 2 are released—documents that show suspicious package handoffs between Sandro Lisi and Rob Ford—Police Chief Bill Blair reveals that Toronto police have recovered the "crack video." Lisi is charged with extortion in connection with attempts to recover the video.

November 5   Rob Ford admits to having smoked crack while in "one of my drunken stupors." He says he won't resign or take health leave.

November 7   A second video of Rob Ford surfaces. The mayor appears impaired and in a rage, pacing around a room and punching the air, saying, "I'm gonna kill that fucking guy. I'm telling you, it's first-degree murder." The mayor maintains he will not resign.

November 18   Toronto City Council strips Mayor Rob Ford of most of his powers, reducing his budget, staff, and authority to develop policy. The mayor declares "war."

PROLOGUE

Mohamed Farah was an hour late.

Once more, I scanned the dimly lit plaza trying to spot him. Maybe he was hiding somewhere, watching us, making sure we had indeed come alone.

I tried to make out the faces of the young men smoking in front of Istar Restaurant, a popular halal joint where diners could see out but you couldn't see in. None of them looked familiar.

Maybe he was inside? It was about 10:30 P.M. Our car was parked at the far end, in front of a bank, as instructed.

"God, he better show up this time," I said to my colleague Kevin Donovan.

This would be our third attempt at seeing the video.

It had been a month, almost to the day, since Farah called me on my cell phone with a cryptic news tip. It was 9 A.M. on Easter Monday 2013, and I'd been trying to sleep in. I shuffled out of bed, irritated that someone was calling so early on a holiday.

"Robyn speaking," I said.

"Robyn Doolittle, from the *Toronto Star*?"

I didn't recognize the man's voice. It was deep and had that nonchalant drawl that young cool guys tend to use.

"Yep. Who am I speaking with?"

"I have some information I think you'd like to see," he said. "I don't want to talk about it on the phone … it's about a prominent Toronto politician."

A week earlier, I'd co-written a controversial piece with Kevin Donovan about the mayor of Toronto's struggle with alcohol. I suspected the caller was talking about Rob Ford.

He claimed to be in possession of a very incriminating video, but he refused to say anything more on the phone. He wanted to meet as soon as possible. "I'll come to you," he offered.

That was encouraging. If he was willing to make the trip, odds were he wasn't completely without credibility.

Shortly before noon, I arrived at a crowded Starbucks in a hipster neighbourhood just outside of downtown Toronto.

"Robyn?"

I spun around to see a clean-cut East African–looking guy who seemed about my age, somewhere in his late twenties, maybe early thirties.

"I'm Mohamed," he said, extending a hand.

He was thickly built, like a football player, and a good head taller than me, wearing a button-up shirt and dark baggy jeans that had a bit of a shimmer to them—hip hop meets business casual. We headed to a nearby park and settled on a bench by the soccer field.

Farah told me he volunteered with Somali youth up in Rexdale—a troubled neighbourhood in Toronto's northwest end not far from where Ford lived—and that he'd read my story about the mayor and alcohol.

"It's much worse than that," Farah said.

I knew this was true. For a year and a half I'd been investigating whether the mayor had a substance abuse issue. To an outsider, what Farah said next might have sounded unbelievable. But not to me.

"The mayor is smoking drugs. Crack cocaine." Farah searched my face to see if I believed him, but I kept a blank expression. "And I have a video of it."

"Did you bring it?"

"I can't let you see it yet. But I brought this." He pulled out a silver iPad.

He thumbed around for a few seconds, then turned it towards me. There was a photo of Ford, grinning and flushed, his blond hair matted and messy, with three men who looked to be in their early twenties. Ford, who was wearing a baggy grey sweatshirt, had his arms around two of them. One of the guys was making a "west side" gesture. Another in a dark hood was flashing his middle finger while gripping a beer bottle. It was shot outside at night. The group was standing in front of a yellow-brick garage with a big black door. There was snow on the ground.

Was this photo part of the video?

No, Farah said, but it showed the mayor in front of a crack house with men connected to the drug trade. And "that one," he continued, pointing to the hooded man with the beer bottle, "is Anthony Smith. He was killed outside Loki nightclub last week."

Farah had my attention.

He put the iPad away and the conversation returned to the video. Farah claimed the footage was shot by a young crack dealer. He swore that it clearly showed the mayor inhaling from a crack pipe, complaining about minorities, and calling Justin Trudeau, the leader of the federal Liberal Party, "a fag." Farah alleged that his friends had been selling drugs to the mayor for a long time, but Smith's death had everyone scared. The dealer wanted out. He wanted to move to Alberta and start over. Farah told me he had agreed to help.

Here came the catch.

They wanted a hundred thousand dollars for the footage.

THAT WAS thirty-three days earlier.

Now, I was waiting in a grungy plaza parking lot in a bad part of town with Kevin Donovan, passing the time by theorizing what was going to happen—if anything. Would they show us the video right there in the car? Would it be a group of people? Or just Farah and the dealer? What if they wanted to drive us somewhere?

The later it got, the more I was convinced we were waiting for no one. Then out of nowhere a black sedan pulled up beside us. It was Farah. He wasn't getting out of the car.

He phoned me from feet away. "Leave your cell phones. No bags. No purses. And get in."

I sat in the front. Donovan climbed into the back. Farah was breathing quickly. He didn't say anything as we turned left onto Dixon Road, a busy street in a part of Toronto called Etobicoke. A few minutes later, he pulled into a dark parking lot behind a six-tower condo complex that looked worse than some subsidized housing in the city. We parked behind 320 Dixon.

Farah called his guy. "He's coming," he told us.

A skinny Somali-looking man in a wrinkled black T-shirt appeared out of the darkness. He got in the back with Donovan. I guessed he wasn't much older than twenty-five. He had a peculiar look about him, his face sort of caved in on itself, with his eyes, nose, and mouth squishing together between a large forehead and pointy jawline. His black hair was cut close to his head, and his arms were pocked with thick scabs. Donovan and I introduced ourselves, but he didn't want to talk and never gave his name. He pulled out an iPhone and hit play.

I thought I was prepared, but I couldn't hide my shock.

There was Rob Ford—and there was no doubt in my mind that it was Rob Ford—the mayor of the fourth-largest city in North America, slurring, rambling, wobbling around in his chair, sucking on what looked like a crack pipe.

BEFORE BECOMING MAYOR on December 1, 2010, Rob Ford had spent ten years as a controversial city councillor. His checkered past included a drunk driving conviction, a domestic assault arrest (which was later dropped), and allegations of racism and homophobia. But Ford's antics had rarely earned ink outside of the Greater Toronto Area, and even two and a half years into his term as mayor, it was unlikely the average Canadian would have recognized him on the street. That would all change on May 16, 2013. That was the night the American gossip website Gawker posted a story with the headline "For Sale: A Video of Toronto Mayor Rob Ford Smoking Crack Cocaine." The *Star* published a few hours later. By week's end, Ford was on his way to becoming internationally infamous, a running gag on American late-night television, and the subject of one of the most astonishing political scandals in the country's history.

ONE

RESPECT
THE TAXPAYER

When the ballot boxes closed at 8 P.M., October 25, the night of Toronto's 2010 municipal election, reporters braced themselves for a nail-biter. Polls showed the leading two candidates in a statistical tie. It looked as if George Smitherman, the former deputy premier of Ontario, had been able to rally a last-minute push for his candidacy, closing a twenty-five-point gap between himself and Toronto city councillor Rob Ford.

That Ford had gotten that far was a shock to most pundits. He was a populist with a temper, a knack for saying the wrong thing, dogmatic views about low taxes and small government, and social sensibilities that were significantly right of the norm. He was the dark horse in a crowded race, which everyone believed would ultimately be a coronation for Smitherman. But by the end of August, Ford had seemed uncatchable. Now, two months later, it looked like a dead heat.

I was at the Toronto Congress Centre, where Ford was scheduled to make his concession—or victory—speech. Hundreds, perhaps a thousand, of his supporters were jammed into the massive room, wearing campaign buttons and T-shirts, waving Canadian flags and "Ford for Mayor" placards. All eyes were fixed on the two giant screens that flanked the stage, tuned to the local news. Four minutes after the polls closed, Ford votes were at 31,000. Smitherman, 19,000. The crowd cheered and clapped and blew train whistles—a reference to Ford's campaign pledge to "stop the gravy train" at City Hall. The councillor was off to a good start. But it was still early—or so I thought.

At 8:08 P.M.—eight minutes in—CP24 television network was calling it. Rob Ford would be Toronto's next mayor. It hadn't been close at all. The Congress Centre exploded. The screens cut to footage of Ford learning the news. He'd been watching at his mother's home, surrounded by family, some staff, and select media. Sitting on the couch beside his wife, Renata, Ford nervously rubbed his knees while the numbers rolled in. When the projection was made, he looked shocked. Everyone jumped to their feet in celebration. Ford hugged and kissed Renata. The premier phoned to congratulate him. Then outgoing mayor David Miller. Then Smitherman.

A little more than an hour later, Ford arrived at the Congress Centre. He was mobbed like a rock star as he pushed through the crowd. People chanted his name and jostled each other trying to snap his photo. He climbed up on stage to uproarious applause. People chanted "Ford! Ford! Ford!" A supporter draped a Hawaiian lei around his neck.

Standing at the podium, Ford grinned, taking in the scene.

"Tonight," he began, "the people of Toronto are *not* divided. We are united. We are united all around this call for change. If you voted for me, I thank you from the bottom of my heart. You voted for change at City Hall. You trusted me, and I will live up to your expectations—guaranteed. Four years, four years from tonight, you'll look back and say, Rob Ford did exactly what he said he was going to do."

He congratulated George Smitherman on a hard-fought campaign, and when some in the crowd began to boo, he admonished them. He said he looked forward to working with Smitherman and the other candidates in the future.

"To the people that didn't vote for me, I will work hard to earn your trust. And I will deliver change that you can be proud of," Ford said to more applause.

What kind of change? He would abolish unnecessary taxes. Cut councillor expense accounts. Make customer service a priority. And get tough with the public-sector unions on the city payroll.

"The party with taxpayers' money is over, ladies and gentlemen. We will respect the taxpayers again. And yes, ladies and gentlemen, we will stop the gravy train, once and for all."

WHEN I WAS SHUFFLED to the City Hall bureau from the police beat in 2010, I wasn't sure if I was being punished. My city editor sold it as something of a promotion. I was young and energetic. Exactly what the paper needed down there, he told me enthusiastically, larding the pitch with compliments about the work I'd done the last two years covering crime. As I envisioned long days of boring committee meetings and agendas and debates about sidewalk widths and tree removal, I boxed up the contents of my office at Police Headquarters and began the grieving process. I thought my days chasing criminals were over.

It was January 2010, and the long municipal election campaign was just getting under way. In those early days, everybody thought Ontario's cranky and openly gay former deputy premier George Smitherman, a.k.a. Furious George, was the easy winner. Up until he quit the provincial Liberal government to run for mayor, Smitherman had been the second most powerful man in Ontario politics. Now he was counting on the fact that Toronto was a liberal city. Not a single Conservative— federal or provincial—had been elected within its borders since 1999. Smitherman had name recognition, a willing electorate, and the keys to a first-class political machine. His only competition was the young hotshot chair of the Toronto Transit Commission (TTC), Councillor Adam Giambrone.

Giambrone was thirty-two, smart, hard-working, a devoted activist, and the successor-of-choice for retiring mayor David Miller. But hubris got the better of him before he even got started. In a profile interview for the *Toronto Star*, Giambrone insinuated he was married, which really upset another young woman, the one he had been dating and entertaining on his City Hall office couch. She contacted the *Star*, claiming Giambrone had promised her that his other relationship was just for appearances, so he'd look more established. (In fact Giambrone wasn't married, despite what he'd told the *Star*.) Giambrone's campaign collapsed, less than two weeks after he announced his candidacy. Once that happened, it looked like the only threat to Smitherman's victory would be if popular conservative radio host John Tory jumped into the race.

Tory, a former business executive, had run for mayor in 2003 and narrowly lost to David Miller. Afterwards, he switched to provincial politics and became leader of the Progressive Conservative Party in the Ontario Legislature at Queen's Park. Tory is a fiscal conservative with liberal values, a well-spoken businessman with a strong social conscience. In Toronto, John Tory is beloved—at least until his name hits the ballot. In 2007, Tory led his party to a disastrous showing in the provincial election after he suggested Ontario taxpayers should be subsidizing all faith-based schools—Islamic, Hindu, Jewish, etc.—since the province funded Catholic ones. Voters revolted. Tory never got beyond Opposition leader. In 2009 he moved to talk radio, which only made him more popular. Every day, callers, political strategists, and city councillors were begging him to take another shot at the mayoralty. On January 7, 2010, Tory held a press conference in the Newstalk 1010 radio station lobby. He would not be running for mayor. He cited the polarized political climate, the eagerness for some to go negative. He wanted to continue to make a contribution to the community— but outside of the political arena.

With that announcement, it seemed that the 2010 municipal election was George Smitherman's to lose.

I'd been on the job two months when Rob Ford, the beefy conservative councillor from Toronto's suburban west end, announced his candidacy for mayor. Like most people in Toronto, I'd heard—and watched on YouTube several times— Ford's speech at city council in which he said "Oriental people work like dogs." I'd read about the Maple Leafs game, when he'd been escorted from the arena by security guards after drunkenly berating a couple in the crowd. And I was the *Toronto Star* police reporter when Ford had been briefly charged with domestic assault. Other than that, I best knew Ford as the councillor to call if I needed an angry quote about a left-leaning policy.

Did I think Rob Ford could be mayor? It seemed like a pipe dream.

The current chief magistrate was a Harvard-educated, thoughtful environmentalist who delighted in developing and debating policy. The contrast between David Miller and Rob Ford was almost comically stark.

At fifty-one, David Miller was tall and fit, with a full head of thick ashy-blond hair. He loved to pontificate in a deep authoritative voice, talking about "city building" and "civic engagement." To a lot of people, Miller came across as arrogant. He was a proud progressive who fed tax dollars into cycling infrastructure, social programs, and the arts. Miller posed in black leather on the front of Toronto's premier gay magazine, *fab*, before the city's annual gay pride festival.

And then there was Ford.

Ford was big. Three-hundred-and-something pounds big. His bulging two-tiered chin pushed outward and upward, jutting out his bottom lip in a way that always made it seem as if he was sneering. Ford was a fanatical right-winger who vehemently opposed community grants, green initiatives, and funding anything cultural. He devoted most of his energy to four issues: slashing office budgets for councillors; battling against community grants; doing away with perks like free food at council meetings; and firing the people in charge of watering the plants in city buildings. "At home, we water our own plants, unless you have a butler or something," he once told council.

But there was another big difference between David Miller and Rob Ford, and it would cast each in the role of champion for one of Toronto's two warring factions—the downtowners and the suburbanites.

In 2009, Toronto celebrated its 175th anniversary. We were a city before Canada was a country. But the Toronto we know today was a drastically different place as recently as 1997. Back then, the region was divided into six municipalities, including the much smaller old City of Toronto, the borough of East York, and four mini-cities: Etobicoke to the west, York, North York, and Scarborough in the east. Each had its own local government with its own mayor, but there was also an overarching regional body to manage issues like policing, which was headed by a chairman. This two-tiered system is how Metropolitan Toronto had been governed for four decades. But in 1997—despite intense public backlash—Progressive Conservative premier Mike Harris's provincial government voted to dissolve the five cities and one borough to form a "megacity" of close to 2.4 million residents as of January 1, 1998. The move was supposed to save money by removing duplication. Why have six finance offices when you could have one? Academics have since concluded that amalgamation was a financial failure. What it did do was drastically alter the political landscape.

Compared with people living outside Toronto's core, downtown dwellers are more likely to rely on public transit and bicycles than cars, more likely to live in a high-rise than a house, and tend to be more liberal. It's not surprising that these two groups, urban and suburban, have different expectations of their local government. Someone in a condo is naturally less invested in Toronto's leaf-collection program than someone from Etobicoke who lives in a house with big trees in the yard. And it only makes sense that that Etobicoke resident cares much less about a multi-million-dollar renovation to a public square in downtown Toronto than someone who lives in a high-rise across the street. This matters at election time, because the residents of the old City of Toronto—which at the time of amalgamation had just over 650,000 residents—are greatly outnumbered. The suburbs account for three-quarters of Toronto's current 2.8 million population.

In Rob Ford's perfect world, a city should have well-maintained roads free of cyclists, streetcars, and gridlock; running water; working lights; punctual, privately operated garbage collection; a well-staffed police service; and as few taxes as possible. It's not hard to understand why this philosophy proved popular in Toronto's suburban neighbourhoods. Why should they subsidize the Toronto International Film Festival, or the National Ballet of Canada, or the Canadian Opera Company when the people actually going to these things, all decked out in their fancy clothes, had money to burn? The downtowners, the original City of Toronto people, could wax poetic about the economic benefits of arts funding—how the return on every dollar could be leveraged to create seventeen additional dollars, how a vibrant cultural sector attracted tourists, packed restaurants, filled hotels, and got people out shopping—but in the suburbs, that all just sounded like elitist malarkey.

Remember, by the summer and fall of 2010, while much of Canada had dug itself out of economic recession, Toronto had not. Many were still out of work and scared. Unemployment was at 10.36 percent, well above the national average of 8 percent. Bankruptcies in and around Toronto were nearly triple the rate elsewhere in Canada. So when Rob Ford vowed to cut taxes without reducing services, by ending the "gravy train," people wanted to believe him. And why not? He had been beating that drum his entire career. "Toronto has a spending problem, not a revenue problem," he used to say.

Ford's colleagues might have regarded him as an inarticulate bumbler who was always losing his temper, but the people who lived in his ward adored him. They loved his crusade against spending. Sure, weighed against a nine-billion-dollar operating budget, a free dinner seemed like small potatoes, but if councillors were wasting money where people could see it, what were they doing behind closed doors? Most significantly, Ford's constituents loved how accessible he was. Ford had a reputation for personally returning residents' phone calls, listening to their complaints, and then showing up at their door with an entourage of bureaucrats to fix a problem that would otherwise have been strangled in red tape. Councillor Ford was so good at his constituent work that people living outside of his ward started calling. So he began helping them too. It was a practice that vexed other councillors. Eventually some complained to the integrity commissioner about it, which merely strengthened the perception in some parts of Toronto that hard-working Ford was the only sane person in office. Over his ten years on council, one phone call at a time, Ford built his base of support, a group that has come to be known as Ford Nation. They're fiercely loyal, standing by their man through every storm.

And there have been many storms to weather. There was the time in 2002 when councillors heard him call an Italian colleague a "Gino boy." In 2005, in a disagreement about potholes, he told a councillor she was "a waste of skin." When Ford opposed spending $1.5 million on AIDS prevention, he rationalized, "If you're not doing needles and you're not gay, you won't get AIDS, probably." Then in 2006 Ford was dragged out of that Toronto Maple Leafs game by security guards after unleashing a drunken diatribe on a couple sitting nearby. It started when the man asked Ford to quiet down. Ford turned to him: "Who the

fuck do you think you are? ... Are you a fucking teacher?" Then
he looked to the man's wife. "Do you want your little wife to go
over to Iran and get raped and shot?" When reporters followed
up, Ford initially claimed he wasn't even at the game, apparently
forgetting he'd been handing out his City Hall business cards.
(This would become Ford's play of choice in a crisis: lie and
deny until someone can provide physical proof.) Most seriously,
in 2008, Ford was arrested for domestic assault and uttering a
death threat against his wife. The charge was dropped due to
inconsistencies in Renata Ford's testimony. When the press came
knocking, Ford answered the door carrying his three-year-old
daughter. He coached her to say "No comment." That wouldn't
be the last time Ford enlisted the help of his children in times
of trouble.

And yet with every scandal, Ford emerged stronger. More
human. More relatable.

On March 25, 2010, the longshot Rob Ford declared his
candidacy for mayor. Within three weeks, he was in second
place. "Rob Ford has reshuffled the deck," Jodi Shanoff,
senior vice-president of polling firm Angus Reid, told the *Star*.
"Depending on what he has to say and, frankly, how he deals
with the attacks that undoubtedly are coming from Smitherman
... those can either expose him for the not-so-serious candidate
that the *Toronto Life* crowd takes him to be, or he can rise to the
challenge and really galvanize his spot as a serious contender."

Even as a candidate for mayor, Ford radiated controversy.
During his campaign, news surfaced that in 1999 he'd been
charged with drunk driving and marijuana possession while on
vacation in Florida. When confronted, Ford denied it. But once
it was obvious that the reporter had access to at least some of the

arrest paperwork, Ford apologized and claimed he'd forgotten about it. He held a press conference the next day and announced he had indeed been charged—with failing to provide a breath sample. That statement was also untrue—he was convicted of drunk driving—and the newspapers pointed it out. The public's reaction? Ford got a 10-point bump in the polls. "The phone would not stop ringing that day," recalls Stefano Pileggi, fundraising manager for the Ford campaign. "People calling in: 'We don't care, Rob. We love you!' It was incredible."

When the *Toronto Star* revealed that in 2001 Ford had been banned from coaching football at a Toronto high school following a heated altercation with a player, he supposedly raised close to twenty-five thousand dollars overnight in campaign donations. When Ford suggested that Toronto close its doors to immigrants until it could fix its current citizens' problems, his office was inundated with calls of support, including from immigrants already here. Meanwhile, former frontrunner George Smitherman was blowing it. His campaign stood for nothing. To voters, he came across as angry and entitled. The Smitherman platform seemed to be built on one thing: he wasn't Rob Ford.

By mid-June, Ford was tied for first. And the momentum continued. He took the lead in August and stayed there until election night. The polls were barely closed before the TV networks announced that Rob Ford would be Toronto's sixty-fourth mayor. A little over half of the city's eligible voters had cast a ballot, and 47 percent of them ticked off Ford's name. The penny-pincher from Etobicoke hadn't just won, he had crushed the competition. Ford finished with 383,501 votes, nearly 100,000 more than sure-thing Smitherman. Deputy mayor Joe Pantalone—who had parachuted in as the progressive candidate after Giambrone's implosion—came in a distant third. Ford won thirty-one of forty-four wards, including every one of the pre-amalgamation suburbs. And while the old City of Toronto electorate stuck with Smitherman, they did it while holding their noses. In fact, Ford had significant support in the land of lattes. The true geographic downtowners went 60 percent Smitherman. But in plenty of old Toronto neighbourhoods, such as Parkdale–High Park, Toronto-Danforth, and Davenport, Ford scooped up more than a third of the vote.

His victory left residents of Toronto's core stunned. In those first days after the election, the confusion was everywhere. On the streetcar heading to work, in line at Starbucks, at the bank, the flower shop, the grocery store, the pub. The most discombobulated were staggering around the corridors of City Hall. One prominent Toronto politics professor sent me a note of apology, having dismissively brushed off my suggestion a month earlier that Ford would win. It was as if a giant protective bubble containing everyone who lived within fifteen kilometres of the CN Tower had been popped.

What it meant to be a "Torontonian" was no longer clear. Three years later—with Ford known the world over as the mayor whose approval rating stayed unchanged after he admitted to smoking crack cocaine—it was even less apparent.

What follows is the story of Rob Ford's improbable rise to one of the most powerful jobs in Canada. It's the story of how the mayor of Toronto found himself ensnared in a scandal so surreal, half of the city couldn't believe it—a scandal with drugs, lies, an attempted cover-up, and extortion, which captivated the globe for weeks. It's the story of a complicated family, wealthy and secretive, with boundless ambition and a sincere belief that its members are destined to lead this country. It's the story of sibling rivalry, an obsession with loyalty, and the never-ending struggle for a demanding father's approval.

A public figure's family life should ideally be private, but in this book it will be impossible to avoid talking about Ford's family. He is who he is because of them. His political philosophy, his strategy in a crisis, his feelings about money, his compulsion to keep dirty laundry hidden—all can be explored through the lens of a fascinating family dynamic. These seeds were all planted on a quiet leafy street in Etobicoke.

TWO

DOUGIE LOVED POLITICS

O ne by one, the four Ford siblings made the trip to the office of Deco Labels & Tags, where Nelson Scharger, a retired Toronto police sergeant, was waiting with a polygraph machine.

It was the last weekend in April 1998, and the family patriarch, Doug Ford Sr., was furious. One of his children had stolen from him. He was sure of it. And now he was going to prove it.

Which of the four, he wasn't sure, but Doug Sr. suspected it was one of the older two. His daughter, Kathy, then aged thirty-seven, was a heroin user. Randy, thirty-six, had spent years in and out of treatment for substance abuse. For their own good, Doug Sr. periodically cut them off financially. Even in good times, he kept them on a tight allowance. Neither held regular jobs.

His other two sons were less likely suspects. Doug Jr., then thirty-three, was married with young daughters and running the family business. The baby of the family, Rob, twenty-eight, wanted to be a politician—just like his old man. Rob had taken a run at city council the year before and lost, but he'd try again in the next election. Doug Sr. didn't think either of these two would steal from the family. From him.

By this point, Doug Sr. was a sitting member of provincial parliament and a millionaire many times over. And yet despite his loaded bank account, he never felt safe without a small fortune in cash at the ready. He had grown up poor. As a young teenager, he would pick up odd jobs in the evenings, work well into the night, then slip his earnings under his mother's pillow. As an adult, even a rich one, Doug Sr. kept a thick roll of bills stashed away in a tin can behind a brick in his basement wall. It was enough cash to buy a luxury car. It was something he'd always done. But then, in 1998, the Ford family had renovations done and the money disappeared.

Was it the contractors? Doug Sr. didn't think so. He demanded that each of his children—as well as Kathy's husband, Ennio Stirpe—take a lie detector test. Everyone agreed.

Scharger, who ran his own polygraph company, set up shop in a meeting room at Deco. The retired officer conducted the short interviews over two days. As each of the Fords and then Stirpe sat down, Scharger explained how the machine worked. He would ask questions, and it would measure each person's breathing, blood pressure, and any nerve activity on the skin. They could leave at any time, he said. But none did.

What do you think happened to the money? he asked each of them. None of the five admitted to taking it.

Did you steal the can of cash?

Randy, Doug Jr., and Rob said no and passed the test. Kathy and Ennio Stirpe were lying, according to the machine. What they did with the money was unclear.

Predictably, the unremittingly strict Doug Ford Sr. lost it.

Kathy and Stirpe split up. She took their baby son and

moved in with her high school sweetheart, Michael Kiklas, the father of her eleven-year-old daughter.

In July of that year, Stirpe broke into Kiklas's home carrying a sawed-off shotgun. Stirpe opened fire on his estranged wife's boyfriend in front of Kathy and the couple's young daughter. The blast hit Kiklas in the chest. News reports suggest he was dead by the time emergency crews arrived. After a three-day manhunt that ended in a high-speed chase, Stirpe was arrested and charged with first-degree murder. He was found guilty of manslaughter and sentenced to thirteen years in prison. Kathy moved back home after that.

DOUG FORD SR., while tough, loved all his children fiercely and would have done anything for them. But he was never able to understand how his family ended up poisoned by drug use. The Ford patriarch had provided his four children with wealth, power, easy career choices. Theirs were extremely privileged lives compared to his humble beginnings.

The year Douglas Bruce Ford was born, nearly one in three Torontonians was unemployed. It was 1933, and the Great Depression had hit Canada hard. After the stock market crash, President Herbert Hoover had signed the Smoot-Hawley Tariff Act, driving up the cost of nearly nine hundred import duties. Canada's prime minister, William Lyon Mackenzie King, retaliated, setting off a tariff war.

It was a catastrophic blow to the Canadian economy. The United States was, and still is, our largest trade partner. The output of Canada's manufacturing sector plummeted by more than 50 percent. Between 1929 and 1932, the cost of lumber dropped by a third. Pulp and paper companies—a staple in Toronto's economy—were going bankrupt across the country. By 1933, workers in Toronto were earning 60 percent of what they had been four years earlier. Two years later, a quarter of the population in and around the city was drawing on social assistance. Commercial and industrial construction ground almost to a halt.

Toronto the Good, as this city had once been known, had become Toronto the Hungry. There was fear, resentment, and ultimately racism. By the early 1930s, 631,000 people were living in Toronto and about 80 percent of them were of British heritage. The two largest ethnic groups, Jews and Italians, weren't welcome on public beaches and at least one city-run swimming pool. By the summer of 1933, the peak of unemployment, Adolf Hitler had become chancellor of Germany. Anti-Semitism was rampant on both sides of the ocean. In Toronto, those racial tensions came to a head on a warm summer night in August on a west-end baseball field. The Christie Pits riot, considered one of the darkest days in Toronto history, broke out after a group of thugs unfurled a black swastika. Hundreds of men, Jews and Italians versus English and Scots, battled for six hours, clubbing each other with whatever they could find—pipes, pokers, bats, and their bare hands.

It was against this bleak backdrop that Doug Sr. came into the world on February 27, 1933. Like many children of the Great Depression, the times he grew up in forged his character. He knew the value of hard work and self-reliance. And he did his best to ensure that his children would know it too.

Doug Sr. was raised in a rundown neighbourhood in the east end of Toronto. He lived in a small house with his mother and nearly enough brothers and sisters—nine—to field a football team. He never met his father. His mother picked up whatever work she could find, usually doing laundry, to try to keep food on the table. It was never enough.

Doug Sr. was not yet a teenager by the time he quit school to start working. Eventually, he got a job as a salesman. He was a natural. Doug Sr. was charming and warm. His good looks didn't hurt either. Standing six feet tall, with his chiselled jaw, thick golden hair, and dashing smile, he looked like a movie star. The girls used to giggle when he walked by. He was a long-distance swimmer. In 1954, he attempted to swim across Lake Ontario alongside sixteen-year-old Marilyn Bell. He didn't make it, but Bell emerged a national celebrity, after nearly 21 hours, 52 kilometres, and 70,000 strokes.

Doug Sr. kept training, and on the side worked as a lifeguard. It was at the local pool that he first caught sight of a beautiful, blond Diane Campbell. According to family legend, Doug Sr. wooed her with a promise: "Marry me and you'll be marrying a millionaire."

Diane Campbell lived in the north end of the city. Her family was not rich, but it was better off than most. Diane's father, Clarence, was a manager with a power plant contracting company. A serious man who used to smoke cigars at his desk, he was not at all impressed by the young man who pulled up on a motorcycle to take his daughter on a date. But Doug Sr., the consummate salesman, eventually won the Campbells over too. Diane and Doug were married on September 1, 1956.

The young couple moved into a modest apartment on Wilson Avenue in the north end of the city near the highway. Next door was another young couple, Ted and Patricia Herriott.

Ted had just finished school and was helping set up a Toronto division of the American-based Avery label company.

Doug Sr. was working as a salesman at a meat packing plant. He would go door to door moving product. And he was good at it, earning Salesman of the Month, month after month. Years later, when Doug Sr. was in the provincial parliament, he talked about those days with a colleague at Queen's Park, John Parker, the member of parliament for York East.

Doug Sr. told Parker that he was one of the best at the company. "And he'd say to me, 'And you know why I was, John? Because I had to be!'

"Doug took great pride in the fact that he'd pulled himself out of poverty," Parker said. "He always said he was just a typical guy, with a bit more hustle than the rest of them. A bit more savvy. He got up earlier. Served the customer better. Somewhere along the line, he developed the credo: you've got to rely on yourself. The only one you can trust is the guy looking back at you in the mirror."

On the home front, the Fords spent a lot of time with their neighbours the Herriotts. Both families had young children. The friendship started with borrowed cups of milk, and soon they were having dinners together. Ted liked Doug Sr.'s spunk. And when a sales job came up at Avery, he recommended his new friend.

In the early 1960s, Ted began getting restless at work. He was tired of making money for someone else. "My wife and I talked about it. We decided we'd rather be the head of a sardine than the tail of a whale," Ted recalled. "I asked Doug if he wanted to go it alone—and he agreed."

At the time, "pressure sensitive labels" was still a new

technology. In the old days, you had a company's logo printed on paper and then someone had to paint the glue on. Avery was one of the first to make the paper itself sticky. And they were making a killing. Avery's markups were big. Ted was convinced that he and Doug Sr. could offer the same quality for a fraction of the price. And if they were lucky, some of Avery's clients would follow them out the door.

The pair spent a year planning their exit. First up: what would they call themselves?

Mohawk had a nice ring to it. Boomerang also made the shortlist. But then one of them, Ted can't remember who, suggested Deco. Short for Decorative. But also because spelled out, Deco was *D* for Doug, *E* for Edwin—Ted's first name—and *Co.* for company. They liked it.

By this time, Diane Ford's dad, Clarence Campbell, had started his own construction business. Clarence had an office at 3077 Bathurst Street, which was just a little north of midtown. He offered his son-in-law use of the basement level. They hired Diane's sister to do some administrative work. Both the wives helped out in the office too. Ted Herriott was the president and Doug Sr. was the secretary-treasurer. Clarence helped out with accounting. At first, Deco Adhesive Products didn't have its own printing equipment. They were forced to rent. But once the business started to take off, they bought their own plant a few blocks west.

The families became as close as two families can get, even though they no longer lived next door to each other. Each had moved to Etobicoke and were only a ten-minute drive apart. Ted and Doug Sr. would work together all day, head home, and then sometimes the foursome would turn around and go to a dinner party. Occasionally, their kids played together. In the evenings and weekends, Doug Sr. played football with the East York Argos. Ted would go and watch every now and then.

The Fords and Herriotts joined up with two other couples and began taking ballroom dancing lessons. It started out at the local YMCA, and then, once they got better, the teacher would come to their houses. The host rotated each week. The instructor would show up with the record player and they would push all the furniture to one side of the room and cha-cha.

"We thought Doug had two left feet," Pat Herriott laughed. "He couldn't dance worth a hat."

Afterwards, they'd sit and have coffee and sandwiches. Occasionally, they would have a drink, although Ted says none of them were big on booze.

Doug Sr. got his first taste of politics in 1963. Deco's lawyer, Alan Eagleson—after taking a run at a federal seat and losing— decided to run provincially as a Progressive Conservative in the southern Etobicoke riding of Lakeshore. Both Ted and Doug Sr. volunteered on Eagleson's campaign. And he won. Looking back, Eagleson doesn't remember Doug Sr. expressing any interest in being a politician himself. "He was too busy working to get Deco off the ground." After serving four years at Queen's Park, Eagleson went on to become one of the most powerful men in hockey. He spent twenty-five years as head of the National Hockey League Players' Association, but he never lost touch with his friends at Deco, even after they parted ways. (In a spectacular fall from grace that shook the Canadian hockey establishment, Eagleson was arrested on fraud charges in both Canada and the United States, spent time in jail, and lost his licence to practise law.)

By 1965, Deco was doing well, but not spectacularly. This time it was Doug Sr. who was growing restless. He wanted to take the company in a new direction, expanding into tags. Ted wanted to stay the course. There was a bit of a "personality clash," Ted conceded.

"We weren't mad. It was just time to move on," he explained. "The friendship had run its course."

The pair had built a shotgun clause into the original business agreement. Accordingly, each made an offer on the company, and Doug Sr.'s was higher. So they shook hands and Ted Herriott walked away to start his own advertising agency. At Deco, Doug Sr. became president, Clarence Campbell became vice-president, and Diane took over as secretary-treasurer. They moved to an office on Martin Grove Road and by 1971 had again upgraded to a space on Greensboro Drive in Etobicoke, where Deco remains today.

Business was booming. Said a close family friend, "As soon as Doug made it, he bought his mother a fur coat." The company needed more staff. Doug Sr. hired his childhood friend Murray Johnson, who took over as vice-president. Doug Sr. was big on loyalty, a trait he passed on to his children, with mixed results. The four Ford siblings, when they were old enough, also got jobs at Deco.

Kathy ran the administrative side. In 1986, she hired a nineteen-year-old named Gary Moody. He started off in the plant and worked his way up to plant manager and eventually general manager once Doug Jr. officially took over in 2002. Around the time Moody started, Doug Sr. was gradually passing the reins to his namesake—Dougie, to those who knew him well. The father stayed on as president and still went into the office every day, but the goal seemed to be teaching his brood the ropes. Kathy was really smart, Moody remembers. "If it hadn't have been for the drugs ..." He didn't finish the sentence.

Randy was in and out of the business, depending on his own personal issues. And by the early 1990s, the youngest, Rob—Robbie—was also at Deco, on the sales side.

"The Fords are just really great people," said Moody. Deco felt like a family.

"Before I started, there were a few wild Christmas parties, so they sort of stopped them. But every year, Doug Sr. would put cash in envelopes and call everyone up, one by one," he said.

"Back then, when you're young and broke and living cheque to cheque, when someone hands you three to four hundred dollars cash, it was huge. It made your Christmas."

Moody left in 2003 to start his own label company.

By the time Doug Sr. was elected to provincial parliament in 1995, Deco employed about forty-five people and was clearing millions of dollars in annual sales. With Doug Jr. taking the lead in the company, Deco expanded into Chicago and New Jersey. About 250 people are currently on the payroll.

Doug Ford Sr.'s story is an inspiring tale of how a child of the Great Depression, with virtually no formal education, built an industry-leading company from nothing, through sheer grit, good instincts, and hard work. But in what would become a recurring theme in their political careers, the Fords could not resist embellishing.

It has become part of the family folklore that Doug and Diane Ford started Deco out of the family basement. It was a story told in the weekly *Etobicoke Life* in 1995, after Doug Sr.

won the Progressive Conservative nomination, and it has been repeated ever since in newspaper and magazine articles about the Fords.

Nowhere is there mention of Ted Herriott, the co-founder, who was as instrumental as Doug Sr. in the genesis of Deco. Business records and official Toronto directories from the time confirm Herriott's account.

Years after their split, Ted Herriott and Doug Ford met at a mutual friend's party. They embraced, and Doug Sr. seemed genuinely thrilled to see his old colleague.

There were no hard feelings, Herriott told me. But I asked him if it bothered him to have been airbrushed out of history.

He considered the question.

"I'll say I've never understood it."

KATHRYN DIANE FORD was the firstborn, arriving on a rainy summer day in July 1960. A little more than a year later, she had competition from baby number two, Randal Douglas. Then, in November 1964, along came another son, Douglas Robert. And the Fords weren't done yet. Twelve years into their marriage, with a growing business to manage, Doug and Diane Ford had their fourth and final child. Another boy. Robert Bruce, weighing in at nine pounds, one ounce, was born at Humber Memorial Hospital in Etobicoke on May 28, 1969.

"I gave my sons names that I thought would look good on an office door," Diane Ford once told a confidant.

In the early days of Deco, money had been tight. But by the time Rob was a baby, the family had moved into the lavish

Etobicoke home where Diane still lives today. Doug Sr. worked
a lot. Diane was a blossoming socialite. She loved to get dressed
up and mingle at the local country club. As their bank account
grew, the Fords continued to climb the social ladder. By the early
1980s they were appearing in the society pages alongside the
elites of the day, the Eaton family, cabinet ministers, senators.

Doug Ford Sr. was a founding member of the Rexdale
Rotary Club and volunteered with the Salvation Army and
Big Brothers. Eventually, he became a board member with the
Etobicoke General Hospital and helped raise $1.5 million so
that the hospital could buy its first CT scan machine.

He was strict with his children. There was no sleeping in at
their household. Every day, the man who had endured grinding
poverty reminded them how fortunate they were. Deco was
doing well. The family could afford nice cars. But Doug Sr.
warned his children to take nothing for granted.

The children worshipped their father and all his eccentrici-
ties—of which there were many. Doug Sr. liked to wear cowboy
hats, sometimes at Queen's Park. He sported a handlebar
moustache and wore fur coats. On his downtime, Doug Sr.
loved to travel, picking up treasures along the way, paintings,
rugs, vases, statues. He was especially fond of items from Asia.
The Ford home became a mini museum, although no one could
ever tell if Doug Sr. had paid ten dollars or ten thousand for
a piece. He didn't seem to care. He liked what he liked. On
the weekends, his favourite pastime was bargain hunting at the
Pickering flea market, east of Toronto. He would never dress up.
"He wanted to see how people would treat him not knowing he
had money," said a family friend.

BY ALL ACCOUNTS, the Ford kids had a happy childhood. No one can really explain what happened next, other than to say it was tragic. As teenagers, both Kathy and Randy started taking drugs. By the time he was eighteen, Randy had a criminal record for assault. He stole a motorcycle then breached his parole. While his younger brothers were just starting high school, Randy was in and out of court, and sometimes jail. Between 1981 and 1987, he was twice found guilty of theft and assault. In 1988 he was found guilty of possession of narcotics. By the time Doug Ford Sr. became a member of provincial parliament, in 1995, Randy had been arrested at least seventeen times, often for multiple offences. Among his dozens of convictions: dangerous driving, mischief to private property, break and enter, driving while impaired, and half a dozen drug offences.

What sons Doug Jr. and Rob were doing at this time is still the subject of considerable gossip in the Etobicoke community, gossip every journalist in Toronto was tipped off about once Rob Ford announced his candidacy for mayor. *The Globe and Mail* was the only news outlet in Toronto to follow up on those rumours properly. And on May 25, 2013, a week after the *Star* published its story about the crack cocaine video, the *Globe* ran a four-thousand-word investigation into the Ford brothers' high school years.

The story, by Greg McArthur and Shannon Kari, alleged that Doug Jr. was one of the go-to hash dealers in Etobicoke during the 1980s. The reporters spoke with ten people—"two former hashish suppliers, three street-level drug dealers and a number of casual users of hash"—who branded the middle Ford brother as a significant player in the Etobicoke hash trade. They alleged that Doug was active from the age of fifteen to about twenty-two. Rob Ford was sometimes around his brother when he was conducting business, but the *Globe* said "he didn't seem to be involved in a significant way," according to sources.

All of the *Globe*'s sources for the story talked on condition of anonymity, although they each spoke on the record to the reporters and several agreed to meet with editors at the paper. The sources said they were worried about reprisals. At least one feared problems crossing the border if his name was attached to a story about buying drugs.

According to the *Globe*'s investigation, Doug Jr. was conducting his drug deals out of his family's basement and a local park. Sources said Doug and his associates called themselves the RY Drifters—a reference to the Royal York Plaza, which was at the end of the Fords' street—and at least ten of them "became heroin addicts, some of whom turned to break-ins and robberies to support their habit." One of Doug's associates was a man named Dave Price, a long-time friend of his. The pair played on the same hockey and football teams. Days after the crack video story broke, Mayor Rob Ford hired Price as his director of operations and logistics. Asked about the hiring, Doug Jr., now a councillor himself, told the *Globe*, "You can't teach loyalty."

The *Globe* story also revealed that, at twenty-four, Randy was charged in connection with the kidnapping of a man named Marco Orlando over a drug debt. A small story about the incident had run in the *Toronto Star* on December 12, 1986.

> Three Etobicoke men have been charged with trying to
> force a man to pay a $5,000 debt incurred by his son.
> Police say the son, Marco Orlando, 28, of Adonis Court,
> was beaten up by a man in the Royal York Plaza on Royal

York Rd. on Tuesday night, then turned over to two other
men who drove him to Bolton and confined him for
10 hours. Orlando was then forced to call his father and
ask for $5,000 for his release. The family called police.
Orlando returned home and police later arrested three
men.

The *Star* story indicates that "[Randal] Douglas Ford, 24"
was charged with assault causing bodily harm. *The Globe and
Mail* article in 2013 reported that "court records retrieved
from the Archives of Ontario show that he was charged with
assault causing bodily harm and the forcible confinement of Mr.
Orlando. The records do not disclose how the case was resolved."

In an exhaustive search of Randy Ford's legal history, I did
not find any convictions relating to an incident in December
1986. The Fords' long-time lawyer, Dennis Morris, is quoted as
saying he does not recall the incident.

Finally, the *Globe* investigation rehashed the fatal shooting
of Michael Kiklas, adding, "Not mentioned in the press at the
time was the fact that Mr. Kiklas was a white supremacist—a
group with which Ms. Ford associated in the 1980s." Sources
told the paper that Kathy never seemed like a true believer in the
movement. Rather, she came across as someone trying to rebel.

After the *Globe* story became public, Councillor Doug Ford
conducted a series of interviews with various media denouncing
the investigation. He called the allegation that he once dealt
drugs "an outright lie" and "sleazy journalism." He admitted to
smoking marijuana as a teenager, "like everyone else."

"Is that the best *The Globe and Mail* has? … They want to go
back when I was in high school," Doug Ford told Global News.

"Why don't we talk about the great things the Ford family has done for Etobicoke and throughout the city? I think that should maybe be *once* the story. About giving back."

He then asked the Global reporter, Jackson Proskow, if he'd ever done drugs. "I'm sure you, Jackson, have smoked marijuana. And God knows what else you've done.… Have you ever done cocaine? I haven't. I've heard a lot of people have done cocaine in the media. People chasing Rob have done cocaine, I've heard." This ploy of accusing the questioners of doing drugs was a tactic Doug would use again. (It's worth noting that in November 2013, after six months of denying the *Globe* story, Doug Jr. told CNN's Bill Weir, "If you want to go calling, you know, going to your buddy and saying, 'Here's a joint for ten bucks,' if that's what you want to call [dealing], so be it.")

In researching this book, I reached out to hundreds of the Fords' former classmates who went to Scarlett Heights Collegiate with the brothers between 1980 and 1988. Because of the age difference, Doug and Rob were only at Scarlett at the same time for one year. Most of the people contacted did not respond. Several former classmates noted that the Ford brothers had a reputation for fighting, especially the eldest, Randy. One person described him as a "terror." But the majority of those who were willing to comment described Doug and Rob as two friendly jocks who used to throw wild parties around the family's backyard pool. They were popular and good-looking. Both devoted their high school years to sports.

Doug Jr. played hockey and threw shot put, but his passion was the gridiron. Football was big at Scarlett in those days. "We probably had the best football team that was out there. There was a [big] conflict between us and Richview Collegiate," said former student Mark Stenoff. One year, Scarlett's Raiders were the better squad, then it would switch.

When kids weren't cheering on their home team, they were partying at someone's house or in the local park. "You know, it was a rock-and-roll school, basically. That's the simplest way I could put it," Stenoff said. "We had a lot of rockers.... You know what I mean? What do you call 'em, long-hairs, I guess. It was a cool school."

In his graduating yearbook, Doug wrote, "Scarlett Heights is nice and hearty every day was a party. I can't believe I'm still alive after five. Make it 3 in a row Raiders."

Once Rob Ford came along, he was immediately cast as "Doug's little brother." When he was in Grade 10, he made captain of the junior football team. The caption on the team photo that year mistakenly read "Doug Ford." Football was everything to Rob. Doug Sr. sent his youngest to a prestigious youth football camp in the US over the summer. Rob was not naturally a gifted player, but he worked hard, beefed up, and became a star on the team. "All I remember is him running the track. You'd drive by after school and you'd see him running the track. He had a lot of heart," said former Scarlett student Bill Gianakopoulos.

"Rob was a good person. He was a generous person," said Dave Miteff, who played two years of football with the future mayor. "The second year that we played, we won the city championship.... [Rob] had a party at his house, and the Fords paid for it all. The father had somebody videotape the game, and he gave us all copies."

Laura Biernat, who had drama class with Rob at Scarlett Heights, remembers him as being shy. "He wasn't at all like the man you see today," she said. "He was a quieter kind of fellow as a teenager."

Outside the classroom, Rob was social, but he didn't seem to have many close friends. He used to run with the "rich kids" in Etobicoke, spending weekends at summer cottages or flying down to someone's vacation house in Florida for a few days. By this point, the Fords weren't yet ultra-wealthy, but they had enough to keep Rob hanging out with the in-crowd. Status was worth the investment.

"He wasn't exactly part of that group, but he hung out with them," said a friend of the brothers from high school. "Robbie was just sort of around a lot. He was friendly with everyone."

Along the way, Rob made friends with a transfer student from nearby Don Bosco Catholic Secondary School named Fabio Basso, said David Profitt, a mutual friend of the two. Basso had long dark hair that covered his eyes. He was laid-back, a "quiet stoner," according to others who knew him. (Twenty-five years later, it was outside Basso's yellow-brick home in Etobicoke that the infamous photo of Rob with two alleged gang members and a murdered twenty-one-year-old would be taken.)

"Robbie liked his weed," said a high school friend. So he and Basso got along well.

Rob spent a few years drifting after high school. He dreamed of a career in football, but never made it past the varsity level. At Carleton University in Ottawa, Ford spent one season on the Ravens' offensive line, but it's not clear if he ever left the bench. One of Rob's former teammates, John Lindsay, explained to *Toronto Life* magazine, "I know it might sound strange now … but Robbie was a little guy." Rob dropped out after a year, went back to work at the family business, and started coaching on the side.

Toronto's future mayor still didn't know what he wanted to do for a career, he just knew he wanted to be successful. "He used to say he's going to be the first in his family to make a million dollars," said one friend.

But in those early days after Carleton, twenty-year-old Rob Ford seemed most committed to "having a good time." After all, he was young, well-off, and his dad was his boss. He started to party. Primarily, he liked to drink and smoke pot, but he dabbled in cocaine as well. Said the high school friend, "What do you expect? He's been around drugs his whole life."

By that time, Randy's substance abuse had worsened. Randy and Doug Sr. stopped speaking for a while. Kathy was not doing well either, and she was no longer working full-time at Deco.

For his part, Rob had never had a strong interest in the family business, but he wanted to be a team player, so he stuck around and joined the Deco sales force. Doug Jr. was running the company, although his father was still officially president for the time being. When the moment was right, Doug Sr. would step back and give the company to his middle son, who had more than proven himself worthy. Doug Sr. was getting ready to retire.

Then fate intervened.

IT WAS EARLY 1994, election time in the pre-amalgamation City of Etobicoke. Long-serving local councillor Doug Holyday had decided to run for mayor of Etobicoke, and he needed help with his campaign signs. A friend recommended Deco Labels.

Holyday was hoping to reuse his old white-and-blue councillor signs rather than print all new ones. He met with Doug Jr., who suggested covering the word "councillor" with a big red sticker that said "MAYOR" in white letters. Holyday loved it. But he got more than just signs that day. Doug Jr. asked if he needed help on his campaign.

Holyday recalled one of Doug Jr.'s first days on the team. Doug Jr. was livid that their political rival was winning the sign war.

"I remember Doug coming down to say, 'You don't have any signs in the Six Points, Kipling, and Dundas area. It's all Bruce Sinclair,'" Holyday said. Doug Jr. vowed to take care of it. "The next day, I drove down Kipling and the area was covered in my signs."

Doug Jr. joined Holyday's steering committee. He attended breakfast strategy meetings and helped with door-knocking. Against the odds, Holyday won, beating out the incumbent Sinclair.

Doug Jr. was hooked. The next year, he encouraged his father to run provincially. Doug Jr. would be his campaign manager.

"Dougie loved politics," said Moody, Deco's former general manager and long-time friend of Doug Jr. "He never talked about running, though. I think Rob had more time on his hands. Dougie couldn't. He was running the business and taking care of his family."

This dynamic would haunt the brothers' relationship for years to come. Doug Jr. had been left with the responsibility of running Deco, leaving baby brother Rob the freedom to pursue his dreams. Both worshipped their father, craved his approval, and spent their lives trying to emulate him. Doug Jr. went the business route. Then Doug Sr. changed careers and decided to run for the provincial Conservative party. A few years later, brother Rob launched his own campaign, at least in part off of his family's business credentials.

Those close to Doug Ford Jr. say that not so deep down, he resented Rob. Glimpses of this tension surfaced during Rob Ford's first year in office, with Doug hijacking news coverage. Friends and former staff go so far as to say that none of the three brothers get along very well. Sometimes they go months without speaking. This is especially true for Doug and Rob, despite the fact that Rob frequently refers to Doug as his best friend, and that Doug is his brother's fiercest defender.

Their loyalty is ultimately to the family name, not necessarily to each other.

ON FEBRUARY 18, 1995, hundreds of people wearing Doug Ford baseball caps and waving Doug Ford placards marched into Scarlett Heights Collegiate to pledge their support for the scrappy tell-it-like-it-is owner of Deco Labels & Tags.

It was the night of the Progressive Conservative nomination for the Etobicoke-Humber riding. The premier of Ontario, Bob Rae, a New Democrat, was expected to call an election in a matter of months. If the polls were any indication, his beleaguered government was going to take a beating.

The early 1990s was a period of recession in Canada. Voters felt that Rae and the Ontario New Democratic Party had mismanaged the economy. The province was running a staggering deficit of twelve billion dollars. In an attempt to tame that beast, Rae had passed an austerity measure in the spring of

1993 that forced public-sector workers to take unpaid leave, or "Rae Days," as they came to be known. In doing so, he became just as unpopular with the left as he was with the right. New Democrat support was barely breathing at 14 percent. All the polls indicated a Liberal sweep. The party, led by Lyn McLeod, had the second highest number of seats in the legislature. They appeared poised to form a majority government.

Enter Mike Harris, the colourful leader of the third-place Progressive Conservative Party. Harris positioned himself as the exact opposite of Rae. He pitched a "Common Sense Revolution" that would cut income tax rates by 30 percent, slash spending by six billion dollars, and force able-bodied welfare recipients to work for their cheques. Harris vowed to do away with affirmative-action programs and get tough with criminals.

Four candidates in Etobicoke-Humber were vying to become soldiers in Harris's revolution. Doug Ford Sr. was up against a lawyer named Tom Barlow, local business manager Alida Leistra, and a small businessman and lawyer named Joe Peschisolido. The winner would take on Liberal incumbent Dr. Jim Henderson, a physician who had represented the riding since 1985.

Doug Sr. won on the third ballot.

It was the first political step by a Ford, and the beginning of a movement that would come to be known as Ford Nation.

THREE

THE CANADIAN KENNEDYS

Chris MacIntyre headed straight home from school on the afternoon of March 31, 2005. The fourteen-year-old was new to the neighbourhood and still making friends. Five weeks earlier, he had moved in with his dad and his dad's girlfriend, Kathy Ford. They lived in an apartment above Kathy's parents' garage, which Doug Sr. and Diane had built for her after she ran into some trouble a few years earlier. The Fords were rich. They had their own label business, and Mr. Ford used to be in the provincial parliament. One of the sons was a city councillor.

Chris figured they were pretty important people.

Kathy, like his dad, wasn't perfect. She'd had a lot of hard years, and she wore every one of them on her face. Both Kathy and Chris's dad had drug problems. Both had criminal records. His dad had spent a lot of time in jail. But things seemed to be better.

Chris had never seen his troubled father so happy. Kathy Ford was forty-five and Scott MacIntyre was thirty-eight, but the age difference didn't seem to bother either of them. Scott said Kathy was "soulmate" material. She was good to Chris. She treated him just as well as she treated her own two children, a seventeen-year-old girl and eleven-year-old boy. Now, the five of them all lived together.

Scott was an excellent cook. In the morning, he would make the kids eggs and hash browns with sausage. Scott would come into Chris's room whisking a bowl of fresh hollandaise sauce, letting the noise wake him up. Kathy took care of the laundry and the cleaning. Some nights they would skip cooking, and the whole gang would go out for Chinese food or pizza. There was a lot of laughter in their lives. Scott and Kathy liked to banter. They would rib each other all day, trading increasingly ridiculous barbs, each hoping to catch the other off guard.

Chris was happy.

This March day, when he got home, he had the apartment to himself. Kathy's two kids were around somewhere, but he didn't see them. His dad and Kathy were with some friends in the kitchen of the main house. A woman—the girlfriend of one of Scott's buddies—was staying with them in the apartment. This was not unusual. People were always crashing for a day or two. Kathy and his dad were generous with their space.

Chris dropped his backpack and headed straight for the television, as Grade 9 boys will do. He was deep into the video game Mortal Kombat when he heard shouting from downstairs.

He dropped the controls and walked to the door connecting to the main house. Something was going on. Chris jogged down the hallway and rounded the staircase to the main level. There were a lot of people in the kitchen. Kathy's daughter was standing by the door. Suddenly, a deafening crack split the air.

The rest Chris remembers in slow motion.

Kathy slumped to the floor. People started to run. Scott put down a 12-gauge shotgun, pushed someone out of the way, and ran to Kathy's side. Kathy's daughter balled up her fists, tilted her head upwards, and began screaming louder than Chris had ever heard anyone scream in his life.

"Kathy! Oh, Kathy! Oh, God!" Chris recalled his dad yelling. "Can you talk to me? What's your name? What's your birthday?"

Her head was gushing blood.

Scott turned to Chris and yelled at him to call 911. Chris ran for the upstairs phone. The screaming didn't stop. By the time Chris got back to the kitchen, his father was gone. He and another man had taken off in Kathy's parents' Jaguar.

The police arrived. Kathy was whisked to the hospital, and Chris was driven to the police station. He sobbed as they questioned him. He knew his dad was in trouble. He wanted to protect him. At first, he lied and said Scott had been at work all day. "He wasn't even home at the time of the shooting," Chris claimed. But the detectives were unrelenting. They told him they already knew everything from Kathy's children. Chris, scared and tired, eventually confessed what he knew.

He emerged from the police station to see Kathy's councillor brother, Rob Ford.

"Rob, please. Please let me stay with you. I have nowhere to go," Chris wept.

Rob looked down at him. "I can't do anything," he said, and turned away.

Chris had to leave Toronto to live with his mom.

Kathy survived. The bullet had grazed her forehead, leaving a scar but no lasting damage. Police tracked Scott down the next day and charged him with careless storage of a firearm, careless use of a firearm, and possession of cocaine. He pleaded guilty to all three offences and went to jail.

Investigators determined that the shooting had been an accident. Scott was trying to break up a fight between his friend and the girlfriend who had been staying with them.

"Somehow or another he was jostled or lost his balance and the gun discharged," Detective Colin Kay told the *National Post*. "I am not of the belief that the victim was the intended target."

The shotgun wasn't Scott MacIntyre's. It belonged to Doug Ford Sr., an avid collector, according to family sources. MacIntyre promised the judge he'd never touch another firearm again. He spent a year in jail.

Once he was released, he and Kathy got back together. They moved into an apartment, for which Kathy's parents were paying, across the street from Scarlett Heights Collegiate. Every few months, Chris would visit the couple. They looked as happy as ever, but trouble never seemed far from Kathy.

DESPITE THE VARIOUS PROBLEMS at home, the Ford family was on its way to becoming a political dynasty.

Doug Sr. had spent just a single term in the Ontario Legislature. The premier consolidated the number of ridings, and Doug Sr. lost his seat in 1999 after only four years as an MPP. But he was still a significant player in the party, plus his youngest son was a city councillor.

In his short time as an MPP, Doug Sr. had made his mark as a staunch conservative warrior, ready and willing to toe the party line even in the face of crumbling public support. His combative speeches at Queen's Park became something of legend. In one famous incident, he began heckling the people who had come to make deputations about not having jobs. It was in 1997, and the legislative assembly was debating Bill 103, the bill that would bring about amalgamation.

"The greatest economist I ever met in my whole life was my mother," Doug Sr. said. "My mother had nine children, and she didn't take any welfare and she had the kind of pride I haven't seen for many, many years."

Someone interjected, "What's that got to do with Bill 103?"

Doug Sr. kept going. "We're talking about living in two rooms with nine kids. The older ones took care of the younger ones. My mother worked every single day of her life. She used to brush my hair, and I used to say to her, 'When I get older, you'll never have to work,' and she used to laugh. Every day, I'd see her go out, and I'd see her come back with a bag of groceries or something. Heating those two rooms—I used to go down to the coal cars, down on Eastern Avenue, take the coal, put it in a bucket, and bring it home on my wagon. Some of you people don't even know what life's all about ... the people over there who are lobbying from the audience every day. I've been listening and I watch them all. I wonder if they've got time or they work for a living. I don't know."

Gilles Bisson, a New Democrat, admonished Ford for attacking the public.

But Doug Sr. pressed on. "Everyone agrees that the status quo is not an option. The mayors, the business community, even the leader of the Opposition all agree there must be change."

By this point, the chamber was deteriorating as people began to shout. The Conservative Party whip gave Doug Sr. the signal to sit down.

Bisson: "The whip is too embarrassed by what you're saying and he wants you to sit down."

Doug Ford: "Why don't you shut your mouth."

Doug Sr. may not have earned himself many friends on the other side of the aisle, but within his own party, his passion, loyalty, and flamboyant charm won people over. They respected his rags-to-riches story. And while Doug Sr. didn't broadcast it, he donated every penny of his political salary to charity.

Doug Ford Sr. became an important fixture in Conservative circles. So, in early 2003, when John Tory, the CEO of Rogers Cable—a division of Rogers Communications, one of the biggest and most powerful companies in Canada—decided he was going to run for mayor of Toronto, he scheduled a meeting with the Fords. Tory was a conservative. And to win an election in Toronto as a right-winger, you needed the suburbs. His advisers explained that the Fords were the gatekeepers to Etobicoke.

"It was 'Fords,' plural," Tory remembered. "I showed up at this restaurant near the airport, and there was Doug Sr., Diane, and Rob and Doug Jr. and Randy."

Looking back, Tory described his lunch with the Fords as "being on show," his moment to explain what he was about and what he planned to do. Diane asked most of the questions, and she was the one who delivered the verdict.

"We like you. You'll get elected, because we're going to help you in Etobicoke," Tory remembered Diane saying. "You'll serve for a period of time, and then it will be Robbie's turn."

Tory narrowly lost the mayoral election to the left-wing candidate, David Miller, but he did take Etobicoke.

According to those who know him well, Rob Ford always knew he would run for mayor once he got elected to council. But he dreamed even bigger. One day, he wanted to become leader of the federal Conservative Party, and ultimately prime minister.

Brother Doug Jr. planned to run provincially and eventually be elected premier. As a councillor, Doug Jr. was open about his plans to move to Queen's Park.

Said a source closely connected to the family, "The Fords think of themselves as the Kennedys. They talk about it. They're the Canadian Kennedys."

Perhaps it's true. The Kennedys had skeletons. And so do the Fords.

ROB FORD WAS TWENTY-NINE years old when he had his first brush with scandal. It was the early morning of February 15, 1999. Ford was on vacation with his then girlfriend, Renata Brejniak, at his parents' condo in Hallandale, Florida, just north of Miami. Well after midnight, for reasons unknown, Ford was driving around a crime-sick slum in downtown Miami known as Overtown. As he passed 12th Street and NW 3rd Avenue, a police officer noticed Ford was driving his gold Crown Victoria without the headlights on.

Officer Timothy Marks pulled him over two streets later. According to the arrest paperwork, Ford was nervous, pink-faced, and reeked of booze. Marks suspected he was drunk and asked him to exit the vehicle for a roadside test.

Ford fumbled his way out of the car, threw his hands in the air, and slurred, "Go ahead. Take me to jail!" He pulled out a handful of cash, chucking the money onto the pavement. The two men, both five feet ten, stood eye to eye, but the driver had one hundred pounds on him. Marks examined the licence. The driver's name was Robert Bruce Ford, born May 28, 1969, and he was in Florida on vacation from Toronto.

Marks pulled out a pen from his breast pocket. He positioned it a foot in front of Ford's face and waved it back and forth. Ford's glassy eyes floated aimlessly around in their sockets, occasionally fastening on the pen before wandering off again. Fail. Next, Marks asked Ford to walk nine steps in a straight line, turn around, and walk nine steps back. Ford made three attempts before Marks moved on to the one-legged balance test. Standing in his summer deck shoes, Ford gingerly raised his foot off the ground and nearly fell over. He hopped up and down, flailed his arms, then gave up. Fail. Finally, Marks asked him to close his eyes, put his hands at his sides, tilt his head to the stars, and try to estimate thirty seconds. Ford listed from side to side, holding out his arms like a tightrope walker on a cable hundreds of feet in the air.

"… Thirty!"

"That was fifteen."

At 2:50 A.M., Officer Marks put Ford in handcuffs. He searched Ford's pockets, emptying the contents onto the hood of his cruiser, and found a marijuana joint stashed in Ford's right back pocket. Back at South Station, Ford blew .124 on the Breathalyzer, well above the legal limit of .08. On the second reading, he wouldn't cooperate. Officer Barbara Shaffner wrote "Playing w[ith] blowing" on the official report, which meant Ford was either trying to stick his tongue in the tube or exhale outside the device.

Ford was charged with driving under the influence and possession of marijuana. He was booked, fingerprinted, and photographed, then driven over to the Dade County jail to sober up.

Never-before-seen arrest documents reveal that Ford has never been fully truthful about what happened that night. After the story broke in 2010, Ford told reporters he had been out celebrating Valentine's Day with Renata prior to his arrest. "I admit maybe I had, you know, a little bit ... one, two glasses of wine or two," he said. "We had a couple of bottles of wine. I wasn't drunk, but maybe I shouldn't have been driving." But Ford's arrest citation paints a completely different picture. Ford told police he had been at a bar called the Players Pub in Hallandale—about twenty-five minutes of highway driving north of Overtown—in the three hours before getting stopped at 2:35 A.M. When asked when he had last eaten something, Ford told investigators he'd had some ribs and potatoes ten hours earlier. He admitted to drinking two large draft beers and two shots of Chivas Regal between 3 P.M. and midnight. (Arresting Officer Timothy Marks said it would take significantly more alcohol than that for Ford to blow what he did.) And it's not clear if Renata was even with Ford at the time, as he has suggested. There is no mention of her in any of the paperwork, and a source close to the family told me she was waiting back at the condo.

Ford initially tried to hide the arrest from his family. When Doug Ford Sr. took public office, the Ford children had been warned there would be strict consequences for any "silliness." This usually meant cutting them off financially for a period of time. It was a punishment that Randy and Kathy knew well. A close family source says that Ford might have successfully avoided the wrath of Doug Ford Sr. if only he had remembered to get rid of his arrest paperwork, which was discovered by another family member at the Florida condo a week later.

Doug Ford Sr. was "absolutely livid," said the source. The tough-on-crime, family values premier of Ontario, Mike Harris, was not going to be pleased if the media learned his backbencher from Etobicoke had a son facing drug and DUI charges. And it wasn't just the Ford family's reputation on the line. Rob's own political future was at stake. He wanted to be a city councillor. He had run and lost in 1997 and was preparing to try again in 2000.

The Fords hired lawyer Reemberto Diaz to work out a deal. On May 14, 1999, Ford pleaded guilty to driving under the influence, and in exchange the state dropped the marijuana charge. Ford agreed to six months' probation, a 180-day suspension of his licence, and $664.75 in fines and court costs. He was also ordered to perform fifty hours of community service and attend a substance abuse program. And that was the end of it.

Shortly after coming back from Florida, Ford announced that he and Renata were engaged.

ON A SUNNY SATURDAY in August 2000, Renata Brejniak married Rob Ford at the All Saints Roman Catholic Church in Etobicoke. She was twenty-nine; he was thirty-one. That evening, there were cocktails, dinner, and dancing at the nearby St. George's Golf and Country Club. They gave a commemorative bottle of wine to each of their guests and looked very much in love.

Renata wore a white dress cinched around her tiny waist, with a sweetheart neckline, short sleeves, and a long flowing train. Her curly brown hair tumbled to her shoulders beneath a veil and beaded tiara. Rob was in a dark suit with a powder-blue tie. Doug Jr.'s four daughters were matching flower girls with blue petals in their hair.

Most people believe the couple had met in high school. A February 2011 *Toronto Life* feature entitled "The Woman

Behind the Mayor: Who Is Renata Ford?" asserts that "what we do know is that Rob and Renata met during high school when they were living a couple of blocks apart." This is what Ford says too, and it's certainly possible. They were only a few years apart at Scarlett Heights. And their childhood homes are in the same Etobicoke neighbourhood. But no one I spoke to recalls Rob having anything to do with Renata until his twenties.

After graduation, Renata went out with a man named Artur Kisicki. He was born in Poland, like Renata's parents, and worked as a cabinetmaker. They got married in June 1993, when Renata was just twenty-two, but separated a year and a half later. A year after that Kisicki filed for divorce. It was finalized in February 1996. Court records do not indicate what led to the marriage breaking down, although a source close to the family says Renata's drinking played a role.

Rob and Renata dated for several years before they got married. Rob had been reluctant to settle down, reportedly, but proposed shortly after his drunk driving arrest in Florida.

It seemed that alcohol continued to be a problem in the Ford household. In July 2005, after giving birth to her daughter, Stephanie, Renata was arrested for impaired driving. Officer Neville Channer also charged her with refusing to provide a breath sample and assaulting a peace officer. The second two charges were dropped, and she was fined six hundred dollars and given one year of driving probation.

In 2008 Renata had a second child, a son named Doug, whom Rob affectionately calls Dougie. Renata's parents help their daughter with the kids most days.

FOR A WHILE, Kathy Ford's troubles continued to haunt the family. There had been a brief period of stability in the mid-1990s. She even ran a political campaign in 1997 for the Conservative nominee in Etobicoke North, Sam Basra. But a year later, Michael Kiklas's killing would devastate her. Kathy moved back in with her parents and eventually into the apartment above the garage. Holding a job was tough. She briefly tried to start a gift basket business out of the family house. But it never really came to anything.

Then she met Scott MacIntyre. He was always grinning and seemed passionate about everything. He made her happy. But in many ways they weren't good for each other. Both were drug users. They would spend time clean, then fall back into it.

Things got bad in late 2003, when the pair went on a rampage stealing from Bell Canada phone booths. On December 10, they were arrested carrying a "pry bar and knife … instruments suitable for the purpose of breaking into a place vault." Kathy and MacIntyre were each charged with thirty-two counts of theft under five thousand dollars for offences between November 4 and 19. In 2004, most of the charges were withdrawn. Kathy got twelve months' probation. MacIntyre, because of his record, spent a few months in jail.

The accidental shooting in 2005 was a brief interruption in their relationship. In 2008, Kathy was arrested for stealing toothbrushes from Zellers. She was also charged with assaulting the person trying to detain her. When she lied about her identity to an investigating police officer, they tacked on an obstruction of justice charge. (The obstruction and assault charges were dropped.) Kathy was given a year of probation for the theft and spent four days in custody.

Through it all, to the surprise and annoyance of her family, Kathy Ford and Scott MacIntyre stayed together.

The night Rob Ford was elected mayor, October 25, 2010, Scott was in the room at the Ford family homestead, alongside immediate family, high-ranking campaign staff, and a handful of reporters.

But fifteen months later, something happened that they couldn't overcome.

It began at 7:30 A.M. on January 11, 2012. Scott drove to the mayor's home and parked around the corner. A neighbour spotted him lurking and spoke to him. She called the police. Another resident asked Scott what he was doing, and Scott answered not to worry, he was family. He then drove into Rob and Renata Ford's driveway and walked in the front door, which was unlocked because, according to court transcripts, Rob had been waiting for a visitor. When Rob came out of his bedroom to investigate the noise, Scott started to yell.

"You owe me money and your sister owes me money," Scott shouted. "If I don't get it, they will kill me!"

Rob ordered him to get out, but Scott kept at him. "You and your family are going to get it, you are going to pay for it."

Scott left and police arrived. An officer reached him on his cell phone. At one point in the phone conversation, Scott told the constable he intended to shoot Rob—who was now the mayor—and cut off his head with a machete.

Hours later, Scott MacIntyre was arrested in a hotel room in Mississauga, just west of Toronto. Police found 2.1 grams of heroin and 1.8 grams of cocaine in his room.

The mayor spoke to reporters later that day: "I can take care of myself. Pretty well told him that.... The whole thing was over pretty quickly." Doug Jr. told the CBC he didn't really know MacIntyre very well. He urged his brother to hire a security detail. Kathy didn't answer her phone that day, but her voice mail greeting still included Scott's name as well as those of her two children. Neighbours said the on-again-off-again couple had spent Christmas together.

But now, to the family's relief, according to sources, it looked like the relationship was finally done for good.

On January 27, 2012, jail security found a letter written by Scott to Kathy: "You and your family have one chance to leave me the fuck alone and stop this shit! Or I am going to start a shitstorm.... You and your family think I should play nice! Fuck you."

While in prison, Scott was "viciously attacked and severely beaten," court transcripts show. It was a case of "jailhouse justice," the judge said, likely related to Scott's relationship with the mayor of Toronto. His teeth were knocked out and he suffered a "catastrophic" injury to his right leg.

Both Rob and Kathy Ford gave victim impact statements. Both said that they weren't worried MacIntyre would try to hurt them and that they hoped he would avoid prison time. Justice Paul French found this to be a significant mitigating factor. The Crown attorney and Scott's defence lawyer agreed on the facts of the case.

Scott was sentenced to five additional months in jail, three years' probation, regular drug tests, and a ban on owning weapons. He was also told to stay five hundred metres away from Rob Ford's home and workplace. Kathy had asked that the court allow her to continue to communicate with Scott to help him with rehab, but Scott's lawyer noted that Kathy Ford "has her own issues. I think that her issues in combination with Mr. MacIntyre's issues are simply a prescription for disaster." The judge agreed. Scott was banned from having any association or communication with Kathy.

Scott MacIntyre was released that fall. In October 2012, he posted on his Facebook page, "I learned a VERY valuable lesson back in January! No matter if you are 100% innocent and have broken NO LAWS you can still be put in JAIL for daring to challenge people who are CONNECTED with the POLITICAL MACHINE!!!!!!" The status update is no longer visible.

I made various attempts to speak to Scott MacIntyre before finally connecting with him through Facebook. (His son, Chris, confirms that Scott communicates primarily through the site.) On July 17, 2013, I wrote Scott a message asking if he would discuss the day he walked into the mayor's home asking for money.

He wrote back two days later. "The Fords as a whole family treated me like one of their own and for the things that I did to them they were more than fair and it would be remiss for me to say any different."

Later he added, "I have nothing to say. And I take full responsibility for my actions. And what I did by going to my ex-brother-in-law's and creating a scene was just stupid and irresponsible. Rob did not deserve the disrespect I caused and I paid my debt to society and have put this all behind me and wish you and all other media would do the same. Why don't you do a story on what a great job Rob has done as Mayor of this City. And the money he has saved the tax payer!!!"

IT MUST HAVE BEEN some relief to the Ford family that Doug Sr. did not witness these sordid dramas. Doug Ford Sr. died on September 22, 2006, at the age of seventy-three—just weeks after his fiftieth wedding anniversary. He had been diagnosed with colon cancer on Canada Day, July 1, and deteriorated quickly. In his will, Doug Sr. made his wife and three sons equal trustees to the Ford estate. To Kathy, he left a million-dollar trust fund, which she could access with permission from her brothers and mother. The money was to be used to ensure her "comfortable maintenance."

Doug Ford Sr.'s funeral was held at Westway United Church in Etobicoke on a Friday afternoon.

A tearful Rob gave a tribute to his father, his "best buddy."

"I affectionately called him Scout, because Scout ran the ship," Rob said. "Sometimes the ship went to the right and sometimes the ship went to the left, but he always seemed to steer it back on course."

Doug Sr.'s niece Sherri Walker called her uncle "the General."

"Doug was never a soldier, but forever a warrior; a warrior in the true sense of the word in all he did," she said. "At the heart of this very complex man was an inner core of absolute, solid rock. The solid foundations he stuck by his entire life: family, integrity, kindness, honour, respect, humility, humour, tenacity and perseverance."

The funeral ended with mourners being asked to sing Doug Sr.'s favourite hymn, the "Battle Hymn of the Republic."

Mine eyes have seen the glory of the coming of the Lord;
He is trampling out the vintage where the grapes of wrath
*   are stored;*

He hath loosed the fateful lightning of His terrible swift
*   sword;*
His truth is marching on.

He was buried at Riverside Cemetery. Etched on his tombstone: "Of Those Who Are Called Few Are Chosen."

FOUR

COUNCILLOR FORD TO SPEAK

Rob Ford was twenty-six years old when he decided he wasn't interested in selling labels for a living. He wanted to be a politician. At the time, his father was a member of provincial parliament under the Progressive Conservative banner. The year was 1997, and PC premier Mike Harris was a year and a half into his Common Sense Revolution. It was a period of painful transition in the province. The Harris government was making aggressive changes to the way Ontario operated. Among other things, it had laid off more than ten thousand civil servants; changed labour laws to discourage workers from unionizing; passed "workfare" legislation, forcing welfare recipients to work for their cheques; and fought for environmental deregulation.

Harris had been upfront about his intentions during the 1995 election. During that campaign, the provincial deficit was around ten billion dollars. In his platform booklet, Harris had said, "If we are to fix the problems in this province then government has to be prepared to make some tough decisions. I'm not talking about tinkering, about incremental changes, or about short term solutions.... It's time to ask ourselves how government spending can double in the last ten years, while we seem to be getting less and less value for our tax money."

Part of that mission involved shrinking the size of government. Harris looked at Ontario's capital city and its surrounding suburbs and saw wasted money. There were too many politicians there, too many bureaucrats doing the same thing for a small geographic area. The premier decided to merge the seven local governments: Toronto, Etobicoke, North York, York, East York, Scarborough, and the regional municipality. His proposal was wildly unpopular. A March 1997 referendum showed that residents in each jurisdiction were overwhelmingly against the move, with opposition ranging from 65 to 81 percent. When the Conservatives passed it anyway, five of the six municipalities took the province to court. They lost. Toronto and its surrounding suburbs were set to join together on January 1, 1998. Toronto would become the fifth-largest city in North America.

The megacity's first council would be decided in the 1997 municipal election. Among the seven governments, there were 106 politicians. Ward boundaries were going to be redrawn, and the number of spots would be cut nearly in half to fifty-seven, including the mayor. To ease the transition, voters would be permitted to elect two representatives in each ward.

Ford decided to try his luck against Gloria Lindsay Luby and Mario Giansante—both sitting councillors—as well as the former mayor of Etobicoke, Dennis Flynn. "I remember hearing [Ford] was really ticked off that Dennis Flynn decided to run again," Lindsay Luby said. "He thought there'd only be the three of us in the campaign, and the odds of getting two out of three were better."

Ford was young and thinner back then, with a full head of blond hair. Even in his youth, Ford was always in a suit and tie. Lindsay Luby didn't know anything about Ford at the time. She doesn't remember debating him or even seeing him much. Giansante, on the other hand, was well acquainted with the Ford family. Both Giansante and Ford had their brothers running their campaigns.

"We're both business people and we met on the street and we got to know each other," said Giansante, a real estate broker. "I guess we sort of had an admiration for one another that worked out well."

Giansante says twenty-something Ford was a lot like forty-something Ford. He didn't change his mind once it was made up, and he saw the world in black and white. As a campaigner, he was a natural. "The showmanship is what really stuck out with me—and not just him, the whole family. The American way of politics." Ford's candidate signs were four feet high by eight feet wide, twice the size of everyone else's. He wasn't big on policy, but he was "flamboyant" and personable. And while Lindsay Luby and Giansante typically canvassed alone or with a few volunteers, Ford would door-knock with a full entourage.

The Fords and Giansantes struck up a bit of a friendship, sometimes sharing information and keeping an eye on each other's signs. Vandalism was a problem. Lindsay Luby, the lone woman in the race, experienced the most harassment. One morning, she looked outside and realized that one of the two stone Labradors at the end of her driveway had been stolen. A few days later a note arrived in the mail, written in cut-out magazine letters. "We have your dog. The ransom is 1000 dog biscuits."

Pictures started arriving showing the dog, in sunglasses and a hat, posed beside a recent edition of the newspaper. Another showed a masked, burly looking man in military garb holding a gun to its head. The next photo had the stone dog's head cut off. It had "what looked like fire burning around its head," Lindsay Luby recalled. The Lindsay Luby family was getting 3 A.M. calls from a Mississauga pay phone. Lindsay Luby went to the police, but no one was ever caught.

When the election ended, so did the harassment, and Lindsay Luby had won. Giansante was second. Flynn came in third. Ford was fourth.

Doug Ford Sr.'s old business partner, Ted Herriott, called the Ford family to offer his regrets.

"So, I guess he's done," Herriott remembered saying to Diane Ford.

"Oh, no, no, Robbie's a career politician."

THEY MET AT A RESTAURANT that doesn't exist anymore in an Etobicoke plaza. Doug Ford Jr. was already at the table when Gloria Lindsay Luby arrived. The conversation didn't last long. She can't remember if they even bothered ordering anything besides coffee.

This was in the early months of 2000, a municipal election year. Lindsay Luby didn't know the Fords very well, except that Doug Ford Sr. was in provincial politics and the youngest son, Rob, had run against her in 1997 and finished fourth. Doug Ford Jr. was his younger brother's campaign manager. She had no idea why he had asked to meet.

"We wanted to know," Doug Ford began, "if you'd be

interested in running in Ward 5. Then Rob can run in Ward 4 and you'll both win."

Lindsay Luby must have looked startled. Doug moved to phase two of his sales pitch. "We've done some polling, and you can win south of Dundas as well as north." And, of course, the Fords would help her with her campaign.

She had been a councillor in central Etobicoke since 1985. Now Doug Ford wanted her to step aside so his kid brother with no experience, whom she didn't even know, could get elected? "They thought they could be so persuasive," Lindsay Luby said, looking back on the conversation.

"Sorry," she told him, "I'm not going to run in another ward. I like my ward. And I don't need your help."

WITH THE 2000 ELECTION fast approaching, and Gloria Lindsay Luby refusing to budge, the Ford camp arranged a meeting with Mario Giansante. More changes were coming to the electoral landscape. Council was set to shrink again. Boundaries were rejigged to form forty-four wards—where it remains today—with one representative per ward, making for a much more competitive game. Now there would only be one seat up for grabs in Etobicoke Centre—in 1997 the ward was called Kingsway Humber—which councillors Lindsay Luby and Giansante currently shared.

"If both of us ran, we knew we didn't have a good chance against Gloria," Giansante said. "If we ran as opponents we'd split the vote and Gloria would win automatically."

So Ford went north to take on incumbent Elizabeth Brown and Giansante stayed back for a rematch with Lindsay Luby.

The *Star* called Ford's bid "a bit of a long-shot." Brown was well liked and was conservative, but her attendance had been spotty around City Hall. She explains that her marriage had been falling apart, then she'd suffered a car accident, and if that wasn't enough, the July before the election she broke her arm.

"Rob Ford actually coached my son's football team at Martingrove. He was the stereotype of a belligerent, bullying coach," Brown said, looking back on the election that changed her life. "To this day, people ask me, 'How did Rob Ford beat you?' They just don't get it."

By the 2000 election, the Ford brand had taken root in Etobicoke. Brown's ward overlapped with part of Doug Sr.'s old provincial riding, giving newbie Ford the name recognition of an incumbent. "People seemed to think that because it was a Ford running in their area, they should vote for him," Brown said. The Ford machine was overwhelming. According to Brown, Ford's campaign was one of the first to use telemarketing technology, something she couldn't afford. The youngest Ford was energetic and full of promises. If Brown hit a neighbourhood after Ford, she'd end up using her face time with voters to deliver bad news. "Rob's telling everybody he's going to put a bus down this street, and I keep telling them Rob has no control over that."

And then there was his secret weapon. Ford vowed to have the "strongest sign campaign in the city." A strong sign game "shows strength … popularity and it also shows that people want new leadership," he told a reporter at the time.

On November 4, the *Toronto Star* endorsed Rob Ford for council. "Ward 2 Etobicoke North: Incumbent Elizabeth Brown's heart is in the right place but she is too often missing in action. We suggest Rob Ford, a local businessman who is the son of former area MPP, Doug Ford."

Brown watched the results from the basement of a bar on Kipling Avenue: Rob Ford 5,750; Elizabeth Brown 4,122.

The three-term councillor quit politics. Ford was sworn in on December 4, 2000.

ROB FORD MIGHT BE A GENIUS—if not of the academic variety, certainly of the kind that matters in politics. He arrived at City Hall wanting to be mayor, and it wasn't dumb luck that delivered his 2010 win. Ford has a natural gift for reading the public mood. In his decade as a councillor, he would pick all the right fights. He knew what he could get away with and what issues stoked his base. Many people assume Ford is a loose cannon, firing at random, but it isn't easy to hit that many targets by accident. Ford seems to understand his intellectual shortcomings. Those close to him say he is aware that he comes across as boorish, a clumsy speaker, and incapable of sophisticated policy motions. So rather than play and lose, Ford changed the game. While the other forty-three councillors battled out their pecking order at City Hall, he spent his time in the ward meeting people. He didn't bother trying to win council votes. Getting an angry quote in the newspaper was the win. Ford knew that the only thing people would remember was that he fought with passion. He knew what he was—a populist stalwart conservative with blue-collar appeal—and he played to that hand. Some of his most controversial comments, particularly the ones with homophobic undercurrents, weren't always a slip of the tongue. Ford's base of voter support was socially conservative. He appeared to be playing for the camera, cultivating a persona, even if he wasn't consciously thinking about it. It seemed instinctive.

In January 2001, at one of Ford's first council meetings, the baby-faced thirty-one-year-old chastised his new colleagues for wasting their office budgets. "We don't have a revenue problem, we have a spending problem," he said, debuting a catchphrase he'd still be using as mayor.

Moments later, he was sparring with left-wing councillor Sandra Bussin after she made a crack about free business cards from a certain family printing company. Ford appeared furious. "If Councillor Bussin ever wants to go out and do what our family did for forty-five years and go out and create jobs which employ a hundred people and meet a payroll every week, she might understand the value of a dollar," Ford said. "[I was] brought up with the mentality that if I'm driving down the highway one day and I look over and see a Mercedes-Benz, I don't think the way some people think: 'Why does he or she have it and why not me?'"

Bussin demanded an apology. Ford refused. And council continued. Later, when the cash-strapped council debated what to do with the decrepit public square in front of City Hall, Ford chimed in, "We have to start today cutting back, not looking for expenditures…. Etobicoke people don't want tax increases. They want services but they don't want [us] squandering hard-earned tax dollars!"

By the time he became mayor, Ford had been repeating the same talking points for ten years. Taxes didn't need to go up. The politicians were wasting your money. Ford argued that he alone could take on the left. He was the one with private sector experience.

And it wasn't just Ford's rhetoric that caught the attention of voters. It was the delivery. The rookie councillor didn't speak his mind, he screamed it, sometimes flailing his arms and banging things, while his face turned redder and redder. His targets were diverse: the size of council, the spend-happy socialists, Toronto's squeegee kid program, unions, bike lanes, free food at council meetings, free parking passes for councillors, plant-watering in municipal offices. He once argued that money spent building suicide prevention barriers on a bridge would be better used catching child molesters, because child molesters were the main reason people jumped off bridges.

Less than four months into his term, Ford's rantings inspired a column at the *National Post* by Don Wanagas.

> What are the four words that people attending city council meetings most fear to hear these days?
>
> The answer: "Councillor Ford to speak."
>
> That's Councillor Ford as in Rob Ford. Young Mr. Ford (Ward 2—Etobicoke North) has only been hanging out at Toronto City Hall for a few months now, but he has already made quite a name for himself. Not for anything he has actually done, mind you. Ford's claim to fame are the outrageously incoherent speeches he likes to make expounding the supposed virtues of neo-Conservatism.

The tirade that inspired Wanagas's column was a soliloquy that meandered between bureaucratic red tape, special interest groups, and the Walkerton water crisis. It ended with Councillor Joe Pantalone shouting, "Prozac, get some Prozac!"

Ambitious politicians usually speak with an irritating amount of caution, fearful that a misplaced word could headline a future attack ad. Ford was clearly ambitious, but he didn't seem interested in following the traditional path to becoming more electable. It was as if he knew that as long as he was consistent, he could be himself. How many times could the press write "Rob Ford said something crazy yesterday" before it looked like they were picking on him?

During his ten years as a city councillor, Ford amassed an extensive archive of politically incorrect quotable quotes which individually could have done in other politicians with their eye on the top job. And he did it during the advent of the YouTube age. In his first year on council, he advocated the environmentally unfriendly position of burning garbage. In 2003, he said, "Homelessness is a cancer. What you're trying to do is spread the cancer across the city." In 2003, he flipped out on Toronto Zoo board chair Giorgio Mammoliti, screaming so loudly that the council speaker threatened to have him removed. "You slithering snake!" Ford shouted. "I know he's a weasel and weasels and snakes belong in the zoo!" He went after his former political opponent and now colleague Councillor Lindsay Luby in 2005, calling her a "waste of skin" and a "lowlife." Then, in 2007, he suggested that cyclists killed on Toronto's roads were asking for it. "Roads are built for buses, cars, and trucks. Not for people on bikes. And, you know, my heart bleeds for them when I hear someone gets killed, but it's their own fault at the end of the day." The remark made headlines, but few were surprised. Ford was not known for his sympathy.

When city council was considering a new harm-reduction drug strategy that would give so-called "crack kits" to drug addicts to help prevent the spread of disease, Ford was harsh in his denunciation. "You're not helping them, you're enabling them," he said. "They're going to smoke that crack whether you give them those crack pipes or not. They're going to shoot that heroin whether you give them clean needles or not. If people want a change, it has to come from within." The Etobicoke councillor added that "tough love" was the only way to deal with drug use.

And then there were the diatribes that veered into homophobic and sometimes racist territory. Of transgendered people, Ford has said, "I don't understand: is it a guy dressed up like a girl or a girl dressed up like a guy?" In 2001, he said it would be "absolutely disgusting" if council helped fund a documentary on gay South Asians. The next year, according to numerous people, Ford was overheard calling Mammoliti a "Gino boy," though he denied making the slur. In 2003, after a male colleague suggested Ford kiss his butt, the Etobicoke councillor shot back, "I believe in Adam and Eve. Not Adam and Steve." Most infamously, in 2006, Ford erroneously stated, "If you're not doing needles and you're not gay, you won't get AIDS, probably." And then, in 2008, while trying to pay a compliment to the work ethic of the Asian community, Ford said, "Those Oriental people work like dogs.... They sleep beside their machines.... The Oriental people, they're slowly taking over."

The comments would always make the news, and sometimes Ford would apologize and sometimes not. For the most part, the public was forgiving, even sympathetic, towards the Etobicoke councillor who was always getting in trouble for saying the wrong thing.

Regular rules don't apply to Ford—which is a good thing, because Ford never cared much for following the rules. He has been officially reprimanded half a dozen times for violating city policy or council's Code of Conduct. Most of Ford's transgressions involve inappropriately leveraging his influence as a councillor—such as when he included his councillor business card in a promotional package for Deco Labels and then distributed the material to members of provincial parliament. But Ford has also been scolded by the integrity commissioner for divulging confidential information about city business on talk radio, wrongly accusing a colleague of unethical practices, and using city resources for personal reasons. On more than one occasion, Ford's temper nearly got him turfed from the council chamber. And the Etobicoke councillor was frequently in trouble with colleagues—especially right-wingers—for skipping afternoon council meetings to coach a high school football team. In 2001, Ford didn't show up for a debate about a new recycling plan, and in 2003 he missed a vote about contracting out cleaning services with the Toronto police. His absence caused a tie, which meant the issue was dead. (As a mayoral candidate, Ford would campaign in favour of this very issue, saying it would save five million dollars.)

Councillor Ford was unrepentant.

In 2006, Ford told Toronto columnist Ed Keenan, "I get criticized a lot, because from September and October every day from three o'clock to five o'clock I'm on the football field. And it drives people nuts. They're like, 'You're leaving council to coach football.' And you know what? I do. I do leave council to coach football for two hours a day and I come right back to council.... My constituents know it, they agree one hundred percent. These kids, it's unbelievable where they come from. But they're playing football, they aren't getting into trouble. A lot of them have been in and out of jail, a lot of them are in gangs, but they're athletes. And if you give them an opportunity to play football ... then it's phenomenal, that they go to university. Because I'm very, very strict. If they don't have a 60 average, they don't play."

Even on the football field, Ford was known for causing trouble. Following the 2001 season, Ford was removed from his volunteer position at Newtonbrook Secondary School in North York after a heated altercation with a player after the teen messed up a play. The chemistry on the team "wasn't great" to begin with, said the school's former head of physical education, John Giuga, who asked Ford to step aside. Ford was already embroiled in a very public feud with school leadership over which division the boys were in. Ford had wanted his charges to compete at a higher level. In 2002, he started coaching at Don Bosco Catholic Secondary School in Etobicoke, and controversy followed him. Two years after he took over the Don Bosco Eagles, the senior squad was forced to drop out midway through the playoffs because Ford had dressed two ineligible players. Nonetheless, the school kept him on. In November 2012, Ford took his team all the way to the Metro Bowl championship but lost. Six months later, the Toronto District Catholic School Board banned Ford from coaching at any of their schools. The decision wasn't related to the festering crack cocaine scandal, officials claimed. Rather, it was the result of an investigation launched by the board after Ford went on Sun News and claimed that many of his players came "from gangs" and "broken homes." This upset many parents and teachers. On previous occasions, Ford had boasted that some of his players would be "dead or in jail" if not for his help.

Oddly enough, it was Ford's private football foundation—which he created in 2008 to help schools start football
teams—that landed him in the most trouble. It all started after
amalgamation, when the city had signed a $43-million contract
for computer equipment with a company called MFP Financial
Services. The costs nearly doubled without council's authoriz-
ation, and an inquiry concluded that improper relationships
between lobbyists and public officials were partly to blame. In
2004, as part of the fallout from the MFP scandal, Toronto
created an "integrity commissioner" position. The commissioner's job was to police councillors' conduct, and the newly
appointed David Mullan took his job seriously.

Ford first dealt with Mullan's wrath in 2005, after he tried to
market the Deco family business to provincial politicians while
highlighting his position as a city councillor. Ford was warned
about mixing business with politics, but the message didn't
stick. In November 2009, a member of the public informally
complained when they received a letter from Councillor Ford
asking for football charity donations accompanied by a Rob
Ford fridge magnet, a sticker from Deco, and the councillor's
city business card. The integrity commissioner, now Janet Leiper,
gave Ford a warning in December 2009. When the issue arose
again in February 2010, she cautioned him once more. Again, he
didn't listen. In May, a Toronto resident filed a formal complaint
after receiving a donation request for Ford's football foundation
on city letterhead. An investigation revealed something more
troubling than improper use of stationery: Ford was soliciting
donations from eleven active lobbyist firms or their clients, seven
of which had either lobbied or registered to lobby the Etobicoke
councillor.

It was exactly the kind of thing that led to the creation of the integrity commissioner position in the first place. On August 25, 2010, on the advice of Integrity Commissioner Leiper, city council ordered Councillor Ford to repay $3,150 in lobbyist donations. He ignored the demand, an act of defiance that would lead him to a legal precipice and nearly cost him his job as mayor.

THROUGHOUT HIS DECADE as a councillor, Rob Ford never cared what anyone at City Hall thought of him. Instead, he was out earning the admiration of his constituents. He toured subsidized housing. He gave out his cell phone number to anyone who would take it. For the first time ever, residents could get their local councillor—not someone in their office—on the phone. In most areas of Toronto, a councillor's assistant would take that call, forward the issue to city staff for investigation, and then the problem would get added to the heavily backlogged capital repair plan. Maybe a bureaucrat would schedule a band-aid solution a few months down the road, but maybe not. "With Rob, they would call, and he'd say, 'How's next Thursday,' then have the guy from public works at your door," said a staffer from Ford's council days.

Why city staff went along with this is hard to know. Ford built relationships with some. Others recognized him as a guy who wanted to help. The former Ford staffer quoted above theorized that it might have been a strategic decision for some city bureaucrats. Councillor Ford was clearly ambitious, and he made no secret of the fact that he intended to run for mayor one day. At Toronto City Hall, the Public Service reports to the city manager, not the mayor. However, the city manager and his deputy managers can all be fired by council. And under usual circumstances, council tends to back the mayor.

Ford Nation was built on those house calls. Through his constituent work as a councillor, Ford spent a decade recruiting volunteers and donors for the 2010 election. Every house he visited, every person he made feel important—whether he addressed their issue or not—became a walking campaign ad, loyal for life.

Soon, news of Ford's first-class constituent work got around Toronto, and he began getting calls from residents living outside Ward 2 Etobicoke North, to the immense annoyance of other councillors. There had always been an unspoken code to stay off each other's turf, but Ford didn't care about that. He helped people in Scarborough and North York and downtown Toronto with the same vigour as he did his own residents. Councillors grumbled and complained. Councillor Karen Stintz recalled the time a resident in her ward had an issue with a neighbour's property where no bylaws were being violated and nothing could be done about it. Stintz's office had a file an inch thick on the issue and had spent months trying to find a compromise. "But it was like they wouldn't accept our answer until Rob Ford said the same thing," she said. Resentment snowballed. Eventually, a handful of councillors decided they needed to do something about Ford's meddling. It backfired on them in spectacular fashion.

It was February 2005. A fed-up council asked the integrity commissioner to review whether it was appropriate for councillors to intervene in matters outside their wards. Ford's critics didn't get the answer they were hoping for. In September, Integrity Commissioner Mullan concluded that there was "no compelling reason" to ban councillors from helping in other jurisdictions. The idea that a councillor's ward was his or her own "personal fiefdom" was "unhealthy." Mullan also raised the point that some constituents might not find a "friendly or sympathetic ear" in their own representative, perhaps because of political differences. Worse, for Ford's opponents, the move came across as petty. It was as if they were accusing Ford of working too hard.

Ultimately, it was Ford's reputation as the topmost tightwad that would come to define him. Even as a first-term rookie, his miserly ways made him one of the most talked-about councillors at City Hall. Six months into his first term, Ford had spent just ten dollars of his annual $53,100 office budget. Contrasted with Giorgio Mammoliti's tab of $43,150, it made for a good news story, again to the immense annoyance of other councillors. Said budget chief David Shiner, "I don't understand how you can be communicating and really keeping in touch with your community for ten dollars." The media did Ford's communicating for him. Every year, the annual expense reports would come out, and every year Ford's refusal to spend tax dollars made the front page. Ford upped the ante when he started posting his colleagues' expenses on his website in chart form, with columns for tickets and donations, food and drink, promotion and taxis, as well as "office." There were zeros across the board for Ford. He delighted in finding items like "espresso machine" and "bunny suit" (for an Easter parade) among his colleagues' receipts. In reality, it was not that Ford wasn't spending money to run his office, he just wasn't spending tax dollars. Ford, unlike most of his colleagues, was a millionaire. He used his own cash. The public didn't care about that nuance. They ate up the sentiment.

"The *Sun* and the *Star* made him," Councillor Doug Holyday said. Before Ford came along, Holyday had always been crowned council's lowest spender, usually billing around $1,500 on basic essentials like paper, pens, and stamps. "These were legitimate expenses," said Holyday. "Ford pays for them all himself. He built a reputation on it. For that $1,500, Ford was buying publicity. It got even worse when councillors started grandstanding about it."

Whenever the office expense debate flared up—which was often—councillors would attack Ford for his low numbers while defending their own purchases. The years-long dispute came to a head in 2007 when council ordered the integrity commissioner to investigate how it was possible for Ford and Holyday to spend so little. "You know what?" Ford told reporters. "I don't know. This is how stupid this council can be." Ford was open about the fact that he was buying his own printer toner and stamps, as well as spending "thousands" on an annual backyard barbecue for constituents. Councillors wanted those expenditures tracked. Councillor Pam McConnell said there needed to be a "level playing field" between regular councillors and independently wealthy ones. Later that year, the city's auditor and the integrity commissioner released a joint report concluding that councillors must disclose their expenses, even if the money was coming out of their own pocket. Holyday was pleased. "That's so a councillor can't spend a small fortune running their office just because they happen to have a small fortune, to make themselves look good politically," he said at the time. Ford mostly ignored the edict.

In 2009, Ford reported spending just $708 of his own money on folders, toner, calendar pads, and a few other items, leaving significant gaps in supplies you'd usually expect an office to need. City council eventually passed a number of restrictions about expense accounts, largely thanks to years of pressure and shaming from Ford. In 2008, councillors agreed to cap their annual restaurant bill at five hundred dollars, not to charge taxpayers for alcoholic beverages, and to post their expenses online on a quarterly basis. (Even as mayor, Ford still didn't disclose all his office expenses, and neither did Doug Ford once he became a councillor. In 2011, Toronto activist Jude MacDonald complained about this to the integrity commissioner. Ford was cleared after he sent in the missing invoices. He blamed delays processing invoices and staff turnover.)

Looking back, Sandra Bussin thinks that this was the issue that made him. "Even then, I thought that the general public would say, 'Well, if he doesn't want to spend it, that's great.' I think that put a huge spotlight on him as this great guy, working hard without spending their money."

THE FIRST SIGN that something serious was happening behind the scenes in the Ford family came in March 2005, when Rob's sister, Kathy, was shot in the head. The shocking story was reported across the country.

Three years later, Ford was charged with assault and uttering a death threat against his wife. His lawyer, Dennis Morris, accused Renata of making up the allegations. On March 25, 2008, Morris said the councillor had come home to a "torrent of verbal abuse," and when Ford refused to do something Renata asked him to do, someone from the home called 911. Ford took the couple's two young children to his mother's home nearby.

The public's reaction was a mix of sympathy, suspicion, and morbid interest. "Now that there is nothing funny about the story of Councillor Rob Ford, every detail of his sickening slide becomes simply awful," wrote John Barber, a columnist with *The Globe and Mail.* Barber noted the distasteful optics of Ford "blandly carrying on business as usual while his lawyer goes on television to denounce the 'irrational behaviour' of the woman he allegedly threatened to kill…. Recent events confirm that the Rob Ford farce is the public face of personal tragedy. Watching is ghoulish, not watching impossible."

I was an intern at the *Toronto Star* at the time. The assignment editor sent me to try to find Renata. I started at the house. Renata's mother, Henryka Brejniak, answered the door. She let me inside. It didn't look like the home of a wealthy man. There were toys and clutter everywhere. The decor looked tired. I asked if Renata was home. Brejniak didn't speak much English. She said her daughter was "getting help" at the doctor's. I asked if she was hurt. Brejniak just said she was "okay." Could I speak with her, to hear her version of what happened? "There's no way she can talk, give her side. She's so upset."

Ford later spoke to reporters with his daughter, Stephanie, in his arms, urging the toddler to say "no comment."

In May 2008, prosecutor Leanne Townsend said she was withdrawing the charges against Ford due to "some serious issues" and inconsistencies in Renata's testimony. Outside the courthouse, Ford said, "I'm just glad this is over," and that he was "glad to be back with my family." He said they were in counselling, doing "whatever it takes."

Once the charges were dropped, the media backed away

from the story. It became apparent that Rob and Renata Ford were dealing with some messy family problems.

With each drama, the public appeared generally willing to give Ford the benefit of the doubt. This had been the case back in 2006, after one of Ford's most egregious missteps. It was April 15, Saturday night at the Air Canada Centre, and the Toronto Maple Leafs were playing the Ottawa Senators. Ford was sitting behind Dan and Rebecca Hope, who were in town visiting from Enniskillen, a hamlet just outside the city. According to the couple, with less than ten minutes left in the third period, the "rather large gentleman" behind them was "becoming extremely loud and obnoxious." He was standing up, waving his arms, and shouting. They particularly remember him yelling, "My sister was a heroin addict and was shot in the head." The Hopes wrote a detailed account of the night to Toronto's city clerk.

> The gentleman continued on in an extremely loud way with his belligerence and obscenities to the point where I turned and calmly asked him to "tone it down a little." He responded, again in an extremely loud way with a verbal assault on me personally. "Who the fuck do you think you are? Are you some kind of right wing commy [*sic*] bastard?" Fearing that the situation would escalate further, I did my best to avoid any conversation and/or eye contact with the gentleman. At one point he shouted the following question at my wife and I, "Do you want your little wife to go over to Iran and get raped and shot" and continued on with other extremely asinine comments.

Security guards eventually removed Ford. The Hopes turned to two men sitting behind them to see if they knew the screaming guy's name. It turned out that Ford had been doling out his city business card. The Hopes went to the City of Toronto website to find Rob Ford's picture. It was him.

When first confronted with the allegations, Ford accused the couple of lying. "This is unbelievable, I wasn't even at the game. So someone's trying to do a real hatchet job on me." The next day, he came clean. Ford told reporters he had lied because he was "completely embarrassed and humiliated about the whole situation."

"I'm going through a few personal problems, but it doesn't justify, you know, getting drunk in public and pretty well acting like an idiot if you ask me," he said. "I was inebriated. I'm not a heavy drinker at all. I guess it hit me pretty hard and it was an unfortunate situation."

The public humiliation didn't hurt Ford with his constituents.

In November 2006, Ford was re-elected in Ward 2 Etobicoke North with 66 percent of the vote. It was just two months after his father had died of cancer.

According to those close to him, this was the moment when things changed—for the whole family. The authoritarian figure was gone. The boys had lost their hero.

Ford would come home at night and drink himself into another world. He sometimes used hard drugs or prescription pills.

Soon, Ford was spending time at Kathy's home, which is just around the corner from the Royal York Plaza and his mother's house. Some old family friends tried to warn him to stop, but he refused to listen. He was increasingly isolating himself from positive influences. This seems to be the period when Ford transitioned to using crack cocaine, although his drug of choice continued to be alcohol.

A convicted heroin dealer who used to sell to Kathy Ford recalls partying one time with her baby brother in a grungy hotel not far from the soon-to-be-mayor's Etobicoke home.

"He didn't like that I was there. He was with a few guys he'd known for years," said the man. "Rob doesn't like strangers."

A MYTHOLOGY ABOUT Rob Ford had taken shape. Average citizens didn't follow the daily dramas in City Hall back then. People didn't know councillors' names, and they knew even less about what any of them stood for. Yet year by year, Ford was able to build a profile for himself. Rob Ford? Wasn't that the guy who never spent any money and sometimes got in trouble? Partway through his career as councillor, Ford landed a Thursday-morning radio segment on AM640's *John Oakley Show* called "What's Eating Rob Ford?" The show gave him unfiltered access to voters, and he used his airtime to slam enemies and promote his work. Ford was controversial, he was shaking things up, and to many that was refreshing.

In a 2004 interview with the *Hamilton Spectator*'s Bill Dunphy, Ford reflected on his early years as a councillor. Dunphy did the interview at the Etobicoke Civic Centre, which Ford sometimes used as a free meeting space.

"I was the laughingstock for the first while," Ford told him. "I got hammered in the papers pretty bad. I got hammered on TV a few times, because of my antics. Did I deserve it? I probably did.... They were out to get me, they got personal. They made fun of my weight, it bothered me, deep down. I sort of flew off the handle a few times, I just lost my temper at council … I just got so mad." Ford said it was "a lonely time. It still is."

The article recounted an incident in which Ford, on being ruthlessly heckled by his colleagues on council, had stood up and bellowed, "Mark my words!," hitting the desk over and over. "Mark my frigging words, I'll be mayor one day."

Everyone had laughed.

"They thought that was hilarious," Ford said. "Anything can happen. In football or politics, upsets happen all the time. You just try your best, let loose with a Hail Mary and you know what? A lot of Hail Mary passes get caught."

Ford would seriously consider running for mayor in 2006, but the climate wasn't right. Torontonians were happy with the job David Miller was doing. Miller—a devoted environment-alist who as a councillor had represented a ward in the core of Toronto—had been elected three years earlier with a broom in hand, vowing to sweep out corruption. It was a time when the MFP computer leasing scandal was still fresh in voters' minds. Miller spent his freshman term as mayor creating accountability safeguards such as the integrity commissioner's office, working to beautify the city's waterfront, and investing in public transit. There were still plenty of left–right squabbles at City Hall over issues like spending, garbage collection, and the future of the rapidly deteriorating Gardiner Expressway, one of Toronto's most important roadways, but for the most part Miller's first three years lacked the kind of lightning-rod issues that garnered much public attention. Miller was a safe choice. The only person willing to take him on in 2006 was an unknown right-winger from East York, Councillor Jane Pitfield. Late in the mayoral race, Stephen LeDrew, former president of the Liberal Party of Canada and future CP24 news anchor, added his name to the ballot. For Miller, it was a cakewalk. He finished with 332,969 votes; Pitfield with 188,932; and LeDrew with 8,078.

By 2010, things had changed. Now the recession, not the MFP scandal, was top of mind. People were looking hard at how their tax dollars were being spent, and they didn't like what they saw. Sole-sourced contracts. Out-of-control expense accounts. Rising taxes. The deathblow for Miller came in the summer of 2009, when he led Toronto into a smelly thirty-nine-day garbage strike. The outdoor workers had walked off the job after the Miller administration went after their union's expensive practice of banking unused sick leave. City parks were turned into temporary dumps. Torontonians were willing to endure the trash if it meant abolishing this extravagant union perk, but then the city caved, opting for a compromise. The "sick bank" would be phased out over many years. It was a significant concession, but after a summer of living in a garbage dump, residents weren't in the mood for middle ground. Miller was already on thin ice with voters. Midway through his second term, he had introduced two unpopular new taxes: the vehicle registration tax—a bill that arrived every year on your birthday—and the land transfer tax. There was a feeling that City Hall was out of touch and wasting money. Miller announced he wouldn't run again.

In January 2010, the Fords commissioned a poll.

The numbers showed that Rob Ford was the third-place choice for mayor. He saw an opening and made a run for that Hail Mary.

FIVE

THE GRAVY TRAIN

Nick Kouvalis pulled into the parking lot at Deco Labels & Tags in Etobicoke unsure of what to expect. He had never met Rob Ford. In fact, until a few weeks earlier, he'd never heard of him. But Kouvalis's business partner, Richard Ciano, had gotten roped into joining the councillor's mayoral campaign by a mutual friend of the Ford family. Ciano and Kouvalis, both in their mid-thirties, owned a political consulting firm called Campaign Research, which specialized in polling, voter identification, and strategy. The Fords wanted them to put together a campaign plan. Ciano had warned Kouvalis that they were in fact dealing with the Fords, plural. Brother Doug was the campaign manager, and he was very, uh, opinionated.

Ciano took Kouvalis through the sales office entrance and up to the second-floor boardroom. There was a wall of windows, a long grey table, some simple chairs, and a whiteboard. It was all very plain. The candidate stomped through the doors in an old black suit, a crooked collar, and a tacky red tie. He was big, nearly as big as Kouvalis had been before losing 180 pounds. "Hey, buddy, nice to meet you," Ford said, extending a hand. "Listen, I just want to let you know, I'm not going to tolerate any cancer on my team." A startled Kouvalis wondered, That's how you greet people? When Ford was out of earshot, he turned to Ciano. "How much are these guys into us for, and when are we getting paid?"

Next, Kouvalis met the brother, who was a slicker, thinner version of Ford. The team was small, maybe ten people. Most didn't seem to have much political expertise. As far as Kouvalis could tell, the majority were just friends of the family. After some obligatory go-team sabre-rattling, Kouvalis got down to business. Where were they with fundraising? What policies were they promoting? He was greeted with blank stares.

Looking back at that first meeting still makes Kouvalis chuckle. "We were there to talk about the campaign and what it would be like. They were talking about door-knocking. They were talking about the lefties and the socialists, the Republican Party and the Tea Party, and their friends in the States who gave them advice. And I was trying to understand the policies."

Despite the rhetoric and shabby suit, Kouvalis liked Ford. They had a lot in common, especially politically. Ford wanted to make the Toronto Transit Commission an essential service, because two years earlier chaos had reigned when the union went on strike. He wanted to cut the size of council in half, because there were forty-four municipal wards and only twenty-two provincial ridings. It would save millions. Ford said the size and cost of the public sector had exploded under Mayor Miller, who was a lefty-socialist who cared only about downtown Toronto. Ford wanted to cut the waste at City Hall.

Kouvalis bought the message, but he wasn't sure how they could win. "They just didn't strike me as normal political candidate types," he said. "I didn't realize, at that moment, that that's exactly the campaign we were going to be running: the anti-establishment campaign."

THE CAMPAIGN THAT Kouvalis and Ciano inherited on April 1, 2010, wasn't really a campaign. Several people involved at the time described it to me as "a train wreck." The Fords had done little more than register a website, make a bunch of T-shirts, and print a few hundred "Ford for Mayor" placards. There was no policy. No platform. No budget. No message. No fundraising strategy. No battle plan. And no real understanding about why that was a problem.

Kouvalis and Ciano needed a team. They recruited a twenty-four-year-old keener named Fraser Macdonald to handle communications. After graduating from Queen's University, Macdonald had gone to work with Ciano at the Manning Centre, a conservative think tank founded by former Reform Party leader Preston Manning. Macdonald was ambitious, smart, and willing to work for peanuts, which is what the Fords were willing to pay.

Mark Towhey was one of the original staffers who had tangible experience. Towhey, a former infantry captain who had moved into the private sector at a crisis management consulting firm, was a long-time staple in Etobicoke conservative circles. Kouvalis and Ciano put him in charge of policy.

Roman Gawur, another Etobicoke conservative, was also assigned to help with policy. His wife and daughter signed up too. Liz ran the office, and young Stephanie became Kouvalis's assistant. Gawur was eventually put in charge of sifting through all the councillor candidates in every ward, pulling out those who would be most likely to vote with Ford. Then they would endorse them, sometimes helping out with signs and strategy. The Fords were essentially trying to put together a slate of like-minded councillors to get around the fact that the mayor had only one vote. It was a new concept in Toronto municipal elections.

Rounding out the early talent was data analyst Mitch Wexler, a political veteran who'd been a Queen's Park staffer during the Mike Harris government and had a résumé stacked with federal, provincial, and municipal campaign experience. As a member of Team Ford, Wexler was to build a voter database. Ford had spent a decade telling people to call him personally if they ever needed anything. And they did. At the end of each day, Ford would get a sheet of blank printer paper and write down every missed call. After returning each one, he'd toss it in a cardboard box. When that box filled up, it would get stashed in a corner. Kouvalis shipped four of these fifteen-pound boxes to his call centre in Windsor, and one of his employees spent two weeks punching the numbers into a spreadsheet. Wexler's job was to extract the value from that gold mine. He logged the numbers into a telemarketing program, and through automated phone polls he built a profile of each voter. If the election were held tomorrow, would they vote for Rob Ford? If yes, did they want a lawn sign? How about volunteering? Perhaps a donation? It could all be done at the push of a button.

Kouvalis and Ciano tackled the organizational charts. The campaign needed a fundraising arm, a communications arm, and a leadership structure. They needed a platform. Kouvalis looked to the voter data. People were unhappy. Transit was one of the biggest issues, and several of Ford's competitors had honed in on it, thinking it a vote-winner. Kouvalis saw something different.

He saw a common theme in the issues. Complaints about unions, potholes, high taxes, congestion, those fancy espresso machines, all suggested one thing: frustration with the way the city wasted money on frills. "The gravy train" was a term Ford had used as a councillor to symbolize this waste, and it resonated with focus groups. It meant something to everyone. There were far more votes to be won by stopping the gravy train than by fixing transit. It would be victory by a thousand cuts.

"Rob won for all sorts of reasons, but this was really important," said Stefano Pileggi, the Ford campaign's fundraising manager. "Nick read the data right where the other campaigns didn't."

Avoiding the transit issue—besides the occasional rant about ripping up streetcar tracks—had another benefit. Ford did not do well in intellectual debates. That wasn't his forte. He was the dark horse, the everyman's man. He wasn't going to talk down to you, or pull that politician's thing of confusing you with stuff like "monetizing assets" or "revenue tools." Straight talk was part of his brand.

The campaign crafted a simple three-point platform. Rob Ford would "stop the waste" by halving the size of council from forty-four seats to twenty-two and slashing councillors' expense accounts. He would "make Toronto a better place to live" by contracting out garbage collection, hiring more police officers, improving customer service at City Hall, and making it illegal for transit workers to strike. Finally, he would "cut unnecessary taxes" by abolishing David Miller's land transfer tax and the vehicle registration tax.

With a framework in place, the next challenge was their candidate.

Ford came with baggage. His ten years in public life had produced an arsenal of attack ad material. The trick was figuring out a way to neutralize his past. "We knew the mainstream media was going to question him harshly. We had to turn it around," Macdonald said. First, Kouvalis and Ciano sat their candidate down for a grilling. Was there anything else about him they needed to know? Any skeletons the campaign should prepare for? Ford was adamant: absolutely not. So the team built a strategy to deal with what was already out there. They felt that all of it—the domestic assault charge, the incident at the Maple Leafs game, the AIDS comment, the comment that "Oriental people work like dogs"—was manageable. If questions came up, Ford would reiterate that he never claimed to be perfect, then turn the conversation back to the gravy train. In fact, no matter what was being asked, Ford's answer was "gravy train."

And the best way to handle unwanted questions from reporters? Avoid the reporters! Ford's team devised a media strategy that sidestepped big news outlets. Kouvalis and Ciano were among the first to use phone-in town-hall forums in a major Canadian election. This emerging technology, popularized in the United States, allowed candidates to take questions from—and speak directly to—thousands of voters all at once, away from the glare of the media. For an unpredictable candidate like Ford, it was an invaluable secret weapon. Campaign staff got to screen which questions made it through to the candidate. Even when they tossed him a curveball—and it was a good place for Ford to practise answering the tough ones—the odds of a reporter being on the line to hear a stumble were slim.

Ford's team started working on the candidate's public-speaking skills. He needed to sound less angry, more in control and reasoned, to show voters he was a leader, not a critic in opposition. His staff gave him talking points to memorize, then techniques to redirect questions back to those key messages. In the safety of a boardroom, Ford did well. But in real-life interviews, he was still easily knocked off script. Sometimes with embarrassing consequences.

Three weeks into the campaign, in a *Toronto Sun* interview, Ford was asked about the domestic assault incident with his wife. "I'm glad you asked me about that," he told columnist Michele Mandel. "I came home one night. She was drunk, and she said, 'If you fucking touch the kids, I'll call the cops and say you hit me.' … I have never laid a hand on a woman in my life." Mandel asked if Ford had ever considered divorce. "I don't bail on people who make mistakes. I've been married 10 years. Is it perfect? No, but we have two beautiful kids … and she supports me."

A senior campaign staffer phoned Ford the morning the *Sun* profile appeared. "We need to think about what kind of information we share with the media. If somebody asks you about private stuff, asks about your family, just say, 'I've said what I'm going to say on that,'" the staffer told him. To the relief of the campaign, there was zero reaction to the story.

Ford had never before been politically coached. He and his family bridled at the control. Macdonald would write speeches that Ford wouldn't read. Doug Ford spent money without asking. He showed up one morning in a giant Winnebago—the Fordmobile—slathered in campaign decals.

The brothers, for their part, struggled with the concept of a city-wide campaign. They knew how to run a campaign in Ward 2 Etobicoke North, which had about 55,000 residents, and to an extent Etobicoke Centre—the provincial riding where Doug

Ford Sr. was forced out in the nomination process in 1999—with its population of about 111,000. But a mayoral bid was an entirely different beast. No political candidate in Canada, at any level, had to win more individual votes than a candidate running for mayor of Toronto. At the provincial and federal levels, people voted once in their own riding for a local member of parliament. In the 2008 federal election, for example, only 38,548 people voted directly for the prime minister of Canada. No one outside of Stephen Harper's Calgary Southwest electoral district even saw Harper's name on a ballot. Premiers and the prime minister were determined based on which party won the most seats.

For this reason, a mayoral race in Toronto was much more like an American gubernatorial or senate race, where voters elected individuals, not parties. And in Toronto, there were 1.5 million votes up for grabs. Yet in the 2010 municipal election, the Fords kept trying to organize door-knocking blitzes, as if they were still campaigning in a small ward race.

"It would help with the area in terms of visibility, but not the bigger goal we were trying to achieve," Wexler said. Worse, the Fords would plan time-consuming canvassing missions without consulting staff. This caused last-minute scrambling and stretched resources, and resulted in higher-priority events getting sidelined.

At one point, staff called in Ford's mother, Diane. She was the only one who could get through to him. According to someone in the room, she turned to her youngest son and said, "You're being ridiculous. Listen to these people, they know what they're doing."

Ford was learning fast, but brother Doug was still interfering. He would often gripe about not being included on the campaign's press releases, "because people are voting for the Ford family brand and the Ford brand is not just Rob." (A few months later, Doug Ford announced that he too would be on the ballot, vying for his brother's vacated Ward 2 seat.)

The campaign antics were too much for Ciano. He quit in May. Kouvalis would steer the ship solo.

NICK KOUVALIS HAS A LOT of enemies. He's built a career in business and in politics with a win-at-all-cost mantra. Standing six feet two with broad shoulders, Kouvalis cuts an imposing figure, although it would be much more intimidating if he didn't always slouch. He's Greek, with olive skin, jet black hair, which he keeps short, and a perfectly manicured goatee. Always well dressed, he takes pride in his appearance, because before Kouvalis became the shrewd strategizer behind Rob Ford, he was a poor fat kid growing up in public housing in Windsor, Ontario.

After a lacklustre academic record, Kouvalis worked blue-collar jobs, eventually landing on the Chrysler assembly line. It wasn't the life for him. When the workday was done, Kouvalis would come home and start planning his escape. He didn't want to spend his life making money for someone else. First, he tried running an electronic sales and repair company. After it failed, he launched a car service. The business showed promise, but Kouvalis was having trouble getting the right kind of insurance. A friend recommended he start associating with some local politicians to see if they could help speed things along. So, in November 2003, he joined the federal Conservative Party. In politics, he found his calling.

Kouvalis started out selling party memberships. He was really good at it. He volunteered with Belinda Stronach's leadership campaign. ("I was new. I didn't know any better," he jokes now.) He thought the plotting, the twists and turns, of politics was fun. He wanted to do it for a living. He dug through campaign financial records and was astonished at how much money was being spent on phone work such as polling and get-out-the-vote calls. He opened a call centre out of his living room with some cheap VoIP (Voice over Internet Protocol) technology. The more work he did with the Conservative Party, the more business came his way.

Kouvalis met his future mentor and business partner, Richard Ciano, during the 2004 federal election. Ciano was managing Peter Van Loan's federal campaign, and Kouvalis was the campaign manager for Jeff Watson, who was running in the riding of Essex, outside Windsor. Kouvalis's and Ciano's candidates both won.

Even in those early days, Kouvalis attracted controversy. Despite his win, Watson had a falling-out with Kouvalis that got personal fast. In the next election, Kouvalis went to work in a neighbouring riding for another Conservative candidate. Hostilities with Watson escalated. In a dramatic climax, Kouvalis was charged in the summer of 2005 with threatening to kill Watson. A year and a half later, he was acquitted. Justice Lloyd Dean said he was "troubled" by evidence that the charges might have been politically motivated.

Kouvalis didn't hold a grudge. Politics was a dirty sport.

Such a combative background meant Kouvalis was well-suited to running Rob Ford's mayoral campaign and trying to control the formidable Doug. He wasn't afraid to say no to the older Ford brother, or threaten to resign if the pushback continued. Once Richard Ciano stepped aside, Kouvalis packed his suitcase and moved into the Deco office. The Fords put him up in an empty room above the factory floor. It had a mattress, an ironing board, a lamp, and little else. He would shower with the factory workers. This would be his home for the next six months. The Fords are cheap, but Kouvalis didn't mind if it meant saving the campaign a buck or two.

Despite the internal campaign hiccups, Ford was doing well with the public. In mid-April, just weeks after declaring his candidacy, he was sitting in second place. A *Toronto Star*–Angus Reid poll put George Smitherman at 34 percent, Ford at 27 percent, and Deputy Mayor Joe Pantalone at 14 percent. The surge caught the competition off guard. During the first debate—held on March 29, four days after Ford entered the race—Smitherman had barely bothered with the Etobicoke councillor. He trained his fire on business executive Rocco Rossi. Rossi, the former national director of the federal Liberal Party, had run John Tory's mayoral campaign against David Miller in 2003. With Tory staying out, Rossi had been hoping to inherit that right-of-centre base. On policy, Rossi was the change people wanted. But on delivery, he couldn't connect. Rossi was polling fourth, at 13 percent, above the only woman in the race, Sarah Thomson. "This is when I first started to get worried," said Stefan Baranski, Smitherman's director of communications. "The trend lines were going in the wrong way."

Smitherman corrected course at the May 5 Toronto Real Estate Board debate. On stage, Smitherman questioned Ford's fitness for the job of mayor after his 2006 comments about AIDS and the gay community. "You said, on the floor of council, 'If you're not doing needles and you're not gay, you wouldn't get AIDS, that's the bottom line,'" Smitherman, a married gay man, shouted. "I'd like you, Mr. Ford, to explain to people how your character, and especially these comments, is justifiable, now that you present yourself as someone who wishes to be mayor of the City of Toronto, one of the most diverse places to be found anywhere in the world." The debate, held at the Toronto Congress Centre, was on Ford's home turf of Etobicoke. People in the audience booed the question.

"Let me tell you what Rob Ford's character is about," Ford fired back. "It's about integrity, it's about helping kids get off the street, helping thousands of kids get out of gangs.... I have a Rob Ford football foundation.... You want to get personal, go ahead ... I'm not gonna play games, like you have, blowing a billion dollars on eHealth when [you were] the health minister."

This was Smitherman's Achilles heel. In October 2009, Ontario's auditor general, Jim McCarter, had released a damaging report about the provincial government's efforts to create electronic health records. McCarter found that since 2002, one billion dollars had been spent developing a system that wasn't being used. Not enough of the right kind of information was available, so doctors and the public still weren't accessing it. The auditor also criticized the province's eHealth agency for hiring pricey consultants without a competitive bidding process. The scandal was a long, messy, and complicated fiasco that spanned both Liberal and Conservative governments. But George Smitherman had been health minister for four and a half of those years, from October 2003 to June 2008, leaving him to bear the brunt of the blame. It was a liability that according to insiders caused him to have second thoughts about running for mayor. His team was still figuring out a rebuttal to the kind of attack Ford was hurling his way that afternoon at the Toronto Congress Centre.

As soon as "eHealth" came out of Ford's mouth, the friendly audience erupted in cheers and applause. Smitherman shook his head and it was on to the next question.

Ford had done well sidestepping the AIDS comment trap, but his handlers were irritated with themselves. They should have seen Smitherman's attack coming and prepared a better response.

Although the narrative was taking shape, the growing pains continued through May. At dawn, a week after the debate, Kouvalis climbed out of bed at Deco and headed to the nearby convenience store for a coffee and the morning papers. To his amazement, on the front page of the *Toronto Star*'s city section, he read, "Mayoral Candidate Tells HIV-Positive Gay Man: 'I Feel Terrible.'" Without telling anyone working on the campaign, Rob and Doug Ford had met with Dieter Doneit-Henderson, an HIV-positive married gay man who had been offended by Ford's comments about AIDS. He had contacted the *Star*, and when the newspaper called Ford for comment, the candidate asked to meet the man. The Ford brothers went to Doneit-Henderson's apartment in an Etobicoke high-rise with a reporter and photographer. "I apologize if I offended you or your husband in any way—that's not my style," Ford said. Brother Doug chimed in, "I've had my gay friends come and visit me in Chicago. Gay men have slept in my bed."

Kouvalis stared at the paper in disbelief and fury. For any other politician, this was the kind of gaffe that could have repercussions for weeks. It was off-message, drew attention to an issue they were trying to avoid, and left readers with images of Doug Ford having sex with men. Kouvalis wanted to scream. Something needed to be done.

Doug Ford was leaving for Chicago that day on business, and Kouvalis offered to drive him to the airport. They made the short trip in uncomfortable silence.

"Nick, I know, I know," Doug said finally as they pulled up to the terminal. "The article was a mischaracterization. It was just supposed to be about how much we love the community."

"Just stop," Kouvalis said. "I bought you a gift." He handed Doug an extra-large box of condoms. "In case any gay men climb into your bed while you're in Chicago."

Doug got the point. But that would not be the last of Dieter Doneit-Henderson.

BY JUNE, FORD'S TEAM had learned to work with the brothers' unconventional behaviour. The campaign had averted some minor crises and could feel some momentum. They hired a new staff member, the charismatic Adrienne Batra, to head up communications. Volunteers were pouring in. Campaign staffer Roman Gawur said, "It was very grassroots. All kinds of people were showing up wanting to work because [Rob] had helped them before." It was starting to seem like the kinks had been smoothed out, like they were a real, functioning, normal political campaign.

It would be a fleeting moment of calm.

One morning in early June, Kouvalis was out jogging with Ford as part of a new routine. Kouvalis wanted Ford to lose weight for the sake of his health, so he was making him exercise.

It helped anchor the day, and it gave Kouvalis quality one-on-one time with the candidate. On this particular run, Ford confided that he'd been talking again to Doneit-Henderson, and that the *Star*'s City Hall bureau chief, David Rider, seemed to know about it. Rider had been the one who wrote the original story with Doneit-Henderson.

"Why would Rider give a shit?" Kouvalis asked suspiciously. Ford shrugged.

Kouvalis got worried. That day, he asked around the press gallery, tested the waters with Rider, pressed Ford some more. By the end of the day, he was able to put it together. And what he saw meant serious trouble for Rob Ford.

The campaign was now operating out of a plaza at 245 Dixon Road in Etobicoke. The office was loud, so Kouvalis liked to sit outside in his car to make calls. "Hey, Fraser, can you come see me?" Kouvalis asked the young communications staffer. When Fraser Macdonald got to the car, Kouvalis was smoking with the windows down. The music was on. This was Nick's office.

Kouvalis looked sombre. "This is serious," he said as Macdonald climbed into the passenger seat. Kouvalis said he believed that that HIV-positive man from the paper, Doneit-Henderson, had been phoning Rob since the interview. Kouvalis suspected they'd been discussing Doneit-Henderson's drug use and that the man had secretly recorded one of those talks, a conversation that may have included their candidate offering to help buy Doneit-Henderson drugs. Macdonald sat wide-eyed. But there was more. It looked like the *Star* had a copy of it. "You've gotta get that tape. I need to hear what's on it," Kouvalis said. "I don't care what you do."

Macdonald went home and got to work. Doneit-Henderson

had a Twitter account and had alluded to the recording in his updates. He'd been boasting that he had "engh 2 destroy th entire Ford Family Legacy." Macdonald decided to befriend him online. He knew Doneit-Henderson wasn't going to open up to a Ford staffer, so he created a fake persona. He pulled a random photo of a woman off the internet and put a Smitherman "twibbon"—a digital campaign button you can pin to a profile photo—on it. She needed a name. He wanted it to sound quintessentially downtown. Someone who would vote for George Smitherman. "Queens Quay" popped into his head, the street that ran along the waterfront at the foot of Yonge Street, the home of the *Toronto Star*. With that, @QueensQuayKaren was born. Macdonald wrote a bio: "Downtown Toronto gal who likes politics, my cat Mittens, and a good book." He started the account that night, June 11. It was duplicitous, yes. But politics was a blood sport and espionage was part of the game.

After posting a few tweets to attract followers and so make the account look more legitimate, Macdonald moved in on his quarry. "@DeiterDH What have you got on @robfordteam? Nothing I'd like to see more than to bring him down!"

Doneit-Henderson responded, and the two started to exchange private messages. Doneit-Henderson told "Karen" about the tape and forwarded a link to a hosting site where the audio could be downloaded.

"I got it—just starting to listen! Who else has heard this???!?" @QueensQuayKaren replied.

Most of the fifty-two-minute recording was rambling and nonsensical. And then Macdonald heard it. Sitting alone in a secluded office at Deco, he put his head in his hands. Ford—a

2010 mayoral candidate—could clearly be heard offering to help Doneit-Henderson "score" OxyContin on the street.

It's over, he thought.

Macdonald called Kouvalis on his cell phone, then Adrienne Batra, newly hired as head of communications. She was downtown with Ford at the time. Kouvalis told him, "Talk to no one about this." Macdonald was to wait at Deco and the other two would meet him there, away from the rest of the staff at the official campaign office. Both arrived within an hour.

The audio file indicated the tape was made on June 4. Doneit-Henderson, who suffered from fibromyalgia, had called Ford for help finding OxyContin, a time-release painkiller that when taken incorrectly can be highly addictive. On the street it's called hillbilly heroin.

> DONEIT-HENDERSON: Can you find OxyContin for me, Rob?
>
> FORD: Huh?
>
> DONEIT-HENDERSON: Can you find OxyContin, so I can get on the medication? …
>
> FORD: I'll try, buddy, I'll try. I don't know this shit, but I'll fucking try to find it.
>
> DONEIT-HENDERSON: How about your brother mentioned your guys' doctor. Did you guys ever look … go into … look into that?
>
> FORD: He said that you've got to come personally.
>
> DONEIT-HENDERSON: Oh, well. Hey, listen, I'm ready to go. I mean, I'd even go down there now in all this pain.
>
> FORD: How much does OxyContin go for on the street— so I have an idea?

· ·

FORD: Leave this with me. Call Doug tomorrow, we'll
see if I can't, uh, I know I won't be able to. But I have no
idea. Fuck, you know, I don't know any drug dealers at
all.

Batra sighed. "Oh, you can't spin that."

But they had to try something. They went over the facts. If
the *Star* had this tape, why wasn't it publishing the story? Was
it possible the paper was saving it for closer to the election? In
fact, there was no *Star* plot to drop the Dieter bomb right before
election day. The *Star*'s city editor was uncomfortable about the
paper having introduced Doneit-Henderson to Ford. The story
had been axed. But the Ford camp didn't know that.

On the surface, things were going well. Ford had just
caught Smitherman in the polls, though a good chunk of voters
remained undecided. It made the tape seem even more like an
unexploded bomb.

Ford took the matter to his lawyer. Was there any legal
recourse to prevent it from being published, given that he had
been recorded without knowing it? Nope. In Canada, as long as
one person was aware a conversation was being recorded, it was
legally admissible.

They knew what they had to do. "We'll have to get ahead
of it, then," Kouvalis said. If he couldn't prevent the recording
from coming out, then the best option would be to orchestrate
its release. The Ford brothers were dead against this strategy.
They wanted to test their luck. Maybe it would never come
out. And in fact, Rob Ford was still denying he'd even made
the comments, even though he knew Kouvalis had listened to

the tape. Eventually, Kouvalis played it for the entire family—
Diane, Randy, and Doug. Rob was embarrassed. The Fords still
wanted to let it go.

Kouvalis wasn't having it. The Ford camp leaked it to a
friendly news organization. *Toronto Sun* columnist Sue-Ann
Levy was the obvious choice. She was one of Ford's biggest
cheerleaders.

The play would be to frame him as the victim. He was just
trying to be nice to an emotionally unstable person. He never
intended to buy the man drugs. And look how he was repaid.
A set-up.

Levy's article, published on June 17, was written with a
predictably sympathetic spin.

> City hall's "enfant terrible"—mayoralty candidate Rob
> Ford—insists he only was trying to help someone in
> trouble when he offered to try to find an HIV-positive
> man some OxyContin on the street.
>
> "I personally feel sorry for him … he needs help …
> he needs something," Ford said Wednesday.
>
> The highly questionable offer comes out in a
> 52-minute conversation Ford had with Dieter Doneit-
> Henderson on the evening of June 4, a tape of which was
> obtained by the *Toronto Sun.*

The campaign held a press conference in front of Deco's office
building the morning the story ran. Up until that point, Randy
had kept a low profile on the campaign, helping with strategy
and signage and volunteering at events. Given the severity of the
situation, Doug wanted his oldest brother involved, to show the

Fords were standing together. So when the candidate emerged, he was accompanied by both of his brothers as well as Batra. (There had actually been a big fight with Randy—who went by the nickname Blackjack—over his cowboy hat. Ford's staff told him it wasn't appropriate for the event. But he wore it everywhere except in the shower and in bed. Eventually, Randy gave in.)

"I feel that I have been set up," Ford told reporters. "There are people out there that will do everything in their power to make sure that I'm not mayor of this great city.... I said what I needed to say to get this person off the phone without provoking him.... His tenor became threatening. I feared for my family. He clearly said on the tape that he could see my house." The matter was now in the hands of the police, Ford concluded.

The public gave him the benefit of the doubt.

No charges were ever laid.

THE FORD CAMPAIGN had cleared one big hurdle, just in time for another.

In mid-July, *Toronto Star* investigative reporter Robert Cribb and education reporter Kristin Rushowy learned that Ford had "quietly [been] asked to stop coaching" football at a Toronto high school after an incident with a player. This was the confrontation at Newtonbrook Secondary School back in 2001, when Ford got into it with a player he thought wasn't performing well. Witnesses disagreed about whether the altercation was physical. The story explained: "Ford, one of his players and an assistant coach at the time deny any physical contact took place. But a parent and another player say Ford aggressively manhandled the student in anger. Ford vigorously denied the allegations saying he's never assaulted a player and called the claims a 'political' attack on his candidacy."

Ford was furious with the story. It went after the thing he cared about most: his work coaching football. The Ford team drummed up a brilliant rebuttal. They completely ignored the substance of the article—that Rob had been fired from the job for losing his temper—and fixated on the physical aspect, which was always in dispute. Adrienne Batra told the *National Post* the story was "outrageous, it's slanderous and patently incorrect."

The campaign team tracked down the former player at a military base and put him in touch with *The Globe and Mail.* "That's completely untrue," Jonathan Gordon, then twenty-five, told the *Globe* when asked if Ford had shaken or slapped him. "Trust me, if he had slapped me I would have beat the crap out of him. No word of a lie." Gordon said Ford had given a halftime speech that he didn't like. He deliberately blew the next play then walked off the field. "Ford lost his temper, started yelling at me," Gordon told the *Globe.* "I took my helmet off, threw it off the field [and] basically told him he 'can go fuck himself.' We got into a heated argument. We were pretty close, face to face, and then we got separated by the assistant coach and that was it."

Ford sent a notice of libel to the *Star*—the first step in a lawsuit, which he never pursued—and an edict was issued to his campaign staff that no one should speak to the paper from then on. Canada's largest newspaper stopped receiving Ford's press releases. It was the beginning of what would become known as the Ford Freeze. According to sources within the campaign, the Freeze was never meant to be permanent, but Ford fans seemed to love it. The man of the people was taking on the elites. The Ford campaign raised tens of thousands of dollars in a matter of days.

Hurdles kept appearing as the weeks went by, and Ford cleared every one.

When John Tory announced he was reconsidering a run, Kouvalis whipped up a cartoon attack ad, partly to try to shake the conservative radio host's confidence and partly to placate Doug, who was demanding the campaign go on the offensive. Tory could have derailed Ford's campaign. The former leader of Ontario's Progressive Conservative Party had all the right-wing bona fides, plus he looked and acted mayoral. Ford had actually been one of Tory's biggest supporters in 2003. "If Tory had got in, he would have won," Kouvalis said. The video started with a speeding gravy train whipping past the CN Tower and knocking out a wimpy-looking Tory, who was trying in vain to stop it. Then superhero Rob Ford swooped in to save the day. It was sort of lame, but it got news coverage. Next, Kouvalis had a staffer anonymously call in to Tory's radio show to question the host's integrity. Looking back, Tory tells me the character attacks had nothing to do with his decision to stay out of the race. "If you look at the campaigns I've been through, my skin has thickened up," he said. The real thing that gave Tory pause was his numbers in the inner suburbs.

Internal polling showed Tory was neck-and-neck with Ford in Etobicoke. Tory had appeal across the city, including in the core, but he wasn't far enough ahead in the old boroughs.

This was what had done him in in the 2003 race against David Miller. Tory had carried twenty-one of the forty-four wards, including most of the suburban terrain, but he didn't win by high enough margins. When the ballots were counted, Miller had edged him out after taking twenty-two wards, with support concentrated in the old City of Toronto. (The fourth-place candidate, John Nunziata, won one ward.)

As veteran political operative John Laschinger explains, conservative candidates running in Toronto need to own the suburban vote, but left-wingers can't build a winning coalition with the downtown alone. "In order to win an election in Toronto, you have to do reasonably well in Scarborough and North York. That's just over half of the total population. You don't have to win them, but you can't lose by more than 20 to 25 points. In Scarborough, you have to win at least 30 to 35 percent or you're toast." (Laschinger, who has worked on dozens of campaigns at every level of government, is the man who delivered Miller's victory in 2003.)

For Tory, his 2010 numbers looked even less favourable. In August he made it clear he was definitely staying out.

With three months to go, the polls on his side, and no John Tory to worry about, it was now Ford's race to lose. This was the time when a typical candidate would ease off and play it safe to avoid making unforced errors.

But the missteps kept coming.

There was the hasty endorsement of a Christian fundamentalist, Pastor Wendell Brereton, who was running for council and believed that same-sex marriage could "dismantle" democratic civilization. In a press conference with Ford and Brereton outside City Hall, reporters asked Ford if that meant he opposed gay marriage. "We're together. We have the same thoughts.... I support traditional marriage. I always have. But if people want to, to each their own. I'm not worried about what people do in their private life. I look out for taxpayers' money."

Sources on Ford's staff say the event was "a bad one for us." Most of the staff heard about the endorsement an hour before the press conference. The Ford brothers had done it on their own. Brereton had not been vetted.

A week later, Ford seemed to step in it again. During a televised debate on CP24, a Tamil in the audience asked how the city should handle immigrant refugees. Ford responded, "We can't even deal with the 2.5 million people in the city. I think it's more important that we take care of the people now before we start bringing in more." His campaign office was inundated with calls and emails. They were messages of support—many from immigrants.

When Ford suggested to the *Toronto Sun's* editorial board—without any specific proof—that council was corrupt, many voters ate it up. The allegation infuriated sitting mayor David Miller and numerous councillors from across the spectrum. Even Doug Holyday, the Fords' old family friend and future deputy mayor, took issue. "Corruption is a strong term, and I think in order to use it, you have to have proof," he said. "I really don't have proof of corruption here and I don't know that anybody else has." It didn't matter. Ford's supporters loved it.

For anyone else, these could have been major gaffes. But the regular rules didn't apply to Rob Ford. On August 12, a week after the Brereton press conference, a telephone survey from Pollstra Research showed Ford had pulled way ahead. He was at 37.6 percent, while Smitherman was barely treading water at 28.7 percent.

A week later, when Ford's 1999 drunk driving and marijuana story surfaced, an Ipsos Reid poll showed he had widened his lead to 11 points. This was when Kouvalis knew they'd won. The momentum continued to election day.

Torontonians knew Ford was flawed, but enough of them

were prepared to accept his rough edges because his message of ending City Hall waste was clear. George Smitherman's director of communications says that focus groups and polling revealed that no one had any idea what their candidate stood for. "We had enough policy to run a small country. There was a substantive plan behind George, but there was also too much policy. It confused our key messages with voters," said Baranski. "We lost the outsider [status]. The 'agent of change' mantra belonged to Rob Ford, and this guy had been on council a number of terms."

Smitherman's campaign manager, Bruce Davis, said he knew they were in serious trouble when at a focus group a woman announced, "If I have to choose between someone who wastes our money and someone who beats their wife, I'll choose the person who beats their wife." Even a last-ditch attempt in which Smitherman scrapped every message except "I'm not Rob Ford" couldn't slow the Etobicoke juggernaut.

In the end, it wasn't even close.

On October 25, 2010, Rob Ford was elected mayor of Toronto in a landslide.

INAUGURATION DAY at City Hall, December 7, 2010.

Hundreds of visitors, mostly of the Ford Nation persuasion, had crowded around a giant projector screen in the ground-floor rotunda to watch the ceremony. Many had camped out for hours. They were wearing Ford campaign buttons and T-shirts. They'd fashioned hats out of "Ford for Mayor" bumper stickers. They were waving Canadian flags, sometimes also decorated with "Ford for Mayor" bumper stickers.

"He's the best Christmas present Toronto could get…. I'm just so excited to be here," gushed Antionette Wassilyn, who had taken the day off work to attend.

Seats in the council chamber were available by invitation only. Standing front and centre was Rob Ford. He was beaming, even blushing, in a crisp black suit, with cufflinks and a white pocket square to match his shirt. His thinning blond hair—slicked straight back for the occasion like his brother Doug's—was the same colour as the stripes of gold on his necktie and City of Toronto pin. Standing next to Ford was a man in a thunderously loud flamingo-pink sports jacket, with an oversized white shirt collar up to his chin and a red rose in his lapel. The man was Don Cherry, a Canadian hockey and broadcasting icon, who was as famous for his outlandish taste and hockey smarts as he was for his knack of offending people. Cherry, a former player and NHL coach, co-hosted a TV segment during *Hockey Night in Canada* called "Coach's Corner." Cherry had used this platform to attack the federal government for not supporting the American invasion of Iraq, to scoff at multiculturalism, and to complain about the "whiners" in French Canada.

Ford had selected Cherry, who lived just outside Toronto, to place the chain of office around his neck. (David Miller had opted for the chief justice of Ontario, Roy McMurtry.) Said *Toronto Life* of the decision, "Aside from the fact that they're both coaches—though not even in the same sport—we can't see what, exactly, is bringing these two together, except for their shared love of speaking without thinking."

Before the big moment, Ford and Cherry offered a thumbs-up to a mob of photographers. Then the city clerk approached with the chain of office. Attached to a blue velvet collar, it was adorned with eight gold medallions—one for each of the seven former municipal governments and one to represent the amalgamated megacity. Ford bowed forward and Cherry carefully draped it around his neck. Councillors left and right were on their feet clapping. Ford walked behind the speaker's chair—which now bore his name—and grinned.

The clerk called on Cherry to give his remarks. There was more applause as Cherry got behind the podium.

"Well, actually I'm wearing pinko for all the pinkos out there that ride bicycles and everything"—eyes in the audience grew wide—"… but, you know, I am befuddled, because I thought I was just doing a good thing coming down with Rob.… I'm being ripped to shreds by the left-wing pinko newspapers out there."

The crowd outside in the rotunda howled their approval, but in the chamber mouths gaped open. Several of the councillors turned their backs on Cherry.

With Rob Ford, "what you see is what you get," Cherry continued.

"I say he's going to be the greatest mayor this city has ever, ever seen, as far as I'm concerned—and put that in your pipe, you left-wing kooks."

That's how it began.

SIX

HE WON'T
GIVE UP THE BLOW

Renata Ford pulls into a Tim Hortons parking lot about an hour north of her Etobicoke home. She's meeting with an acquaintance, a former drug addict, to get some advice. She's worried. Her husband, Rob Ford, has recently been elected mayor. She knows this new status is going to put her family under intense scrutiny. Renata doesn't have many friends, but she met John—not his real name—through someone in her small circle. He'd faced addiction and come through it. She's hoping he can give her some tips to bring Rob on side. What she doesn't know is that John is secretly recording the conversation.

"Hey, Renata," John says as she climbs into his front seat. "You want a coffee?"

"Oh, no, no."

"You sure?"

"Yeah."

Renata trusts him completely. John steers the conversation into incriminating territory. He brings up Rob.

"He still thinks he's going to party," Renata says. "He thinks that he, oh, you know, 'I'll get off the pills, but I'm not giving up the blow.'"

"He's a public figure, for Jesus Christ," John says. "There's a lot of people after him … that's why you've got to be very careful."

"I know that," Renata says. "I told him, 'Fuck, you could ruin your whole fucking life.'"

"If someone wants his ass, they're going to get him."

"I've been trying to tell him that."

No one gets her, she says. She's tried to talk to people before, but they can't help her. She can't trust them.

"I got two kids. I've gotta, you know, I've gotta get this shit together. And like you said, we're in the public.… You know, it's just time. It's fucking time," she says. "So I really appreciate the help."

John gives her some advice about methadone, withdrawal symptoms, and clinics that will be discreet. She thanks him again.

"I can trust you, because I know you've gone fucking through it," she says before heading back to her car.

This is the other side of Rob Ford's world, the one that even his most trusted staff didn't fully know about until the crack cocaine scandal. For two and a half years while running the city, the mayor managed to keep it secret.

IT WAS NOVEMBER 2010, and councillor-elect Jaye Robinson was on her way to meet the mayor-elect. Robinson walked to the west elevator bank at City Hall and pressed 16. The transition team had summoned her. For now, they were working out of the tower offices until David Miller packed up and vacated the mayor's digs on the second floor. The group was small and mostly made up of familiar faces. There was Nick Kouvalis and Mark Towhey from the campaign. Brother Doug. Two former councillors, Gordon Chong and veteran conservative Case Ootes, former city bureaucrat Claire Tucker-Reid, and a man named Amir Remtulla. Remtulla was the director of government relations for brewing company Molson Coors, but before that he worked as Ootes's executive assistant at City Hall.

The transition team's work would be done by December, but many of its members would take up roles in the new Ford administration.

Robinson was one of fourteen new councillors, although City Hall wasn't new to her. She'd logged twenty years as a bureaucrat, most notably as the director of events. Many of Toronto's most treasured cultural initiatives—the Nuit Blanche art festival, the Moose in the City statues, and the culinary event Winterlicious, among others—were Robinson's work.

The team was trying to meet all the councillors, both veteran and newly elected. Each had been asked to fill out a form indicating which of the seven standing committees—parks and recreation, economic development, public works, etc.—he or she was interested in joining. The most prestigious was the mayor's executive committee. Robinson signed up for everything. "I figured, I'm not going to be a city councillor forever. I wanted to roll up my sleeves and get really involved in charting the course of Toronto," she said.

She entered a nondescript boardroom on the sixteenth floor. Three people were waiting for her: Rob Ford, Nick Kouvalis, and Doug Ford. She did a double take. Why was the mayor's brother here? The conversation lasted less than thirty minutes. The mayor-elect barely opened his mouth. Doug Ford, who was "extraordinarily friendly," did most of the talking. Later, he would turn on her, but that was still two years away.

Kouvalis had three questions for Robinson. Would she support privatizing garbage collection in the city's west side? Would she vote to make the Toronto Transit Commission (TTC) an essential service? And would she help kill the vehicle registration tax? "If you're comfortable with these three issues," Kouvalis said, "then we're happy to move forward with you being a member of our executive."

Robinson was thrilled. All three issues had been part of her platform. But now she had a question. If she joined the executive committee, would she be expected to vote with the administration on every matter all the time? She said she couldn't commit to that. She considered herself an independent centrist. According to Robinson, Kouvalis made it clear that her allegiance was required only on those three issues. Kouvalis flatly denies this. He says every executive member was made aware that they were expected to vote with the administration on every issue. If a mayor couldn't rely on his team to support him, the agenda would never get passed, Kouvalis explained to me.

City Hall doesn't work like other levels of government. Ford would get just one vote on council—one out of forty-five. Unlike in some American cities, the mayor of Toronto doesn't get to veto policy. The strength of the office is rooted in the individual mayor's powers of persuasion. On any given issue, Ford would need to woo twenty-two councillors to support him. And that wasn't necessarily going to be easy. About a third of those elected were hard-core lefties. Another half a dozen identified as centrists, and while the rest leaned right, only about ten were as conservative as the mayor-elect. Ford would need to bridge the vote gap. The mayor's best bargaining tool was that he got to pick the chairs of each standing committee as well as the members of the all-important executive. City councillors wanted these positions. It gave them profile and power. For members of Team Ford, that power would come at a price.

From the outset, the Ford administration took measures to try to ensure that its agenda was supported. Ford staffers began to distribute "cheat sheets" to like-minded councillors, with suggested votes on dozens of issues. Robinson says it got so bad that members of the executive were expected to show solidarity on simple procedural votes, such as whether someone could speak for three or five minutes during a debate. And it wasn't just executive committee members who felt the administration's muscle. The mayor's office frequently used aggressive tactics to bring centrist votes on side. For example, the administration tried to bully Councillor Ana Bailão to fall in line by holding up, of all things, the installation of a traffic light she had requested for her ward. Councillor Josh Colle, the leader of the so-called Mighty Middle, said of the tactic, "If it's a strategy to sway votes, I don't think it's a productive strategy." Later in that council meeting, Ford caused problems for a project in Colle's ward. The mayor relented after the councillor backed Ford's controversial plan to rip up a major bike lane.

Like Robinson, Councillor Karen Stintz says that when she accepted the TTC chair position, she didn't think she had signed up for four years of following orders. "Nick [Kouvalis] had one question: Would I support making the TTC an essential service? I said, 'Yes, sure.'" Stintz didn't need selling on the broader Ford agenda. She was a stalwart fiscal conservative. Under the previous

Miller regime, she had been a leader in a group of centre-right councillors who formed an unofficial opposition called the Responsible Government Group.

For his part, Councillor Paul Ainslie said he understood right away what he had gotten himself into. "They talked about running it in a cabinet style," typical of federal and provincial politics, where members are expected to vote as a bloc. Ainslie was offered the chair of the government management committee and a spot on the executive. He had been shut out from leadership during the Miller years, and now he had a chance to shape policy. He couldn't pass it up. But not long after he accepted, he received a letter distributed by Ford's staff to each member of the executive requesting him to pledge support for the Ford agenda. Each of them was to sign and return it immediately. "Some of my colleagues were saying, 'Well, wait a second. We're not a cabinet-style government here. We didn't run on a Rob Ford ticket. We ran on our own tickets.'" Everyone started asking for amendments, and eventually the pledge was abandoned. But the tone was set.

Robinson now admits she was a bit naive. "I took a huge pay cut to take this job. I wanted to effect change. I thought we were going to do that. Turns out that wasn't the case."

ON ONE OF HIS last days as mayor-elect, November 29, 2010, Ford unveiled his team. There wasn't a single left-winger or downtown councillor in the mix, and only two women had made it onto the executive. Both were rookies. In fact, eleven of the twelve councillors represented the former boroughs. David Miller had stacked his executive with enough sympathetic councillors to ensure his agenda would get through, but he was also mindful of geography, gender, and ideology. One conservative and three centrists served on his team, and fewer than half represented wards from pre-amalgamation Toronto.

Ford claimed that his approach reflected a new direction. "This is not about left or right. This is about bringing respect for taxpayers back to City Hall. They're hard-working, they understand customer service, and that's the bottom line," the mayor-elect told reporters as his de facto caucus looked on. Doug Holyday would be deputy mayor; Karen Stintz, chair of the TTC. Suburban councillor Frances Nunziata was Ford's choice for council speaker. And the comically cantankerous Mike Del Grande, a right-winger from Scarborough, would be budget chief.

Case Ootes said the transition team felt it was important to have "unanimous support" for the mayor's agenda. Former mayor David Miller might have had a few more centrist councillors, Ootes said, but he didn't invite any staunch conservatives onto his team either.

"The mayor was elected on a platform to end the gravy train. The overwhelming majority of people wanted an end to the spending that was happening under Miller. The councillors on Ford's executive reflected that. Why would you put a guy like Adam Vaughan on the executive committee?" Ootes said. Vaughan, a former journalist, was a downtown councillor and one of Ford's most passionate critics.

"We did take into consideration male–female representation and tried to balance that out in some form or another—like Karen Stintz with the TTC—and that was a challenge, because, as you know, there are more men on council than women," especially on the right, Ootes said.

With his team in place, Rob Ford used his first press conference as mayor to kill one of the pillars of Miller's legacy, Transit City. At a cost of $8.15 billion, and seven years in the making, this massive transit expansion plan was funded almost entirely by the province, apart from one arm of light rail in Scarborough, where the federal government was kicking in $330 million. The network relied heavily on above-ground light rail trains, or LRTs. Where subways cost $300 million per kilometre to build, above-ground LRTs come at a bargain $100 million per kilometre. But in Rob Ford's Toronto, the car reigned supreme, and anything that slowed drivers was bad.

"Ladies and gentlemen, the war on the car stops today," Ford said. "We will not build any more rail tracks down the middle of our streets." He called TTC general manager Gary Webster and instructed him to halt work on Transit City and start investigating how to build subways.

The new chair of the TTC was incredulous. Karen Stintz didn't believe the administration actually intended on ripping the whole thing up. "In my mind, we would kill Transit City, which was a David Miller plan, and rebrand it something else that was the Ford plan," she said. Scrapping the whole project wasn't financially prudent, and perhaps not even possible. The provincial transit agency, Metrolinx, had already spent $137 million on the project and signed a $770-million contract for the trains. Subways require high population densities to ensure sufficient ridership to pay back some of the increased costs, and many areas, particularly in Scarborough, didn't have the densities to support one. Most significantly, the Fords had no idea how to pay for it. Stintz thought killing off Transit City was just political showboating from a new mayor eager to demonstrate his authority.

During the election, once it became apparent Rob Ford might win, some left-wingers warned he would never be able to govern. "This man can't even convince five people to vote with him. So if disaster happens and voters are sucked into this tale, the other members of council will steer the ship," progressive councillor Pam McConnell told me at the time.

But at the first meeting of city council in mid-December 2010, Ford proved his critics wrong. He scored a trio of quick victories with votes to spare. Council voted 39–6 to repeal the vehicle registration tax, 28–17 to make the TTC an essential service (the Ontario government had to approve of the change, which it did), and 40–5 to reduce councillors' office budgets from $50,445 to $30,000.

The momentum kept up in the New Year with his first budget. As promised, Ford balanced the books without service reductions or tax increases. "This is the beginning of a new era," he boasted. In truth, the mayor's maiden budget was an unexceptional, stay-the-course document that relied, ironically, on surpluses from the Miller years. Partly acknowledging this, Ford cautioned that the real hunt for waste, or "gravy," as he had memorably called it during the election, would start in March. The city was going to hire outside experts to comb through each department searching for efficiencies. They would leave "no stone unturned," and if managers pushed back, "then we will have to find new managers."

On the surface, the Ford administration looked well-organized and professional. Pull back the curtain, and it was a different story. Stintz caught her first glimpse during budget discussions. The mayor's office had signed off on a ten-cent fare increase, so the TTC built its numbers around that revenue.

Then, the night before the budget announcement, Kouvalis phoned. "The mayor doesn't want a fare increase," he told Stintz. "Go figure it out." Officials spent the night altering months of work by hand. There would be no increase.

It got worse from there. After the fare turnaround, Stintz was called to the mayor's office in late January for a brainstorming session on the new transit plan. Upon arrival, she learned that they already had one: cancel the proposed LRT along Eglinton Street in the middle of the city and use that money to turn the proposed Sheppard LRT line in the north into a subway. Stintz looked around the room to see if they were serious. She was the councillor for Ward 16 Eglinton-Lawrence. "I invited them to replace me as chair. I also explained this was never going to get through council." Eglinton impacts half a dozen wards on the east side of the city, meaning half a dozen councillors would be unlikely to support axing transit expansion along this corridor. Kouvalis, Towhey, the mayor, Doug Ford, and Stintz's assistant were in the room. Rob Ford didn't say much. Doug kept insisting the private sector would "give us billions!" to pay for subways, which Stintz said was completely unrealistic. "I left that meeting thinking, These guys are nuts. And you can put that in your book."

AS A CANDIDATE, Ford pledged to run a transparent government. But as mayor, he was astoundingly secretive. His office refused to release his daily schedule, something most political leaders do, including Ford's predecessors. My colleague Daniel Dale tells of calling staff in the Chicago mayor's office—we frequently use the Windy City as a comparison in stories: Toronto does x, Chicago does y, Montreal does z—and having Ford's schedule come up in conversation. Dale mentioned that Ford didn't release them, and the aide in Chicago was lost for words. "But, but then how do you know where to go to cover him?" Exactly. In 2013, when asked about a misbehaving member of his staff, Ford laid out his views on the public's right to know: "It's actually no one's business what happens in my office."

Given that Ford's staff continued to freeze out the *Toronto Star*, reporters from the paper relied on Twitter to keep track of the mayor's whereabouts. Sometimes our colleagues in the City Hall press gallery would give us a heads-up about an appearance, and sometimes not. All considered, it wasn't as big a problem as you might expect. The mayor of Toronto almost never spoke to reporters, which, if it needs saying, was extremely unusual. Meanwhile, Doug Ford had become the de facto spokesperson for the administration. (To the annoyance of Ford's staff, Doug still took the *Star*'s calls, because he couldn't help himself when asked for his opinion.) The problem with that arrangement was that reporters could never tell if Doug Ford was speaking for himself or the mayor. One of the first things Doug did after being elected was to contact city staff to see about installing a door in the wall between his Ward 2 office and the mayor's office. This would give him round-the-clock access without anyone seeing him come or go. City staff put the kibosh on the idea, largely because of the expense, but door or no door, title or no title, Doug was as much a part of the mayor's office as the chief of staff. Doug acted on behalf of the mayor in meetings with business leaders, city staff, and councillors. As far as he was concerned, Rob might be mayor, but it was the Ford family that was running the city. (This led to numerous blow-ups with Nick Kouvalis, the chief of staff. Kouvalis was fed up. He quit two months after the inauguration.) This caused a great deal of tension between the Ford brothers, sometimes publicly.

This was the case in mid-February 2011, when Doug suggested the mayor should have more power so that the office wasn't beholden to council. In some American jurisdictions, such as Chicago, mayors can veto decisions that don't have a two-thirds majority. Asked about the comment, Rob Ford said Doug had been spending too much time south of the border. (Before getting elected, Doug Ford split his time between Etobicoke and Chicago running Deco Labels.) Reporters pressed the mayor about why Doug seemed to be doing all the talking. Was Ford avoiding the media? "My brother is not the mouthpiece," Rob said. "I'm always available. I tell you, it's pretty hard to hide three hundred pounds of fun."

Nevertheless, Rob Ford continued to be MIA.

A little more than a month later, the *Star*'s Daniel Dale, through freedom-of-information requests, was able to obtain Ford's daily schedules for the first ten weeks of his reign. They showed Ford had been slated to attend more than 110 events in his first sixty-nine days. They ranged from a Christmas party at the elite Albany Club to a championship spelling bee to Chinese New Year events. The documents revealed Ford had semi-regular meetings with councillors, provincial and federal politicians, and business leaders. Dale checked up on as many of the items as possible. In some cases, Ford had never shown up. In a few others, Doug had taken the mayor's place. Another interesting tidbit gleaned from the schedules was that Ford still had a foot in the family business. On January 24, 2011—the day Ford's budget was to clear the committee level—his schedule said "DECO ALL DAY." And of course, football was in there too. In one reference, on Thursday, February 3, Ford was scheduled for a "locker room meeting" at 10 A.M. Yes, football—during a Canadian winter.

After Dale's story, Ford's staff began stripping specific names from schedules so that no one could verify his attendance. Several former staffers tell me that releasing a daily schedule would have been challenging, because they were never sure if Ford would show up. Says Adrienne Batra, who after the election became Ford's press secretary, "It's fair to say I didn't know where he was about half of the time."

Rob Ford's open disdain for the press shouldn't have been a surprise. His mayoral campaign was designed to avoid the mainstream media. Whether it was strong-arming councillors or ignoring reporters, Ford was unapologetically doing things differently. And the people who had it the worst were the staff at City Hall.

UNDER PREVIOUS REGIMES, the opinions of city bureaucrats were more valued, their years of institutional knowledge and expertise routinely put to use. Managers and department heads were more or less treated as partners. The Ford administration had a different style. When marching orders to find reductions were handed down, pushback was not tolerated.

Deputy city manager Sue Corke resigned in March 2011. She later told me, "There was a lack of civility. The environment wasn't as professional as what I had been used to in thirty years in the public sector. I'm used to a professional environment in which civil servants are provided with respect and where they provide the best advice to their political masters." She said the mayor's staff—and brother—sometimes ignored advice that didn't fit with their "right-wing ideology." It was too frustrating a work environment for Corke, who believes social policy should be based on evidence, not ideology.

Another senior manager who left in 2012, and who asked for anonymity to protect remaining staff, told me, "Clearly, there is a lot of influence and persuasion, and I'd even say bullying, to have city staff do the will of the mayor's office."

Within the first year, more than a dozen high-level managers left City Hall, some voluntarily, some not. In 2012, Toronto ombudsman Fiona Crean released a report that accused the mayor's office of interfering in the process of selecting citizen members for the city's boards and agencies.

Crean—who holds one of the four "accountability" positions created after the MFP scandal—was attacked for five gruelling hours at council when she presented her findings. Councillor Giorgio Mammoliti, once Ford's mortal enemy, now his caucus whip, accused her of having "political motivations." Councillor Michelle Berardinetti, a member of Ford's executive, questioned her objectivity. Councillor Doug Ford said her findings were based on "hearsay."

Council eventually voted unanimously to adopt Crean's recommendations. Three months later, the administration denied Crean's request for an additional full-time investigator. "The evidence certainly points to this being a political payback for her reports," left-leaning Councillor Joe Mihevc told the *Star* afterwards. "Budget time is the time to get back at people, and it seems like this is the play."

Many felt the Ford administration was too harsh with staff. Others say that drastic change meant there would be casualties. Ford got elected because Torontonians believed the public service at City Hall was bloated and wasting money. And whether you loved or loathed the mayor, whether you supported or opposed his methods, City Hall became a leaner operation on Rob Ford's watch.

Press secretary Adrienne Batra recalled, "Managers were coming to us proactively with budget reductions. Rob Ford set a tone that changed the culture."

THE GREAT GRAVY HUNT began on March 21, 2011, the day the executive approved a three-pronged investigation of city services. Council then agreed to pay external consultants three million dollars to drill deep into every department, agency, board, and commission to locate the waste Ford promised was there. Phase One: separate "core" programs from "discretionary" ones. Phase Two: find the flaws, the overlaps, the duplications in delivery of services. Phase Three: determine if people were paying enough for them.

Findings from Phase One, which were prepared by consulting firm KPMG, came out in July 2011. It turned out that most of what the city did was "core." In fact, the bulk of what the city provides is mandated by the province. The consultants did identify lots of non-essential nice-to-haves, like fluoride in the water, bike lanes, recycling programs, late-night bus routes, and some snow plowing. But most people thought, unsurprisingly, that dental health and being able to drive in the winter were pretty important.

Some backlash was inevitable, but things might have gone differently if the review had steered clear of the library system. This was the issue that, ultimately, galvanized the public and council against the mayor. And it was all Doug Ford's fault.

On the third week of the core-service-review reports, KPMG presented its findings on the library system to the executive committee. Page 76 left the public baying for blood: "The Library Services could be reduced by reducing the number of branches [there were about one hundred] and/or constraining the hours of service." Doug Ford threw gasoline on the inferno. "I've got more libraries in my area than I have Tim Hortons," he said, referring to the ubiquitous coffee shops. Beloved Canadian author Margaret Atwood poked back on Twitter: "Twin Fordmayor seems to think those who eat Timbits [doughnuts], like me, don't read, can't count, & are stupid eh?" Atwood rallied her 220,000-plus Twitter followers to patronize their local library, then hold book club meetings at their local Tim Hortons. Rather than ignore the jab, the mayor's brother doubled down, saying he would close a library in his ward "in a heartbeat." And as far as Atwood was concerned, said Doug, "I don't even know her. If she walked by me, I wouldn't have a clue who she is." His advice to Atwood? "Go run in the next election and get democratically elected. And we'd be more than happy to sit down and listen to Margaret Atwood."

It was the first time Karen Stintz split publicly with the Fords. In a letter to her constituents, she announced, "I value the Toronto Public Library and can assure my constituents that these are not the type of cuts that I will support." Speaker Frances Nunziata was next, saying that if anything libraries should be better equipped to deliver city services. On July 28, the executive committee held a marathon twenty-two-hour meeting to hear from the public. Only three of the 169 members of the public who spoke supported cuts.

Rob Ford seemed to be taking it all in stride, but beneath his confident demeanour he was starting to come apart. The mayor couldn't rely on his own team. His message was being lost. He knew Doug was getting out of control and irritating his staff, but how could he get rid of his own brother? Looking back, two members of the mayor's staff at that time told me it was apparent the stress was getting to him.

ROB FORD IS STUMBLING down Front Street near Blue Jays Way, his drenched shirt hanging loose, the collar unbuttoned around his neck, a Slurpee cup in hand. A bachelorette party is on the sidewalk in front of him. He pushes past.

The girls watch as he starts to cross the street. Doesn't he look familiar …? Then it clicks. "That's Rob Ford!"

They chase after him, asking for a photo. He seems to say no, waving his arm and muttering "aaaaah." But the girls crowd around him. Ford's eyes are shut and he doesn't quite manage a smile. One of the girls puts her arms around Ford's neck and asks for someone to take a photo while she kisses his cheek.

Jason Hebert and two friends were standing next to the young women when Ford came by. The twenty-six-year-old got in touch with the *Star* and came into the office shortly after. "He stunk like booze. He was definitely drunk." The photo with the girls made it online, but the media largely left it alone.

"This was the first time anything like this had happened," said a member of the mayor's staff. Ford wasn't supposed to be by himself that August night. He should have been watching the Ontario varsity football championships at the Rogers Centre with a young aide, but he hadn't shown up and wasn't answering his phone. The game was nearly done, so the staffer went home. Then Ford decided to go after all. From then on, the mayor's office instituted a new rule: the mayor's designated handler on any given day had to wait at City Hall until 10 P.M. in case Ford called—even if he'd been MIA.

BY THE END OF AUGUST 2011—just weeks away from the big showdown at council over service cuts—Rob Ford's honeymoon with voters was winding down. The public was angry. The mayor had promised he could slash the budget without cutting services. But so far, the core service review had yet to find the gravy. The agenda was unravelling. And tensions were mounting on Team Ford. It was at this fragile time that Doug chose to hijack the limelight.

During a morning interview with CBC Radio's *Metro Morning*, the mayor's brother triumphantly announced that he had secretly been developing a plan for Toronto's eastern waterfront, a plan he had recently revealed to a group of stakeholders. "We had fifteen people in the room, and everyone's jaw just dropped when they saw it. It is spectacular, just spectacular." There would be a sleek monorail, a 1.6-million-square-foot megamall, with a Nordstrom and a Bloomingdale's and a Macy's department store, a Venice-style hotel that you could sail up to by boat. And overlooking the whole utopia would be a Ferris wheel so big it would put the London Eye to shame.

It turned out to be more of a political Hindenburg.

Doug Ford's scheme jettisoned an existing plan for Toronto's eastern shoreline, a plan more than a decade in the making and which had already cost eight hundred million dollars. To handle the project, all three levels of government had joined to form Waterfront Toronto. After years of studying and planning and assessing and surveying, the agency had designed a vibrant mixed-use community, with stores, parks and public spaces, bistros and cafés. It was a slow process for a host of reasons—the soil was contaminated, the area was prone to flooding, and there were a number of parties to please—but the Fords weren't interested in hearing about it.

The reaction to Doug's scheme was fierce.

Councillor Jaye Robinson was the first member of the Ford bloc to denounce Doug Ford's plan, followed by Stintz, Michelle Berardinetti, and John Parker. Councillors' offices were inundated with calls from angry citizens. In an open letter to the administration, nearly 150 academics, planners, activists, architects, and designers, including the celebrated Richard Florida and Paul Bedford, denounced the scheme as "ill-conceived" and "reckless." If adopted, it would "result in irrevocable harm to the City, as well as higher costs and further delays." Even the centrist councillors—who at this point were still trying to avoid public fights—took a stand against it. All this while the administration was supposed to be selling people on its budget.

CUPE Local 79, which represents city employees, seized on the chaos and commissioned one of the biggest polls in Toronto's history—a telephone survey of thirteen thousand people—to test the public mood. The poll revealed that more than three-quarters of residents wanted their city councillor to "vote in the interests of protecting city services in your community, even if it conflicts with the wishes of Mayor Ford." Only 27 percent said they would vote for Rob Ford if an election were held the next day.

By mid-September 2011, the mayor was backtracking on service cuts and Doug Ford gave up on his Ferris wheel.

In November, the mayor pitched a drastically scaled-back budget that hinged on a ten-cent transit fare hike, a modest property tax increase, and savings generated by 2,300 layoffs. The city had pulled in a $154-million surplus in the current year, but Ford still wanted cuts to daycare service, transit, ice times at city rinks, and leaf collection, as well as a few homeless shelter and swimming pool closures. Council wasn't having it. Centrist leader Josh Colle orchestrated a deal between progressives, independents, and some conservatives that required using a small chunk of the unexpected surplus to save many of the programs Ford wanted cut. He took the deal to his embattled mayor, saying, "You can take it. It can be your win," but Ford refused.

Colle's compromise budget passed 23–21.

The Ford brothers voted against it.

It was the beginning of the end in terms of Ford setting the agenda at City Hall. City council pretty much ran the show after the budget coup. The mayor did score one more important victory—albeit with council's blessing—on the labour front. In early 2012, the Ford administration negotiated new contracts with the public-sector unions that garnered significant concessions around job protection as well as an estimated $139 million in savings.

It would arguably be his greatest achievement as mayor.

From then on, the Ford administration descended into side-show territory.

I WAS IN MEXICO covering the Pan American Games when one of the more bizarre events of the Ford mayoralty occurred. It was October 2011. I had been dispatched to Guadalajara for three weeks because Toronto would be the next host city in 2015. I wasn't there for the sports; I was there to see what it was like during the Pan Ams. The traffic, security, the impact on the local economy, whether people were interested enough to buy tickets. Ford was supposed to visit a few days before the October 30 handover ceremony, when the mayor of Guadalajara would pass the Pan Am Games flag to the mayor of Toronto. At the time I headed for Mexico, Toronto Pan Am organizers confessed to me that they still had no idea if Ford was going to show.

Then, just days before Ford was supposed to leave, news broke that the mayor had called 911 when a comedian from CBC's *This Hour Has 22 Minutes*—Canada's version of *The Daily Show*—showed up in his driveway. Actress Mary Walsh, dressed as her alter ego Marg Delahunty in a red warrior-princess costume, accosted the mayor as he was about to get into his van around 9 A.M.

"Ford! It's me, Marg Delahunty!" the fifty-nine-year-old Walsh shouted in an exaggerated Newfoundland accent. The mayor looked furious. "Can I go into my car, please? Can I go into my car, please?" he said, growing more and more agitated as she touched his arm. "Oh, Mayor Ford, please, I came all the way from Newfoundland to talk to you, honey." At this point,

Ford got out of the driver's seat and headed back inside. "One good thing about being stubborn, though, Mayor Ford, is you always know what you're going to be thinking the next day," said Walsh. "God love ya! Take care of yourself, now."

The Marg Delahunty ambush is a well-known, some might say treasured, comedy sketch in Canada. Walsh's long list of victims includes former Ontario premier Mike Harris, former prime minister Jean Chrétien, Prince Philip, and Governor Sarah Palin. Most have gritted their teeth and played along. Instead, Ford called the police. Later, the mayor claimed he had no idea who Walsh was and that his daughter was afraid, although there's no indication the girl was outside at the time.

The story took a sinister twist later in the week. The CBC reported that multiple sources had told them the mayor lost his temper on the phone to the 911 dispatcher when he felt they weren't moving fast enough. According to the CBC, Ford said, "You ... bitches! Don't you fucking know? I'm Rob fucking Ford, the mayor of this city!" Ford categorically denied using the slur or leveraging his title, but he admitted to using "the F-word." The fiasco inspired American TV host Keith Olbermann to feature Ford on the "Worst Persons" segment of his show. The police refused to release the tape, but both Toronto Police Chief Bill Blair and Ontario Provincial Police Commissioner Chris Lewis said they had listened to the recording and that the CBC report was inaccurate. (Adrienne Batra, the mayor's press secretary at the time, told me after she'd left his office that "[Ford] absolutely doesn't say ['bitches' or 'Rob fucking Ford']. I promise.")

I made some calls from Mexico. The source I finally got a hold of didn't know anything about the tape, but he had another tip—one that would ultimately shape my reporting for the next two years. "From what I hear, that wasn't the only time 911 got called from that address that day." Rumour was, there had been a domestic dispute between Ford and Renata. And it wasn't the first. Confirming something so sensitive from Mexico was going to be impossible. It would have to wait until I was back.

Meanwhile, with controversy brewing in Toronto, Ford decided to make the trip south, and unusually he brought Renata with him, although she mostly stayed at the hotel. One night, Ford and I ended up at the same party. It wasn't the right moment to ask about a domestic dispute. "Hi, Mayor Ford!" I said. "We should get a photo." He looked over and smiled warmly. "Sure." I realized he had no idea who I was. "Great! Just to confirm, it's me, Robyn Doolittle, from the *Star*." His eyes got wide and he shook his head. "Oh, nah, sorry." I handed my camera to someone standing nearby. "No, no, no," I said. "We're doing this." He relented, and we both flashed big grins. It's a lovely photo. I sent both the mayor and Doug a copy. For the next year, Doug referred to me as Rob's "girlfriend."

At the handover ceremony in Guadalajara, Ford conducted himself like the mayor of a major North American city. Organizers told me he was nervous about getting up in front of fifty thousand screaming people, but when the Canadian national anthem started to play, he sang along and smiled. In a sharp black suit and fresh haircut, he beamed as Guadalajara's Mayor Jorge Aristóteles Sandoval Díaz handed him the Pan Am flag.

As soon as my plane touched down in Toronto, I got to work on the domestic call story. I contacted sources in police and emergency services, as well as some folks in Ford's neighbourhood. The trick would be catching the next incident shortly after it happened.

I got my break at 8 P.M. on Christmas Day. I was at my parents' place three hours outside of the city.

"Robyn?" It was a police source I had gotten to know during my crime reporting days, and he was whispering.

"Hey. What's up?"

"Look, I can't talk. I just wanted to let you know there was another domestic dispute at Ford's place this morning. Apparently, he was drunk and taking the kids to the airport to go to Florida or something. The wife's parents phoned it in."

"Any idea what time?"

"Sometime between 4 and 5 A.M. I gotta go."

There was no sense calling the police division for comment. All they'd do is tell headquarters that the media was asking questions. None of my people were going to talk over the phone. I'd head back to the city early the next day and start chasing it then.

CANADIANS MIGHT NOT REALIZE IT, but they live in one of the more secretive countries in the developed world. In 2013, Canada ranked fifty-sixth out of ninety-five countries in an annual transparency report card produced by the Centre for Law and Democracy. The Halifax-based human rights organization helped develop an internationally respected method to assess countries with "right-to-information" laws. In the inaugural ranking, Canada came in at forty-second out of eighty-nine countries. We're now in the bottom half, below Mongolia, Russia, and Romania. So what does that have to do with City Hall reporting? When it comes to Toronto's mayor, rumours and gossip are as common as football references. The problem is, you can't separate fact from fiction under our archaic access-to-information laws.

"Canada is utterly behind. It's not because of anything we're doing, it's because other countries are getting better," said Toby Mendel, the centre's executive director. And at this rate, he added, we will continue to slip.

In 1983, Canada became one of the first countries in the world to adopt access-to-information legislation (the first being Sweden in 1766) under Prime Minister Pierre Trudeau. The provinces followed suit in subsequent years, and municipal freedom-of-information laws were crafted by the provinces. With a five-dollar cheque, Canadians were suddenly able to demand that public institutions release internal documents such as budgets, letters, memos, and staff reports. But over the years, we fell behind. There are huge gaps in the Canadian system. The requests take too long to process, and bureaucrats have too many excuses to deny access.

This lack of transparency has made it extraordinarily difficult for journalists to confirm basic information about public figures like Rob Ford. Even the mayor's schedule, something routinely released by previous mayors, must be obtained under a freedom-of-information request. And what does get released is largely incomplete. Huge chunks are marked "private." Ford himself has conceded that these schedules are only "a tidbit of what's really going on."

If that wasn't bad enough, Canadian access laws don't cover the judicial system. Most paperwork filed in Ontario's court system, such as transcripts and case "information"— essentially a summary of the allegations, court appearances, and any outcomes—is supposed to be public. In reality, it's not that simple.

As the law stands, someone trying to access a public document in our publicly funded judicial system is at the mercy of whatever court clerk happens to be on duty. While records filed in court are supposed to be accessible, you can only get them if you have exact details about the case, such as the incident date, the charges, and the accused's birthday. For a reporter following up on a lead, this is information you are likely hoping to learn from the document you're requesting. To recap this absurd situation: to get the paperwork, you need to know information that can only be learned from the paperwork. It's a Catch-22.

When I explained this problem to Ontario's information and privacy commissioner, Ann Cavoukian, she was aghast. "That offends me, because people hide behind privacy. That has nothing to do with privacy. Ultimately, the information is accessible, if you have the right key."

This isn't the way it works in "best practices" countries. When news broke about Rob Ford's 1999 drunk driving arrest in Florida, reporters immediately contacted the Miami-Dade courthouse. Within a few hours, a clerk emailed us a PDF of the police affidavit, along with details of the sentencing.

As for police documents, every jurisdiction has restrictions on access because of the sensitive nature of the information, when no charges are laid. But few are as secretive as Canada. In the United States, for instance—which ranks forty-second out of ninety-five countries in the 2013 annual access rankings—even in sensitive cases journalists are usually able to obtain some information. In New York State, if police are called to someone's home, it is a matter of public record. The address and the nature of the call must be disclosed, and if someone is charged, then the arrest report and the names of those involved become public. In Ontario, if police investigate an incident, it can be kept entirely secret, including whether the call occurred, whether officers were sent to investigate, and the names of any suspects.

Months earlier, after I began hearing about a handful of incidents at the mayor's home through various emergency services sources, I filed a freedom-of-information request for a summary of all the 911 calls made on the mayor's street over a five-year period. The document I got back was twenty-nine pages of a heavily redacted list of calls. There were no addresses and no dates.

Camille Jobin-Davis, the assistant director of New York State's Committee on Open Government, was shocked when we spoke about the challenges of crime reporting in Canada. So police in Canada wouldn't even confirm if they had gone to a house? Nope. Or why they were called? Nope. "That doesn't quite make sense to me, because I can tell when there's a police car driving through my neighbourhood. There's nothing private about that.... Our logic is that by merely indicating the nature of the call, we're not releasing anything about who was present or what the allegations are," Jobin-Davis said. "I think the checks on use of public resources is a valuable one, and I think the checks on the behaviour of those officials who have police authority over our lives is also a valuable one."

I wish Canadian lawmakers felt the same way.

On December 29, 2011, when I phoned Toronto police for details about the Christmas Day incident at Mayor Rob Ford's home, I was told they could not confirm or deny anything, because that information was private. I contacted the ranking officer in the Fords' Etobicoke North ward, who also happened to be a friend of the family.

"Anyone, if it's you or I, they have a right to privacy if someone calls the police and it's a domestic related issue," Superintendent Ron Taverner said. "We don't go around talking about that. That's their personal business. I don't think anybody would want that."

I, of course, was expecting this. And by the time I phoned Taverner, I'd already confirmed that the service was investigating an incident at the mayor's Etobicoke home that took place early Christmas morning. I had also confirmed that they were looking into a separate domestic complaint involving the mayor on October 25, the call I had heard about in Mexico. That was the one made hours after the mayor had phoned 911 on CBC comedian Mary Walsh. I learned that the investigating detective was Jacqueline Baus, who was with the Youth and Family Violence Unit. When I got her on the phone, all she would say was that the cases were open. She refused to give details. I would need to dig those up on my own.

Over the next few days, I met a source in a coffee shop, then another in a downtown bar. They allowed me to read an official synopsis of the Christmas morning incident, and a high-ranking police source gave me an account of the October call.

Two sources with knowledge of the October incident said it was Renata who called 911, at 10:17 P.M., after she and Ford got into a shouting match. On Christmas morning, it was Renata's parents who had phoned. The Brejniaks said the mayor had been drinking, and he was heading to the airport with his children.

He planned to take them to Florida against Renata's wishes. My sources were clear that, as far as the police knew, Renata had not accused Ford of being violent.

Nevertheless, the situation was troubling. Rob Ford was essentially Toronto's CEO. The mayor—or a designate acting on his behalf—has a seat on the Toronto Police Service's civilian oversight board. In fact, four of the seven board members are city appointees. By choosing the chair of his budget committee, and through appointments to the board, the mayor has a say in the police budget. In 2011, the service was on the verge of a massive 10 percent cut to its 2012 budget. After Chief Bill Blair paid a personal visit to Rob Ford's office, the service ended up with a modest increase. Political and police sources said it was the mayor who made that happen.

This dynamic leaves Toronto officers in a quandary when they are called to investigate the man who is, at least indirectly, their boss. According to the letter of the law, Toronto police are under no obligation to disclose any details about an ongoing investigation. But they can, and do, use their discretion. In my experience, in cases where there is heightened public interest, nine times out of ten they will release basic information about an incident. In my two years as a crime reporter, I would often call and ask about a stabbing or break-and-enter. I can't recall a single time when a police spokesperson refused to provide me with a short synopsis and some vague details about the people involved, such as the age and sex of the victim, or a brief description of a suspect. But when it came to the mayor, it seemed as if he was being afforded more privacy than the average citizen.

When I had the details of the latest 911 calls nailed down,

I put in my official call to Toronto police. True to form, they refused to comment. I asked police spokesperson Mark Pugash whether the police investigating the mayor were placed in a conflict because of Ford's position. "The procedures don't take into account the social position or occupation of a person being investigated or charged," he said.

The story "Rob Ford 911 Calls Raise Questions" ran on the *Star*'s front page on December 30. Later that day, the Fords emailed the *Toronto Sun* a photo of the mayor playing with his children in a swimming pool. The caption read, "Mayor Rob Ford and his children Douglas and Stephanie having fun in Florida this week. (Courtesy the Ford family)." *Sun* columnist Joe Warmington, one of only a handful of writers the mayor will talk to, called Ford at the family's condo in Hallandale.

> My first call was to a cellphone and the familiar voice on the other end answered on the second ring.
>
> "Happy New Year, Joe," the mayor said jovially from Florida, with his kids laughing in the background.
>
> Turns out Ford had not heard of the media report but said everything was now fine.
>
> "We have had a great couple of days down here," he said of he and his young children Stephanie and Douglas. "There's no problem at all."
>
> His brother Doug, who was with the mayor in Florida and like him returned home Friday, said "Rob was not drinking as reported. It's just inaccurate."
>
> In fact, a source close to the investigation told me that while alcohol was an issue none was consumed by the mayor.

For a man who frequently accused the media of going after his family, it was surprising how often Ford seemed to use his wife and children as a political shield.

SEVEN

THE BIER MARKT

Leo Navarro was wandering in a daze, not sure if he could trust his eyes. He needed air. A moment to think. Someone could handle his tables for a few minutes. He ducked out of the Bier Markt's side door and bumped into a server named Jenna sitting by the door, smoking. He seemed rattled.

"What's up with you?" she asked.

He looked at her.

"I think I just saw the mayor do blow."

THE BIG RED QUEEN STREETCAR rolled up to City Hall a little after 8:30 A.M. I clambered out the rear doors, trying to keep my coffee in its cup rather than on the newspaper tucked under my arm. It was the second day of the March 2012 library strike. Hundreds of kind-looking women and pasty-looking men in Tilley hats were marching in a circle around Nathan Phillips Square, placards draped around their necks, some singing "Row, Row, Row Your Boat" to pass the time. The Ford administration was targeting the public sector, but the unions had an ally in Mother Nature. The forecast predicted sunny weather all week, which was pretty remarkable for Toronto in March.

It was going to be a busy day. In addition to the library strike, top lawyer Clayton Ruby had just launched a lawsuit accusing the mayor of a conflict of interest, which the press was still trying to figure out. Most importantly, city council was about to debate a cornerstone of the Ford administration's agenda—whether Toronto would build a subway or an above-ground light rail system in the northeast end of the city along Sheppard Avenue. The mayor wanted "subways, subways, subways," and getting that vote through council would either solidify his authority during a time of turmoil or expose his weakened leadership. It seemed as if everything was at stake. By the end of the day, none of it seemed important.

I was sitting at my messy desk in the press gallery when my land line started to ring.

It was my city editor, Graham Parley. Parley looked exactly how you would expect an old-school print guy to look. He was a gruff-talking Brit, with frizzy grey hair, a thick moustache, and zero tolerance for slackers.

"What's up?" I said.

"It's sort of sensitive," Parley said quietly, which was unusual. "We just got a tip that I want you to look into. Apparently, Ford was at the Bier Markt on St. Patrick's Day this weekend. Showed up totally hammered. We heard that someone walked in on him snorting coke in some private room and then he got kicked out by security."

"Wow," I said. I'd suspected Ford had a drinking problem, and there were always rumours about drugs. But cocaine? In a crowded bar?

"Here's the thing: the place is on lockdown. Staff aren't supposed to talk about it. Can you call some police sources and check it out?"

I knew the Bier Markt well. It was a five-minute walk from the *Star* along the Esplanade, a strip of bars and pubs just off Yonge Street. By day, it was one of the nicer and more expensive places to eat in the St. Lawrence Market district. After dark, it transitioned to a trendy nightclub that was popular with young professionals and university students.

I punched out a few cryptic text messages to some police contacts who had been helpful on my stories about domestic calls to the police from the Ford home. No one had heard about the mayor being in trouble. I logged into Twitter. It didn't take long to find photos from Saturday night of Ford looking woozy in a bright-green tie, linked arm in arm with random groups of people on the street. In one, Ford was standing in front of a coffee shop that I knew was just around the corner from the Bier Markt. I also realized a weekly paper called *The Grid* (which is owned by the same company as the *Star*) was already on the story. Earlier that day they'd published their regular roundup of Ford sightings over the last seven days. The writer, Jonathan Goldsbie, put it together by trawling social media. Apparently, Ford had arrived at the Bier Markt with a group around midnight. They were moved to a private room. "According to a server," wrote Goldsbie, "the group looked like they had already been somewhere earlier, and said they'd wanted to get out and cut loose for the night."

Goldsbie had obviously been poking around, which accounted for the "lockdown" our tipster had warned us about. I wanted a bit more information before heading to the restaurant myself. People are always more likely to talk when they think they're confirming something you already know rather than digging for dirt you're not sure is there.

The next afternoon, I walked over to the Bier Markt for lunch and took a seat near the window at a small table draped in white linens. I was one of about a dozen people in the place—not an ideal backdrop for a sensitive conversation.

The waitress came by to take my order.

"Um, I'll have the cheese fondue please."

"Great," she said, starting to turn away.

"Oh, hey." I scrunched up my nose and whispered, "So, like, what's all this stuff on Twitter about the mayor? Was he really here on the weekend?"

The muscles in her face tightened. "Sorry, I haven't heard anything about that."

I ate my lunch and left. I would need to come back at night when it was crowded. I texted a friend of mine named Will. "Hey. What are you doing Thursday? Think you could sit with me at the Bier Markt for a few hours while I work? The *Star* will buy drinks." He was in.

We grabbed a bar table just off the dance floor. Every twenty minutes, I'd wander around looking for a staff member who was alone and didn't seem to be management. No one was very chatty, but bit by bit, pieces started to come together. Ford had arrived "out of it." He was put in the back, away from everyone, and he stayed there for less than an hour. Eventually, he was urged to leave. On his way out, he "stormed the dance floor," and there was supposedly security footage of this. As for what happened in the private room, only one person had seen it.

Will and I went back Friday night and then Saturday. By

then I knew I was looking for an olive-skinned bus boy. But I could feel my window was closing. The Bier Markt was big, but my questions were starting to draw attention. I could see bartenders gesturing my way and whispering. Then I saw a young Spanish-looking guy in a black apron walk by with a handful of dirty dishes. Will and I looked at each other. I got up and followed him to the kitchen, where he briefly disappeared. In seconds, he flew back into the busy club carrying steaming plates of something. He was heading to the far side of the room, where a wall divided tables from the nosy bartenders. Now was my chance.

"Hey," I said, loud enough that he could hear me over the booming music. "Look, I'll be quick. I'm trying to find the guy who walked in on Rob Ford supposedly snorting coke."

He smirked and half chuckled. "Yeah, that was me."

"I thought it might be," I said. "I'm Robyn from the *Star*. Can we talk?"

His name was Leo Navarro, and he would meet me at 2 A.M. after his shift. I headed back to my table, downed the rest of my beer, and emailed Graham Parley: "Found him."

I WAS WAITING on the sidewalk a bit down the street when Navarro came outside. We started to walk west and eventually hopped in a cab. I'd promised to drive him home. Navarro didn't mind if I taped the conversation, but he asked me to keep his name out of it. He was a college student and he needed this job. The restaurant would definitely fire him if they thought he was talking. I agreed to keep his identity confidential until he instructed otherwise.

According to Navarro, Ford and an entourage showed up around 11:30 P.M. on March 17 and were taken to the private room in back, the Merchant Room, which is curtained off. One of the club's security guards was outside the entrance. Someone else was serving the room. Navarro was just there to deliver a plate of poutine. As he pulled back the red curtain, he saw the mayor with "some really young girl right beside him." Ford leaned towards her and "snorted something off the girl's hand." Then "he kinda just wiped his nose right after," jerking his head up. Then the woman curled forward, sniffed, and threw her head back. He never saw any powder. There weren't any lines on the table. Ford didn't say anything or even acknowledge him. When the mayor had arrived at the club, "he was already hammered. So, I mean, he really had googly eyes, and he wasn't paying attention."

Navarro left the room and tried to process what had happened. He didn't say anything to anyone for at least ten minutes. He finally had to get some air out back. That's when he told Jenna and then a bartender about what he'd seen. He never told a manager, and he hadn't heard about the mayor being asked to leave. He did show me a business card belonging to one of Ford's young aides, Brooks Barnett.

"There's one other thing I should probably tell you, in the interest of full disclosure," Navarro said. "I supported Smitherman in the election."

A FEW DAYS AFTER I tracked down Navarro, a DJ called in to the *Dean Blundell Show* on 102.1 The Edge, claiming he had been working at the Bier Markt when the mayor showed up. He told the radio host his booth had been set up beside the private room where Ford, two assistants, a few buddies, and two women around the age of thirty were partying. "I'm trying to do my thing, and then I hear all this noise in the background," the DJ said. Ford was "slamming the table, saying that he's this, he's that." He was "bickering, arguing, just loud-mouthing." He told Blundell that the mayor was "starting fights with his buddies and acting like an idiot."

When I contacted the DJ's entertainment company, Freshstone, the owner, Rob Stone, mistook me for someone from the Bier Markt's head office. "I already gave his number to someone this morning," he said. When I identified myself as a reporter, Stone would not put me in touch with the DJ and made a note of saying he wasn't a regular staff member.

The Bier Markt operating partner, Robert Medal, denied everything in an email to me. "On March 17 [2012], Mr. Ford was an exemplary guest enjoying a fun night out at the Bier Markt. At no time was Mr. Ford or any member of his group ever asked to leave the premises. When he and his group chose to leave the restaurant, our staff let them exit via a private dining area for their convenience. I did want to further clarify one point. Guests at the Bier Markt who do not adhere to the law or requirements laid out by AGCO's [the Alcohol and Gaming Commission of Ontario's] Smart Serve program are promptly exited from the restaurant."

Staff had been warned not to talk to media, and in fact Navarro was punished for even mentioning what he'd seen to other staff members. The restaurant had been in trouble a few times with the AGCO.

I moved on to my contacts within the mayor's circle. The more pieces I uncovered, the stranger the story became.

Rob Ford didn't have a typical political staff. Most of his hires were chosen for their loyalty rather than political experience. You could count his senior aides on one hand. The majority of the roster was dominated by "kids," as they were called in the office, fresh out of university. They were his "special assistants." Some focused on the mayor's football teams. Others answered email and returned constituents' calls. The veteran aides sometimes got to help with policy files. The one thing everyone had to do was take turns being Ford's "body man."

The night of St. Patrick's Day, it was Brooks Barnett's turn. He'd gotten a call to go to City Hall around 7 P.M. When he arrived, the mayor was crouching like a football player and sprinting around his office. A scantily clad woman was there whom Barnett didn't recognize, as well as a friend of the mayor's. Ford was "talking quickly," "slurring," and seemed generally "out of it." Barnett texted a senior staffer for advice. Earl Provost, who managed councillor relations, rushed to City Hall. The mayor said he "wanted to party."

I heard they headed to the Bier Markt after that, and once they got kicked out they returned to City Hall. That was when the mayor flew into a rage, pushing Brooks Barnett hard enough that he lost his footing. There was also some suggestion that Ford had driven drunk or high later on. One former staffer told me Ford had almost run Earl Provost over with his car.

It was more than a year before I learned the full details through police documents and additional interviews. It turned out it wasn't just Provost and Barnett there that night. Two other staffers, Olivia Gondek and Isaac Ransom, had also been called in. When Ford decided he wanted to head to a bar, the group got into two cabs and made the short drive to the Bier Markt. En route, the mayor started heckling the cab driver, calling him a "Paki" and mocking his accent. After it became clear the restaurant staff was ready for the mayor to leave, the group returned to City Hall. That's when things really deteriorated. Ford was wild, aggressive, and talking irrationally. One staff member thought they saw the mayor pop an OxyContin pill. When he announced he wanted to start phoning constituents back, staff members unplugged his phone. Confused and frustrated, Ford turned to Barnett and told him, "I hate you!" The mayor shoved Barnett, who fell onto an office couch. "Fuck this," Barnett said, and walked out.

At 2:30 A.M., Ford stumbled down to the City Hall security desk carrying a half-empty bottle of St-Rémy French brandy. He was sweating and slurring his words. He told two guards that he wanted to leave but his car had been stolen. Ford asked one of the men, Davood Mohammadi, to call the police.

"I reminded the mayor that he did not drive to City Hall and that his car was safe and sound at his place," Mohammadi wrote in an incident report after the fact. (The city refused to release this report until November 2013, denying a freedom-of-information request filed by the *Star*.)

Things were out of hand. Ford continued to wander around, yelling and swearing. Staffer Isaac Ransom overheard the mayor tell a female security guard he was "going to eat her box." He also claimed to have heard Ford tell his colleague Olivia Gondek, "I'm going to eat you out" and "I banged your pussy." (Gondek denies this.) Eventually, Provost got the mayor into a cab and headed for Etobicoke, but once they pulled into his driveway, Ford announced he wanted to go out again. He got into his own car. Provost jumped out of the cab to try to block the driveway. The mayor's car nearly hit the cab as it peeled out of the driveway and disappeared. No one heard from him for a full day.

His most senior staff huddled the next morning for a meeting. They were sure it was over. But reporters were never able to nail down the story. Navarro hadn't seen any powder. I'd confirmed that Ford was drunk at the Bier Markt and that he'd been walked out by security, but that wasn't quite enough for a story. It was St. Patrick's Day, after all. As for the stuff about City Hall, which would have been in the public interest, the details were still sketchy for me. At the time, I had only two sources, and neither had seen it with their own eyes. I had more work to do.

Back at City Hall, Ford apologized to Barnett. The young aide, fresh out of university with aspirations for a future in politics, reluctantly accepted. (In November 2013, when many of these details first surfaced publicly through police documents, Ford threatened to sue former staff members as well as Navarro from the Bier Markt for what they had told police about that night. As of year's end he hadn't followed through on the threat.)

One former staff member who was working in the office at the time told me that the St. Patrick's Day incident was a turning point. From then on, the mayor became more and more erratic.

"We knew he drank," said one former staffer, "but this was the first time we heard about drugs."

The more I dug, the more obvious it was that something bigger was happening. According to three former staff members and a close confidant, senior staff had been trying to get Ford into rehab for more than a year. They believed his drinking was affecting his job. He was arriving late at the office and sometimes not at all. More and more, he couldn't be relied upon to show up at events. More and more, he wasn't answering his cell phone. With the mayor missing in action, his administration had lost control.

While many councillors identify with a political party, the municipal system is independent. Votes are won on an individual basis. A personal call from the mayor can help sway a fence-sitter. Those conversations weren't happening at City Hall. A group of centrist councillors had seized power. At one point, there was talk among the mayor's staffers about organizing a fake vacation during which he would go to a treatment centre. Ford refused. As a last resort, they tried to hook him up with a prominent person in the city who had also struggled with addiction, just to talk. Ford refused.

"That's the story you should be looking into," a high-ranking former staffer told me at the time. "He's going to die otherwise."

MY FOCUS SHIFTED AWAY from the Bier Markt incident to the drinking and rehab. Photos of the mayor buying mickeys of vodka—almost always the cheap Russian Prince brand—had been popping up on Twitter for weeks. I'd been taking screenshots and filing them away in a just-in-case folder. Most of the sightings ended up in Goldsbie's weekly *Grid* roundup. Now I started reaching out to these Twitter paparazzi for more details.

As the story got further along, the head of the *Star*'s investigative unit, Kevin Donovan, got involved. He was soon able to deliver a key source to further confirm that the mayor's staff was hoping to get him into a rehabilitation program.

The story was coming together. We were confident that

the mayor had a drinking problem and that his staff wanted him to get help. The next part was proving the public interest. Rob Ford was not the first political leader to struggle with alcohol. That private battle becomes public news only after it begins to impact the official's job. This clearly seemed to be the case for the mayor. With the Ford administration refusing to release the mayor's daily schedule, the *Star* and other organizations were obtaining them through freedom-of-information requests. Analyzing the latest batch against the same period a year before clearly showed that Ford's workload had been cut in half. I began compiling a list of events where the mayor was a no-show. A VIA Rail speaking engagement; a meeting with Calgary's Mayor Naheed Nenshi; official greetings of foreign dignitaries. Many of Toronto's most influential city-builders hadn't met the mayor in more than a year: United Way Toronto CEO Susan McIsaac; Board of Trade president, Carol Wilding; CivicAction's CEO, Mitzie Hunter; the list went on. His own committee chairs acknowledged they hadn't met with Ford in months. Toronto's city manager was dealing with the chief of staff, Amir Remtulla, not the mayor. The only time Ford could be 100 percent relied upon to show up was at a monthly council meeting, an executive committee meeting, and every football practice and game.

I spoke with a dozen prominent, non-partisan civic leaders in Toronto who expressed serious concern about the mayor's truancy. Rob Ford was the head of Canada's sixth largest government. He oversaw an annual operating budget of nine billion dollars, and he was the CEO to fifty thousand city employees. When he opened his mouth, he spoke for 2.8 million people. (And it's worth noting that every year, taxpayers write the mayor of Toronto a cheque for $170,000 as compensation for his work.) Ford's absences troubled many.

By the end of April 2012, Donovan and I had formally looped in the mayor's office about our investigation, giving them adequate time to respond. We spoke to staff in person, left phone messages, sent texts and private notes on Twitter. A detailed email with all the allegations went out to senior staff as well as the mayor. A few days later, I bumped into Ford's chief of staff near the security desk in the rotunda.

"When's it coming?" Remtulla asked.

"Soon, I think. Maybe in a few days."

He simply nodded.

The *Star*'s in-house lawyer had been through a draft story. The mayor's office had declined to comment. On May 2, Donovan and I met with the *Star*'s senior editors, the lawyer, and the publisher, John Cruickshank, in the paper's fifth-floor boardroom overlooking Lake Ontario. I had to give a presentation detailing everything I knew and how I knew it. I used ten four-foot-long sheets of white paper and a pack of Magic Markers to outline my case. I broke down each source, how they knew what they knew, how it fit into the larger narrative, and then taped these sheets around the walls. I was grilled about each one. I left work that night on edge but excited. This had been my life for a month, and now we were close to publishing. A friend took me out to dinner in the east end of Toronto.

A little after 9 P.M. my cell phone rang. It was Daniel Dale calling from a *Star* land line. Daniel and I had been interns together, and he had moved to our City Hall bureau a year and a half earlier. He was, and is, one of my best friends.

"Hey, D," I said. "What are you doing at work so late?"

"Robyn!" His voice was shaking. "I can't— You will not believe what just happened. I can't believe it. I'm so sorry."

ONCE I'D HEARD DALE OUT, I rushed in to the *Star*. By now, I was shaking too. I found Dale in the newsroom. There was no colour in his face. Everyone was being very quiet. He spotted me and got up from his desk. We walked around a corner.

"Are you okay?"

"I'm okay," he said, but he didn't look okay.

"I just don't get it. What happened?" I asked. "Did you call the police?"

Dale started at the beginning.

Earlier that day, probably around the time I was taping those sheets of paper to the boardroom walls, one of Dale's sources called with a story idea. The mayor was trying to buy a chunk of city parkland that was next to his Etobicoke property. It was an unusual request. In a letter to the Toronto and Region Conservation Authority, Rob and Renata Ford had said they needed it to build a fence around their home for "safety" reasons. This perplexed Dale. The Fords' backyard was already fenced. He wondered how the parcel of land would help with security.

Most reporters would have just written around that hole in the logic. But Dale isn't most reporters. He wrote an early story to be posted on the *Star*'s website and drove to Etobicoke to see for himself the land Ford wanted to buy. He was irritated about having to miss a documentary he'd bought tickets to weeks before.

It was 7:30 P.M. and Dale was in the park behind the Fords' fenced backyard, trying to identify the piece of parkland in question. The summer sun meant it was still bright. Standing about fifteen metres from the back of the Fords' property, Dale tried to take a photo of a group of trees he thought might be on the right spot—maybe he would post it on Twitter—but his BlackBerry died before the photo saved. Moments later, the mayor came barrelling around the corner, wearing a white Team Ford campaign T-shirt, sweatpants, and flip-flops. "Hey, buddy," he hollered. "What are you doing? Are you spying on me? Are you spying on me? Are you spying on me?"

Dale was confused. Astonished. He explained that he was there to look at the parkland Ford had applied to purchase. The mayor kept coming at him, screaming about him spying. Then Ford cocked his fist and charged in a full-out sprint.

"Mayor Ford," Dale yelled, "I'm writing about the land! I'm just looking at the land! You're trying to buy the TRCA land!"

Dale fumbled for his recorder. He wanted to document whatever was about to happen.

Ford yelled, "Drop your phone! Drop your phone now!"

Dale tried to run, but Ford shuffled left, then right, blocking his path as if it were some sort of football game. Finally, Dale threw his phone and recorder to the ground—"Take them!"— and made a break for it.

The moment Dale fled, Ford went back to his house and called staff. They saw an opportunity and began calling friendly media. Ford held a press conference in his front yard to announce he had caught Dale standing on cinder blocks, looking into his backyard, taking photos of his children. "It was, like, unbelievable what he was doing. And I caught the guy cold. It's unbelievable what he did. And I'm not gonna put up with it.

I've got the police here, and if I have to press charges I will. And it's pretty emotional. It's tough on my neighbour. It's tough on my family."

The next morning, Ford elaborated on Jerry Agar's Newstalk 1010 radio show. "My neighbour knocked on my door at about eight o'clock. I was helping my daughter with her homework, and he said—my neighbour's a senior, he's about seventy-five years old—and he said, 'There's some guy taking pictures out in your backyard.'"

In the mayor's version, he had calmly asked Dale what he was doing. "He starts throwing everything on the ground. 'Oh, don't hit me, don't hit me.' He was, like, in panic mode. Like a deer caught in the headlights.... [I said], 'Hey, I'm not touching ya.... But what are you doing? Like, you know, taking pictures of my kids? Of my family? You know, are you a sicko? What's your problem?'... He was standing on cinder blocks. Up against my, the back of my fence."

Ford claimed he had security footage that showed Dale's "head bopping up and down." Agar asked the mayor about Dale's claim that Ford had ordered him to drop his phone. "He voluntarily gave this stuff up. So, it wasn't like I, you know, stole his money or his keys," Ford said. "Honestly, I was so upset, I didn't know if I was gonna hit him or not. And I said, No, no, keep your cool, Rob.... As the mayor, you can't do that. You have to have control."

The bottom line, Ford concluded, was that the *Toronto Star* couldn't be trusted. "They are liars."

The Twittersphere dubbed the fiasco #Fencegate. (Most of Ford's scandals earned a Watergate-inspired name on Twitter.

There would later be #Assgate, when former mayoral candidate Sarah Thomson accused Ford of groping her, and, of course, #Crackgate.)

Back at the paper, Dale wrote a first-person account which was posted online that same night. But almost all of the coverage went with the mayor's inaccurate version. The headline on the *Toronto Sun*'s story was "Mayor Nabs Reporter: Ford Furious After Catching *Star* Correspondent Taking Pictures of His House from Backyard." Respected CBC anchor Anne-Marie Mediwake asked the mayor the next day, "I want to start with the issue of private security. You've said in the past that you don't want it. But do incidents like this prove that maybe you need it?" Global TV anchor Kris Reyes tweeted, "Your reaction to Daniel Dale and the Rob Ford story. Mayor's reax, justified?"

Given Ford's history of taking liberties with the truth when his back was against a wall—the Maple Leafs game, the marijuana charge, for example—the media coverage was exceptionally frustrating.

A week after the incident, the police closed the case. The police found no photos of the mayor's family—or his backyard, for that matter—on Dale's phone, which had been in their possession since that evening. Security footage proved that Dale did not look over the fence. In fact, he'd never been close to it.

Dale had been completely exonerated, but it didn't get the same coverage. A lot of people tuned in only to that first press conference in the mayor's front yard, where Ford's account had gone unchallenged. For the next year, many pundits, columnists, and Ford supporters were still talking about Dale snooping around the mayor's backyard. (In December 2013, a year and a half after the fence incident, Ford was forced to admit he'd made it all up.)

The furor was strong enough that my story about staff counselling the mayor to enter an alcohol rehab program was shelved. Dale felt awful; he'd guessed from the start what the result would be. With the *Star* a player in the latest mayoral controversy, it wasn't the right time. "It will run eventually. Something else will happen," my editor, Graham Parley, predicted.

I whittled my investigation down to a piece about the mayor's dwindling workload, with the "why" left unanswered.

Meanwhile, the night after Ford confronted Dale, the mayor went down to Sullie Gorman's pub at the Royal York Plaza, near his mother's home. It was the kind of tucked-away watering hole where everyone knew everybody, and people, usually, kept their mouths shut.

According to someone who was there that night, Ford started the evening at a Bank of Montreal ATM. He was meeting a well-known cocaine dealer in Etobicoke. "He was trying to take out five hundred dollars, but it wouldn't let him. He was getting really, really angry." Next, the patron says, Ford was inside, offering to buy shots for a group of women.

He was "dancing up a storm" and kept making trips to the washroom. Outside the bar, Ford was stumbling and rambling— mostly about wanting to fight a *Star* reporter. He lit up a joint in the parking lot.

"It wasn't like he was hiding it or anything," said the patron.

EIGHT

THE DIRTY DOZEN

With two minutes until showtime, Councillor Doug Ford bounded into the Newstalk 1010 studio, giddily clutching a newspaper article he had torn out of the *National Post*. He pushed it up against the glass for the half-dozen reporters who had made the trip uptown to watch the show live from the control room. Satisfied that everyone had their shot, Doug Jr. settled into his black swivel chair beside the mayor and popped on his headphones.

At 1:06 P.M., the familiar jingle boomed from the speakers and the smooth-talking radio announcer introduced the pair: "You're listening to *The City* with Mayor Rob Ford and Councillor Doug Ford on Newstalk 1010." It was their first show back after a nearly three-month hiatus.

"Well, Rob," Doug said, "how was the summer? Uneventful?"

The quip earned a chuckle from those looking on.

It was September 16, 2012, and Rob Ford was in all kinds of trouble. His job was in jeopardy. Earlier in the year, Clayton Ruby had taken him to court for allegedly violating municipal conflict-of-interest laws. As a councillor, Ford had used city letterhead to solicit donations from lobbyists for his football charity.

He had been ordered by the previous council to repay that money, but never did. As mayor, he had asked the current council to undo that penalty, and it obliged. However, Ford had cast a vote in his own favour, and if a judge agreed that his vote constituted a conflict of interest, the penalty was mandatory removal from office. The trial had just finished, and Ford's testimony had not gone well.

That was just one of the problems the mayor was dealing with. Days earlier, *The Globe and Mail* had revealed that Ford was using his staff and city cell phones to help run his football team. Never mind that this use of taxpayers' dollars undermined the bedrock of the Ford platform, the mayor's bigger problem was that a week earlier he had testified under oath that he no longer used city resources for football activities. The mayor was also embroiled in a six-million-dollar defamation lawsuit, a case that would soon be in court. Plus, his campaign finances were being audited.

It was all too much for brother Doug. "You know, folks, let's jump on this right from the get-go," he said into the radio microphone. "There's a double standard now." In his garbled fashion, Doug said that environmentalists—"the tree huggers association"—had lost their grants and were bent on revenge. They were to blame for Rob's court problems.

He held up the *National Post* article. "They're all interconnected here, folks. It's the unions," he said. "It's just a big circle. I call 'em the dirty dozen."

The Fords had a habit of blaming the media for their troubles. But on this front, the councillor had a point. Most of Rob Ford's legal problems did in fact intersect with a small group of brainy left-wing activists who knew the city bylaws, understood the mechanisms to have them enforced, and revelled in any opportunity to use those rules against the mayor.

Leading that charge was a twenty-something labour relations officer with a mouthful for a last name. Or, as Doug Ford calls him, "that little prick."

ADAM CHALEFF-FREUDENTHALER was not a typical twenty-six-year-old. By early 2011, he had been taking on people in power for the last decade, and he understood how to work the media. As a teenager, Chaleff-Freudenthaler was a member of the Toronto Youth Cabinet. He parlayed that experience into a position on the Toronto Library Board. In 2010, Chaleff-Freudenthaler had run, unsuccessfully, to be a school board trustee. In high school, he co-founded a province-wide network of student activists. By sixteen, he had been arrested with three others while protesting against then-premier Mike Harris. Police tossed the group in the back of a van and held them for more than nine hours without charge, including three hours in a cell. After a formal complaint, the police service was forced to apologize and Chaleff-Freudenthaler was awarded twenty thousand dollars. Chances are, between 2001 and 2006, if students were fighting against something—Pepsi in public school vending machines, the invasion of Iraq, loopholes in tobacco advertising laws, raises in tuition fees, school funding cuts, public space restrictions—Chaleff-Freudenthaler had a hand in it. A decade ago, Toronto's left-wing weekly *NOW* magazine named him one of "10 Teens Taking Over." In the magazine's Q&A, he was asked, "Why are people over 20 full of shit?" Chaleff-Freudenthaler answered, "They're not full of shit. They're just broken by the myths and lies used to oppress Joe/Jane Citizen." He was exactly the kind of "left-wing kook" Don Cherry had been talking about. And he was one of the "dirty dozen" included in that *National Post* clipping Doug Ford had been waving around at the radio studio.

He had begun his journey onto Doug Ford's so-called dirty dozen list the morning of April 6, 2011, when he read a *Globe and Mail* story by freelance writer John Lorinc which claimed that the Ford family corporation, Doug Ford Holdings, had spent $69,722.31 on mayoral campaign expenses such as salaries, polling, and fundraising overhead. Corporations and unions are not allowed to donate to municipal campaigns, and candidates are allowed to borrow money only from banks or other recognized lending institutions. What troubled Chaleff-Freudenthaler most was the possibility that Deco Labels had given Ford's mayoralty campaign an improper loan.

Chaleff-Freudenthaler was intrigued. He emailed his friend Max Reed, who had recently graduated from law school. "Any interest in making [an] application to the Ontario Superior Court on Rob Ford's improper campaign finance accounting tricks?" Reed replied twenty minutes later: "Sounds like fun. Can you send me the name of the relevant bylaws? If you're serious, there's a number of things to talk about."

The pair headed to City Hall to sign out the Ford campaign's thick stack of financial records. They sat at a small wooden table in the clerk's office and spent two hours rifling through pages of receipts, invoices, time sheets, donor records, and official paperwork, and checked them against the monthly spreadsheets. They researched the Municipal Elections Act and realized what they were dealing with: penalties for some of the alleged offences included removal from office. Neither of these rabble-rousers thought that would ever happen, but it could generate some headlines.

In May 2011, Chaleff-Freudenthaler and Reed submitted their findings to the compliance audit committee, a panel of three citizen experts. To the immense annoyance of the mayor, the three-member panel voted unanimously to audit Ford's campaign expenses.

Chaleff-Freudenthaler and Reed ended up filing eight other audit requests against four councillors—including Doug Ford for his councillor campaign, a request that the compliance audit committee rejected—and four unelected candidates. The duo's work inspired them to co-found the accountability watchdog Fair Elections Toronto.

ON JULY 13, 2011, two months after filing the audit requests, Chaleff-Freudenthaler was at City Hall to watch a council meeting. He had just finished chatting with a councillor near the entrance to the council chamber and was making his way to the elevator when an angry Doug Ford spotted him.

"Hey, you're the guy with the audits," Doug said. Chaleff-Freudenthaler just stood there, startled. "Well, buddy, [you] better make sure you get your facts right."

Chaleff-Freudenthaler tried to walk away, but Doug kept at him, demanding to know if he was the person launching all the campaign audits. Chaleff-Freudenthaler said he was.

"What goes around comes around," Doug said.

"[Are you] threatening me?" Chaleff-Freudenthaler asked.

The councillor seemed to realize he had crossed a line. He turned and walked away.

Chaleff-Freudenthaler, true to form, responded. He wrote a letter to the integrity commissioner in which he accused the mayor's brother of violating the Code of Conduct for members of council. "All members of Council have a duty to treat members of the public, one another, and staff appropriately and without abuse, bullying or intimidation, and to ensure that their work environment is free from discrimination and harassment," the Code of Conduct reads. Six months later, on January 30, 2012, Integrity Commissioner Janet Leiper concluded that the mayor's brother should formally apologize. It was one of those little Ford sideshows that gets a lot of attention on Twitter. But something much more serious came out of the integrity commissioner's office that day. Something that would set off a chain of events that, briefly, cost Rob Ford his job.

The same day Leiper slapped Doug Ford on the wrist, essentially for his aggressiveness, she released a separate report reprimanding the mayor. In a meeting in August 2010, at the integrity commissioner's request, city council had ordered Councillor Rob Ford to repay the $3,150 in donations he had solicited from lobbyists for his football foundation. Over the next thirteen months Leiper contacted Ford six times to see if this had been done. Ford finally responded in late October 2011 with letters from three donors indicating they didn't want their money back. Leiper was not impressed. She wanted to bring the issue back up at the next council meeting and demand Ford "provide proof of reimbursement" by the beginning of March 2012. But there was one big difference between the council meeting in August 2010 and the one coming up in February 2012. Rob Ford was now the mayor.

It's important to note that the City of Toronto has a fraught history with lobbyists. In the aftermath of the MFP computer leasing scandal, a public inquiry revealed that city officials were being wined and dined—with lavish dinners, golf games, expensive hockey tickets—by MFP salesman Dash Domi, the brother of hockey star Tie Domi, the famous Toronto Maple Leaf. Madam Justice Denise Bellamy concluded that there had been "inappropriately close relationships" between lobbyists and public office holders. As noted earlier, MFP is the reason Toronto now has an integrity commissioner and strict rules about accepting gifts from lobbyists. That's why Ford was sanctioned in the first place.

At the February 7 council meeting, Doug Ford was up first with item CC16.5, his forced apology to Chaleff-Freudenthaler. The young activist was watching in the chamber's upper decks near the media. Doug grimaced as he stood up. He spoke directly to the speaker. "Just so this won't continue on and it won't drag out forever and ever and ever … I apologize if I acted unparliamentary. If I offended the complainant. Doug Ford apologizes." The room applauded. Chaleff-Freudenthaler felt two hundred pairs of eyes on him—although none belonged to Doug Ford—and was eager for the moment to be over.

Now it was Rob's turn, item CC16.6, which concerned his refusal to repay $3,150 in lobbyist donations.

"I want to explain how my charity works, because I think a lot of people don't understand it. I—and it's not about me, this is about kids, more specifically teenagers between the ages of fourteen and eighteen—I'm very, very passionate about helping these kids. And I will do anything for these kids. And my foundation was set up to help these kids play football. And it's not— We don't pay coaches, we don't pay gas, we don't pay food.

It goes for the football equipment itself. And it costs about four hundred dollars to outfit one player.... So a team starts off with about fifty kids. So therefore fifty times four hundred, you're looking at twenty thousand dollars. I go approach the school, any school.... If you wanna start a football team, I will pay between five thousand and ten thousand dollars to help you out."

He continued, rhyming off twelve schools in eleven different wards that had received seed money from his program. His football work extended well beyond the boundaries of Etobicoke. The implication seemed clear for the councillors with Ford-sponsored teams in their areas: if you vote against me, you're going to have angry parents knocking on your door.

"Folks, everybody I see I talk about my foundation. The money goes directly to the Toronto Community Foundation"—a not-for-profit agency that handles the collection and distribution of donors' money so that they can get tax receipts—"I don't touch the money ... [the TCF] cuts a cheque. I do not sign the cheques. I have nothing to do with the money.... If there's anything that's more clear and above board, I don't know what this is. And it's the kids—and it goes on. There's so many stories about the kids that have [come] out of these football programs. It would bring tears to your eyes."

Ford argued that his foundation kept children in school, attracted post-secondary scholarships, and sometimes paved the way to a professional football career.

"If it wasn't for this foundation, these kids would not have had a chance. So, and then to ask for me to pay it out of my own pocket personally? There's just no sense to this. The money is gone. The money's been spent on football equipment.... At the end of the day, I'll leave it up to you. I'm gonna continue coaching. I'm gonna continue to help kids. I'm gonna continue to fundraise. And my goal is to get a high school football team in every single school in the city. And we're well on our way.... I've fundraised probably close to a hundred thousand dollars in the last few years. I don't know how much, what else, I can say. It's crystal clear."

It was an argument that resonated—and not just with Ford Nation. It was easy to overlook the principle that politicians shouldn't ask lobbyists for favours, because, well, the money went to help kids in poor neighbourhoods play football. What was the harm in that? The majority of council certainly didn't see any. They voted 22–12 to rescind Leiper's earlier sanction. The only problem was, one of those twenty-two was Rob Ford. Not only did he speak to a motion that directly benefited him, he voted on it.

Watching from his seat in the public gallery, Chaleff-Freudenthaler thought this was wrong. A lawyer he knew called a few days later with a tip: it wasn't just wrong what Ford had done, it might be illegal. So what would you do if you were Chaleff-Freudenthaler and thought public officials were flouting the rules? You'd call up Max Reed, your lawyer friend, find a copy of the Municipal Conflict of Interest Act, discover that elected officials who broke the rules were automatically removed from office, and recruit a high-profile lawyer to take the case.

Clayton Ruby was their first pick. Ruby was one of Canada's most respected attorneys and an expert in constitutional law, with a history of taking on high-profile cases pro bono. He was also already involved with Chaleff-Freudenthaler and Reed's Fair Elections Toronto. Reed fired him off a two-page summary of the case and the relevant sections of the act. Was he interested? The reply was simply, "Yes."

THE MEDIA-SAVVY Chaleff-Freudenthaler thought that, given his role with the compliance audit, it would be better if he and Reed watched this show from backstage. (He also didn't want a judge to see his name, learn about the audit, and think the case was politically motivated.) He recruited an old family friend named Paul Magder to be the Joe Citizen face of the lawsuit. Magder had helped on Chaleff-Freudenthaler's school board trustee campaign. He was a well-read, soft-spoken fifty-seven-year-old who managed an electronics manufacturing lab outside Toronto. The married father of two grown children had dabbled in civic activism just once before. The previous September, Magder filed a complaint with Toronto's lobbyist registrar concerning Doug Ford's botched waterfront takeover. Magder complained that the mayor's brother had met privately with an Australian shopping-mall developer without properly documenting the meeting. (This requirement is another by-product of the MFP scandal.) The matter was dropped when the company belatedly registered the meeting.

When it came time for the press conference on March 12, 2012, Magder stood by awkwardly in a light-grey sweater vest, mostly staring at the carpet, while the eloquent Clayton Ruby laid out the mayor's offences, punctuating each point with a jab of his pen.

"You can't, as a city councillor, speak to a motion, vote on a motion, that benefits you personally," Ruby said, standing in front of a four-foot sign that played on Ford's campaign slogan: "Respect Taxpayers, Respect the Law."

Yes, the act was strict, Ruby said, but it was strict for good reason. "Because if you don't catch conflict of interest [on] the small things—and this is not that small—there's a real danger that you will, in fact, encourage corruption on a wider scale." As a veteran councillor, Rob Ford should have known better, Ruby said. "'I'm sorry' is not enough. It doesn't get you off the hook for a minute."

The media turned to Magder. Who was he, and why was he involved? "I'm fed up with all the stuff I see going on in politics, basically," he said.

BY THE SPRING OF 2012, Rob Ford was fighting for his job on two fronts. He was embroiled in one court case about his election expenses, and at the same time in another case about a possible conflict of interest.

Now, a third legal battle was making its way to court.

During the election campaign, city council had voted to extend the lease and exclusive vending rights of a waterfront restaurant for twenty years without taking outside bids. Technically, council had agreed to do this three years earlier, against staff's advice. City bureaucrats wanted to put the Boardwalk Pub's lucrative deal out to tender, but council had a soft spot for the father-and-sons operation. The Foulidis family had secured the rights along Toronto's eastern beach back in the 1980s. They had mortgaged their homes to finance construction and laid most of the bricks themselves. If another company—say a multinational restaurant chain—won the bid, the family would be forced out of their business, which was built on city parkland. Council voted with its heart, not its head, to extend the lease.

But by 2010, the agreement still hadn't been signed. The city and the restaurant owners—their company was registered as Tuggs Inc.—were still haggling over the annual rent. Critics saw an opportunity to reopen the deal. It was a good issue for councillors looking to get their name in the paper. Many beach-going Torontonians had a beef with the Boardwalk Pub. Being a seasonal operation, the prices were higher. People liked to gripe about the food. But the main issue was political. During the first extension vote in 2007, the local councillor at the time, Sandra Bussin—the council speaker and a close ally of Mayor David Miller—spoke on the Foulidises' behalf. Her political enemies in the ward pounced. They pointed out that members of the family had contributed to her campaign. It was common for businesses to donate to the local councillor's re-election efforts, but not every business operated with exclusivity rights that banned little girls from selling lemonade on a hot summer day. Not that the Foulidises were shutting down lemonade stands, but that was one of the wild rumours going around. Soon, some people had the (wrong) idea that they weren't allowed to bring their own food to the beach. Despite the bad press, the Boardwalk Pub was able to keep its deal in a 21–14 vote.

The lease extension might have been settled, but the Foulidises' problems were just getting started. The fiasco was a perfect issue for the Ford campaign. Wasted money, the taint of campaign donations, a lefty maybe behaving badly, and—bonus—the public already angry. Rob Ford made a pledge to stop sole-sourced contracts. In July of 2010, he took it a step further. When asked by Newstalk 1010 radio host Jerry Agar if he believed anyone was getting money under the table, Rob replied, "I truly believe they are, and that's my personal opinion, and when I see all these donations, going through campaigns, it stinks to high heaven."

The following month, the *Toronto Sun* ran a front-page story with the headline "Council 'Corrupt.'" The story, by Jonathan Jenkins, began, "City council's decision to award an untendered, 20-year contract to Boardwalk Pub operator Tuggs Inc. smacks of civic corruption, Councillor Rob Ford says. 'If Tuggs isn't, then I don't know what is,' Ford told the *Toronto Sun*'s editorial board. 'I can't accuse anyone or I can't pinpoint it, but why do we have to go in camera on the Tuggs deal? These in-camera meetings, there's more corruption and skullduggery going on in there than I've ever seen in my life.'"

Ford brushed off the Foulidises' demand for an apology. George Foulidis, on behalf of his family, filed a six-million-dollar defamation suit against Ford just before the election. Representing Foulidis was Brian Shiller, a litigator with the boutique law firm Ruby Shiller Chan Hasan.

Yes, that Ruby.

(And for the real conspiracy theorists, Shiller was the lawyer who negotiated Adam Chaleff-Freudenthaler's twenty-thousand-dollar settlement with Toronto police after his wrongful detention.)

NINE DAYS AFTER CLAYTON RUBY announced that "sorry" wasn't an adequate response to breaking municipal conflict-of-interest laws, news got around that Rob Ford had hired one of Canada's most skilled and expensive lawyers to defend him. Alan Lenczner was a sixty-nine-year-old living legend known for his ego, creativity in the courtroom, and ability to win when a loss seems unavoidable. As retired Supreme Court of Canada judge Ian Binnie explained the night Lenczner was named Ontario's civil litigator of the year, "He is the lawyer you go to when your goose is just about cooked." Lenczner's former clients included Conrad Black and one half of the feuding McCain brothers of french-fry fame. When the Fords recruited Lenczner, it was the first indication that the conflict-of-interest business might be more than a media stunt.

The morning of the trial, September 5, 2012, saw reporters lined up outside the court building at 361 University Avenue long before the doors opened at 8 A.M. Courtroom 6-1 is supposedly the largest in Ontario, and every seat was occupied, as journalists, Ford-watchers, university kids, and city staff crammed inside. Chaleff-Freudenthaler was there too, off and on.

Ruby's team arrived first. Then Lenczner's. They unpacked their legal boxes with gusto, smiling and relaxed, obviously anxious to get in the ring. The mayor looked less enthused. He wore a dark suit, geometric-patterned tie, and blue shirt. He seemed anxious. He sat at one of the front tables and immediately pulled out a pen with which to fidget. His newly minted chief of staff, Mark Towhey, press secretary, George Christopoulos, and brother Doug sat with him. Hearing the case would be Ontario Superior Court Justice Charles Hackland, who was brought in from Ottawa to avoid any perception of bias. At sixty-one, Hackland was the senior regional judge in his area—one of eight in the province—and the go-to choice for politically sensitive cases. "In most disputes both sides are happy to get him because they know they're going to get a good hearing," Ottawa defence lawyer Mark Ertel told the *Star*.

Hackland won over the media when he announced that "Twittering" would be allowed. Audio recording was also approved for the purposes of accuracy in reporting, not broadcast, but there would be no photography, which is standard, or phone calls, obviously.

Ruby was up first. He set the stage with a quick rehash of the MFP scandal—"Toronto has suffered from the activities of lobbyists"—then cast Rob Ford as a character who delighted in flouting the rules. The mayor, Ruby said, would argue that he'd made an honest mistake and that he hadn't realized he was in a conflict-of-interest situation. But how could someone with twelve years of experience on city council argue he didn't know the rules? "Mayor Ford wants this hearing to be about the kids and the good work he does by directing donations to the high school football teams that work with them. That is not what this hearing is about.… The only person hurt in all of this was Rob Ford. He had to pay back the money to publicly correct his breach of city integrity and he just did not want to do that."

Lenczner's turn. "My submissions to you at the end of the case will be more about the law." His defence strategy hinged on a complicated legal dance around jurisdiction. Lenczner explored how the three sets of rules in the case—the City of Toronto Act, the Municipal Conflict of Interest Act, and council's Code of Conduct—worked together and how they didn't. Two gave council authority to punish rule breakers, but the penalties outlined in each of those were different. One said council could only hand down a reprimand or suspend pay, the other gave five additional options, including "repayment or reimbursement of moneys received." Lenczner argued that council referred to the wrong set of rules. And so, if council didn't have the authority to make Ford repay $3,150, it didn't matter what he did later on. And just in case Hackland didn't buy that argument, Lenczner fell back on an "error in judgment." Ford would testify that he didn't realize he was in a conflict of interest. (If Judge Hackland believed there was an honest mistake, or that the amount of money was too small to influence him, he could let Ford off.)

At 10:51 A.M., Robert Bruce Ford put his hand on a Bible and swore to tell the truth, the whole truth, and nothing but the truth. Things got tense in a hurry. As Ruby grilled him, Ford kept coming back to the same rehearsed statement: "How I define a conflict of interest is if it's both financially beneficial to the city and financially beneficial to myself or there's a financial interest with the city and a financial interest with myself."

Ruby challenged him on this, noting that in Ford's twelve years on council he had a duty to be well aware of the rules. Ford had been elected four times—in 2000, 2003, 2006, and 2010—therefore, he'd sworn a declaration four times to "disclose any pecuniary interest direct or indirect in accordance with the MCIA."

Ford testified that he had never read the councillor handbook and didn't even remember getting one. And he had never attended orientation as a councillor, because "some councillors like myself ... the son of an MPP, knows how the provincial government works and knows how City Hall works and knows how the federal government works, so I didn't think I needed to attend."

RUBY: "What steps if any [did you take] to find out what the Municipal Conflict of Interest Act required of you?"

FORD: "None."

RUBY: "None, that's your answer?"

FORD: "Yes."

At one point, Ruby read Ford a passage from the Conflict of Interest Act. When a member of council had a "pecuniary interest direct or indirect in any matter," read Ruby, they should "disclose the interest" and "not take part" in the "discussion" or "vote."

RUBY: "You're familiar with that?"

FORD: "I've never read that before."

RUBY: "You had to have read that before. That's the Municipal Conflict of Interest Act."

FORD: "I've never read this before."

The courtroom erupted in giggles.

Judge Hackland: "Excuse me, we don't need any outbursts. Thank you."

Ford changed his shirt during the lunch break. But things didn't get any better for the mayor. By the time the trial ended, most legal experts were predicting that Judge Hackland was not going to buy the "honest mistake" argument. The "insignificant amount" exception was also dead in the water, because other Ontario politicians had been kicked out for far less and Ford himself had testified that he thought $3,150 was a significant amount of money. As for Lenczner's assertion that the Municipal Conflict of Interest Act somehow didn't apply to all code of conduct violations, well, "that's ridiculous," said one prominent lawyer I was consulting at the time. Lenczner's final gambit,

The three Ford brothers, Randy, Rob, and Doug, pose in front of a portrait of their late father, Doug Sr., at the family business, Deco Labels & Tags. March 22, 2010. © David Rider/ *Toronto Star*.

Mayoral candidate Rob Ford and his brother (and campaign manager) Doug Ford meet with Dieter Doneit-Henderson (left)— an HIV-positive gay man—and his husband, Colville (right), during the 2010 campaign. Ford was there to apologize for comments he had made about people who contract the virus.
© Rick Madonik/ *Toronto Star*.

Mayor-elect Rob Ford celebrates his landslide victory alongside his mother, Diane, and wife, Renata. October 25, 2010.
© Lucas Oleniuk/ *Toronto Star.*

Controversial hockey commentator Don Cherry poses with Rob Ford on inauguration day at City Hall. December 7, 2010.
© Tannis Toohey/ *Toronto Star.*

Nick Kouvalis, the architect of Rob Ford's winning campaign and later his chief of staff, during an executive committee meeting at City Hall. December 8, 2010. © Carlos Osorio/ *Toronto Star*.

Mayor Rob Ford talks with his brother, Councillor Doug Ford, during a compliance audit committee meeting. The committee opted not to prosecute Ford for campaign spending violations. February 25, 2013 © David Cooper/ *Toronto Star*.

An intoxicated
Mayor Rob Ford
greets other
St. Patrick's Day
revellers on his way
to the Bier Markt
bar in downtown
Toronto in 2012.
Courtesy of
Jennifer Gordon.

Mayor Rob Ford's high school football team, the Don Bosco Eagles,
wins the semi-final match. They would go on to compete in the
Metro Bowl. November 21, 2012. © Richard Lautens/ *Toronto Star.*

Rob Ford poses with Anthony Smith, Monir Kassim, and Muhammad Khattak in front of an alleged crack house at 15 Windsor Road. The *Star* was given this photo by the men trying to sell a video of the mayor smoking what looked like crack cocaine. Early 2013.

Kevin Donovan and I (Kevin is in the back seat) meet with Mohamed Farah to watch footage of the so-called crack video, May 9, 2013. © Dale Brazao/ *Toronto Star*.

Mayor Rob Ford and Alexander "Sandro" Lisi (far right), his friend
and occasional driver, at a Toronto Maple Leafs game. May 8, 2013.
© Joe Warmington/ *Toronto Sun*.

Investigative reporter Kevin Donovan defends the *Toronto Star*'s
coverage of the so-called crack video at the Ontario Press Council.
September 9, 2013. © Colin McConnell/ *Toronto Star*.

Chief Bill Blair announces that the Toronto Police Service has recovered the video of Rob Ford appearing to smoke crack cocaine. October 31, 2013. © Andrew Francis Wallace/ *Toronto Star*.

After the mayor admitted to smoking crack cocaine, his sister, Kathy Ford, and mother, Diane Ford, sit down with CP24 news to defend him. November 7, 2013. © CP24.

Mayor Rob Ford drags his wife, Renata, through a throng of reporters after apologizing for making vulgar comments. November 14, 2013. © Steve Russell/*Toronto Star*.

City councillors turn their backs to Mayor Rob Ford after he refuses to step down. November 14, 2013. © Mark Blinch/REUTERS.

that Ford's vote in his own favour on February 7 didn't matter because council should never have imposed the fine in the first place, was interesting but still a long shot.

Hackland promised a quick decision and was true to his word. On November 22, 2012—less than three months after the hearing—an email went out to reporters: Hackland had reached a decision. It would be released Monday morning.

On November 26, dozens of journalists lined up outside the clerk's office at 361 University. We killed time rehashing the case and speculating on the ruling. "Do you think he'll actually be removed?" we asked each other, over and over again. Most, myself included, were skeptical.

Shortly after 10 A.M., a court staffer—with an excellent poker face—emerged carrying a stack of papers that came up to her chin. We pounced like jackals. The *Star* was second in line. I grabbed mine and flipped to the back.

Page 23: "I declare the seat of respondent, Robert Ford, on Toronto City Council, vacant."

"Whoa. He's gone," I said.

The mandatory removal provision was "a very blunt instrument," the judge wrote, but there was no wiggle room. He did not buy Lenczner's argument that the act didn't apply; he believed council had broad authority to impose a financial penalty; and he rejected the "error in judgment" claim.

"There must be some diligence on the respondent's part; that is, some effort to understand and appreciate his obligations. Outright ignorance of the law will not suffice, nor will wilful blindness as to one's obligations," he wrote.

Everyone—journalists, councillors, the Twittersphere, even Ford himself, according to sources—was shocked. It wasn't that people thought it was the wrong decision; it was that few thought a judge would take the political risk. Reaction was mixed, but most seemed to think Ford had brought it on himself.

Wrote Marcus Gee from *The Globe and Mail*, "Rob Ford says 'left-wing politics' are to blame for his ouster as mayor of Toronto. Nonsense. This wound was entirely self-inflicted. If he had paid even the slightest attention to the rules—if he had even bothered to learn them—he would not be in the fix he is today."

Others were uncomfortable with the fact that an elected mayor had been removed by a judge because of a few thousand dollars. Said Simon Kent of the *Toronto Sun*, "The judiciary being asked to decide a matter involving an amount of petty cash going to charity is taking an elephant gun to hunt a field mouse.... This matter should have been decided at City Hall. It was not a serious or systemic case of corruption under investigation, just one man's vote."

The next day, the *Toronto Star* ran a profile of Chaleff-Freudenthaler. "History will write him up as a hero," said left-wing city councillor Joe Mihevc, who had known him since he was a kid.

Shaken, Ford spoke to a horde of reporters camped outside his office. "It's more disappointing than surprising.... I'm going to appeal it and carry on with my job. I'm a fighter." Ontario Superior Court Justice Gladys Pardu agreed to let him keep his job until that appeal was settled. Those close to Ford, including staff, confidants, and allies on council, say he was devastated and convinced he would never win his appeal. "I know the stress affected him," said Deputy Mayor Doug Holyday.

BACK IN MID-NOVEMBER, when Ford was waiting for Judge Hackland to render his decision, the mayor was dealing with a different matter at another University Avenue courthouse. The libel suit launched by restaurateur George Foulidis had made it to trial. This time, Ford was being represented by Toronto lawyer Gavin Tighe.

Tighe's battle plan was to argue that the law gave politicians considerable leeway to speak freely on controversial issues with significant public interest. In his opening arguments, Tighe said, "It is critical, in my submission, to a free and democratic society that people know frankly where candidates stand on issues." This time, Ford's team would use the MFP case to its advantage. "We can't divorce ourselves from the historical perspective," Tighe said. "All of this comes in light of the Bellamy report and the MFP scandal, where sole-source contracts and non-competitive bid processes dealing with the City of Toronto were the subject of substantial political and public issue."

Taking him on was Clayton Ruby's colleague Brian Shiller, a highly regarded constitutional lawyer in his own right, with a hefty résumé of libel and defamation experience.

Shiller painted his client, George Foulidis, as a hard-working entrepreneur who became a political football during a divisive election campaign. His business had suffered. His family was being harassed. Strangers would show up at the restaurant wearing T-shirts that said "Bribe." All so Rob Ford could score political points. "Mr. Foulidis was left with no choice but to go public" following the "blatant attacks on his integrity," Shiller said. The plaintiff gave emotional testimony. In tears, Foulidis said, "My wife was distraught over it ... my daughter was ten at the time. She asked me if I had done anything wrong."

Referring to the *Sun*'s article in which Ford was quoted as saying the Tuggs deal "stinks to high heaven," Foulidis said he felt "humiliated. I felt like a criminal."

Shiller's main hurdle was convincing Judge John Macdonald that Ford had in fact accused George Foulidis of corruption. The most damaging sentence in the *Sun* article, the one with the *c* word, was paraphrased by the reporter. Tighe argued that "we don't really know" what was said, since there was no tape of the interview. With the evidence as it was, the dots weren't quite connected.

And then, on the second day of the trial, Foulidis caught a huge break. A former editor at the *Sun* had located a tape of the interview, and it was clear that Ford had in fact suggested the deal was corrupt. It was a "curveball," Tighe admitted at the time.

The mayor stuck to his guns. He testified that he had never specifically accused Foulidis—a man he had never met—of corruption. Just the deal itself. He'd received some anonymous phone calls that "money was being exchanged." For two merciless hours, Shiller poked, provoked, and attempted to unnerve the mayor.

Was he accusing Tuggs Inc. of corruption?

Ford: "The deal in general."

By "corruption," did he mean something that could attract jail time?

Ford: "Not following the process, to me, is corrupt. However you want to define that, that's how I'm defining that."

Shiller pressed harder, and the mayor started to crack.

Ford: "They [councillors] don't follow the process. So staff said, 'You should go out on the Tuggs deal for competitive bids.'

They said no. I saw the local councillors work the room to try to get the votes to give the sole-source contract to Tuggs.... At council there was a lot of rumours going around that this deal does not smell right. Other councillors were saying it. The public was— I was getting called. I heard it over and over again, numerous times."

Shiller: "My question is … when you say, 'and if Tuggs isn't, I don't know what is,' what [you're] saying is, 'if Tuggs isn't an example of corruption and skullduggery,' I don't know what is?"

Tighe objected, but the judge said he wanted to hear the answer.

Ford: "I'm going to repeat myself the best I can to explain and answer you. Here, I don't agree with how the Tuggs deal was done and I used the word, when they don't follow the process, and when staff recommends a [request for proposal] and you ignore it, I call that skullduggery and corruption, that's the answer."

On December 27, 2012, Judge Macdonald ruled in favour of the mayor, saying Foulidis had not proved that Ford's comments were directed at him. Foulidis was ordered to pay a portion of Ford's legal bills, which is customary in Canadian civil cases and intended to help discourage frivolous lawsuits. Foulidis has appealed, and at the time of publication that case is still working its way through the system.

THE NEWS THAT HE HAD WON the libel lawsuit failed to lift Rob Ford's spirits. He was still facing removal from office over alleged conflict-of-interest violations and was due back in court on January 7, 2013, for the appeal.

This time, the backdrop was an opulent courtroom at Osgoode Hall, where a three-judge Divisional Court panel was hearing the case. Chaleff-Freudenthaler snuck in at the last minute, taking a spot in the back.

This arena wouldn't feature the colourful back-and-forth of the trial. The mayor would not testify and it would last only a day. This was a battle rooted in legal minutiae. Lenczner once again made his argument that council had no authority to impose a financial penalty, that it had acted "ultra vires," beyond its power, and so everything Ford did after that was "a nullity" and could not be used against him. (One municipal lawyer watching the case likened the rationale to that of a criminal investigation, where police can't use evidence if it was obtained improperly.) Ruby fought back with an equally technical argument. The mayor was trying to mount a "collateral attack," which essentially meant challenging an earlier decision to win a current one. If the mayor believed council had overstepped back in August 2010, he should have said so at the time. He couldn't go back now and say it was wrong.

Regional Senior Justice Edward Then promised a prompt decision.

Less than three weeks later, on the morning of January 25, 2013, the mayor was summoned to Lenczner's downtown office at 130 Adelaide Street West. The verdict was to be released at 9:30 A.M. Both Rob and Doug Ford arrived, along with a few select staff members. The small group made nervous chit-chat as the minutes ticked by and they lost track of time. Lenczner was out, and his colleague Andrew Parley, who had helped argue the case, was watching the firm's email inbox.

The decision arrived unbeknownst to the others. Parley scrolled to the bottom. "We won," he said.

The appeal judges had agreed that council overstepped its authority.

Ford froze in disbelief then looked around the room. The group exploded in cheers, hugs, and high-fives. The mayor was essentially let off on a technicality. Even though it was a conflict of interest for him to have voted at council that day, the penalty should never have been handed down in the first place. Everything he did after that was, legally, null and void.

Soon after, the mayor headed to City Hall to give a statement. The experience had been "very, very humbling," he said.

A month later, the city's compliance audit committee voted 2–1 not to pursue non-criminal charges against the mayor. An auditor did find that the Ford campaign appeared to have broken the law in numerous instances, including when it accepted a $77,722 interest-free loan from Doug Ford Holdings, the company that runs Deco Labels, but the panel didn't think the contraventions were serious enough to call in a special prosecutor.

Apart from the slim-chance libel appeal, Ford cleared his final legal hurdle in June 2013, when the Supreme Court turned down a request from Clayton Ruby and his client Paul Magder to get involved in the conflict of interest case.

Miraculously, it seemed, Mayor Ford had survived three serious court challenges to his leadership. It was his personal demons that would soon lead him into deep trouble once more.

NINE

THE GARRISON
BALL

It was business as usual in the City Hall press gallery. The Ford administration had won its fight with the unions, but lost a vote on a Scarborough subway, and the Toronto and Region Conservation Authority rejected Ford's request to buy the land adjoining his property. I kept adding to my just-in-case folder when stuff popped up online, but the off-hour sightings of Ford dropped off dramatically. Staff sources told me the special assistants were now making the mayor's runs to the liquor store.

In July 2012, I was sent to cover the Summer Olympics in London. The *Star*'s editor-in-chief, Michael Cooke, who is from England, was also there for a few days. One night, the whole *Star* Olympic team and Cooke went out to the pub.

"So where are we at with that Ford story?" he asked me.

A THING OR TWO about the editor of the *Toronto Star*.

Michael Cooke is a tabloid man. He came to Toronto in 2009 after stints running the *New York Daily News* and the *Chicago Sun-Times*. With his arrival, the *Star* changed almost overnight. Cooke loves exclusives and investigations, splashy stories that demand attention. To me, he has always seemed better suited to an era when newspapers were sold on street corners by kids hollering, "Extra! Extra! Read all about it!" Cooke, now in his early sixties, cut his teeth on London's famous Fleet Street. In 1974, he took a trip to Toronto, stopped by the *Star* newsroom, and was offered a job.

From the *Star*, he moved to increasingly senior positions at three major Canadian dailies in three provinces before heading south to become editor of the *Chicago Sun-Times*. In 2005, Cooke took over the *Daily News* in New York, where he went head to head with Rupert Murdoch's *New York Post*. After about a year, he was back in Chicago. And that's where he stayed until 2009, when he was lured back to the place his North American career began, the *Toronto Star*.

Almost every profile I've ever read about Cooke describes him as being ruthless in pursuit of a story. That partly comes from his time at the helm of the *New York Daily News*. While there, he was part of a short-lived Bravo TV reality show called *Tabloid Wars*, which documented the battle between the *Daily News* and the *New York Post*. In one of Cooke's more spectacular quotes, he described the rivalry with the *Post* as follows: "We put our foot on their throat every day and press down till their eyes bulge and leak blood, but still they won't die. We just have to keep at it until they do die."

OVER BEERS THAT NIGHT in the London pub, I promised Cooke I'd stay on the Ford story. I arrived back in Toronto in late August 2012. I hadn't missed much.

The mayor's various court dramas occupied the press

gallery until the end of January 2013. Former staffers say Ford spent these months crippled by stress. He believed he was going to lose his case and be removed from office. In that event, council would either have to appoint a new mayor or hold a by-election, and Ford was focused on winning his seat back should that happen. (If for some reason Ford was banned from running in a by-election, which was one possible punishment, brother Doug was ready to step in and hold the seat until the 2014 election.) Every scenario meant that Ford needed to act mayoral. He switched to campaign mode. He made a point of being seen at City Hall in the morning and afternoon. He began routinely making himself available to answer questions from the press. And while I'd still get the odd tip about the mayor being spotted out on the town, information I continued to file away, things were mostly quiet on the after-hours front. The threat of losing his job seemed to have scared Ford straight. But once that threat was gone, things unravelled.

The first sign came on March 7, 2013, when former mayoral candidate Sarah Thomson made an astounding claim on her Facebook page. "Thought it was a friendly hello to Toronto Mayor Rob Ford at the CJPAC [Canadian Jewish Political Affairs Committee] Action Party tonight until he suggested I should have been in Florida with him last week because his wife wasn't there. Seriously wanted to punch him in the face. Happy International Women's Day!" She posted a blurry photo of the two of them from the event. Ford looked like a frat boy at his first keg party. His mouth was hanging open, his eyes were shut, his cheeks, chin, and forehead were glowing red, and there was a big wet stain on the front of his white shirt.

The story got worse. "He told me he was in Florida and I should have been with him because his wife wasn't there," Thomson told the *Star* the next day. "I didn't expect that. Rob doesn't normally act that way towards women, so I was a little bit shocked, and then we posed to get our picture taken and he grabbed my ass during the pose."

The mayor's office issued a press release addressing the allegations. "I can say without hesitation that they are absolutely, completely false. What is more surprising is that a woman who has aspired to be a civic leader would cry wolf on a day where we should be celebrating women across the globe." On his Sunday radio show, Ford added, "I've always said, I don't know if she's playing with a full deck."

It was hard to know what to believe. Thomson was the forty-five-year-old publisher of *Women's Post* magazine and a married mother of two. When she had announced she was running for mayor in 2010, she had little presence. Rightly or wrongly, she was rescued from the fringes because she was a credible woman in a field of middle-aged white men. Her gender got her in the door, but her impressive campaign kept her there. Thomson was likeable and had a plucky charisma. She did well at the debates. And she presented the most realistic plan, by far, to build transit in Toronto. Alas, Thomson never stood a real chance of winning, and towards the end she bowed out to join George Smitherman's anyone-but-Ford campaign. She impressed the provincial Liberals, and in October 2011 ran as their candidate in a downtown riding against the long-time New Democrat incumbent. Thomson narrowly lost, which was sort of a victory. The near miss solidified her position as a player in Ontario politics.

But almost as soon as people started to take her seriously, Thomson seemed to go a bit loopy. She replaced her French roll with Rasta dreadlocks, traded in the power suit for hippie skirts, and began speaking a bit too freely, posting a bit too much personal stuff online for someone with political ambitions. She seemed to be chasing the spotlight. The medium she used to make the allegation against Ford didn't sit well with people. Why did she use Facebook to broadcast the incident? Why didn't she make a formal complaint through the proper channels, by calling the integrity commissioner or even the police?

Over the next few days, Thomson escalated her claims. In an interview with KiSS 92.5 radio, she said that Ford had been "completely wasted." In a pre-interview, she told a producer she thought the mayor had been high on cocaine. The host asked her about this. "Did you think that he was on cocaine? Is that what you had said to our producer?" Thomson replied, "I thought he was, yes. But I don't know.... I went back and looked up, you know, what are the signs of cocaine use. I looked it up [on Google]. And, you know—sweaty, talking quickly, out of it … all these things were on there."

It was bizarre. Groping and cocaine aside, it did seem that the mayor had shown up at a political event in a state unbecoming of an elected official. People at the fundraiser confirmed that much. Ford once again avoided the press. That day, he brought his son and daughter to City Hall. Come evening he walked out of his office, past the waiting reporters, trailing his two young children behind him. It was as if he was daring someone to ask him about cocaine in front of them.

That afternoon, I saw the editor-in-chief in the newsroom.

"You know," I said, "if we're ever going to resuscitate the Ford drinking story, now might be the time."

The whole team was back around a conference-room table later that week. The Bier Markt piece was almost a year old. We would need to return to the original sources. The Thomson story was too shaky for a news hook, but it was useful in the sense that it had people talking.

Then we got the tip we needed. Through a source, the *Star* learned that Ford had shown up at a military gala rambling, sweaty, and stumbling. But the information was second-hand. I needed to find one of the players involved.

The Garrison Ball is the kind of black-tie affair that makes the society pages. In 2013, it was held on the last Saturday in February at the elegant Liberty Grand banquet hall near the western waterfront. The minister of national defence, Peter MacKay, the chief of defence staff, General Tom Lawson, and the commander of the Royal Canadian Navy, Paul Maddison, were among the distinguished guests. The invite list was a who's who of Bay Street and Toronto money, but mainly it was a night to honour a few hundred members of the military and their families, including soldiers, sailors, and air force personnel. The gala was also a fundraiser for the Wounded Warriors charity. Mayor Ford had been expected the year before but never showed. It was a snub that had irked many of those involved. For the 2013 gala, one of Ford's closest political allies and a friend, Councillor Paul Ainslie, was on the organizing committee. Ainslie convinced the other organizers to give the mayor a second chance. They agreed.

On the night of the ball, February 23, 2013, it looked like Ford was once again a no-show. The cocktail hour and silent auction had come and gone, and still no mayor. Ainslie checked in with Ford's chief of staff, Mark Towhey.

"We've got a problem," Towhey told him.

"Okay. Where's the mayor?" Ainslie asked.

"Well, he's on his way. But he's not quite himself …"

Indeed, when Towhey connected with Ford before the gala, the mayor had been muttering incoherently, flushed, and breathing heavily. More perplexing, he had his two young children with him, as well as two friends. One of them was Bruno Bellissimo, a crack addict who had met Ford in high school. The other was Alexander "Sandro" Lisi. He was the one driving the whole group to the Liberty Grand in his Range Rover.

Towhey was suspicious of Lisi. He'd been told that Lisi was a friend of the Ford family, but he suspected there was more to it. He was right, although he wouldn't learn just how toxic the relationship was for several more months. On the night of the Garrison Ball, Towhey was just trying to get in and out without causing a scene.

Lisi pulled up to the Liberty Grand shortly after 7 P.M. One of the mayor's young staff members, who was also at the event, took the two Ford children to McDonald's while Towhey tried to figure out what to do. Ford insisted on going inside. So, as eight hundred guests in ball gowns and tuxedos were being served salad, Ford stumbled through the front doors. Towhey directed the mayor to the downstairs coat check. Ford tripped on the stairs, and one of the event staff caught him. He was heaving and disoriented.

Around this time, one of the ball's thirteen organizers decided to make a washroom run. The organizer spotted the mayor and Towhey hanging around at the bottom of the stairs. Upon getting closer, the organizer noticed something was wrong. Ford, tie askew, sweaty and red-faced, seemed to be high or having some sort of medical emergency.

"We know each other, and he stopped me to say hello," the organizer said. "He was babbling. I couldn't understand him. He was talking really fast, something about flooding issues in Etobicoke. It was totally incoherent. He was making no sense. But I never smelled any booze.... He wasn't even really looking at me. He would giggle."

The organizer approached the mayor's staff and Councillor Ainslie several times to see about "helping the mayor to make a dignified but early exit." According to the organizer, the staff said, "'No, no, it's okay.' ... It was bizarre."

Rather than leave, Ford and his small entourage went to sit at their table. At that point, Ainslie went to speak with Towhey himself, urging the chief of staff to get the mayor out of there. (Towhey denies this.) Ford left about an hour later.

For a few weeks, news of the mayor's bizarre appearance at the Garrison Ball stayed within a tight group of organizers and military personnel. But after the Sarah Thomson incident, people began to whisper about a developing pattern.

The Garrison gossip made it to my desk the second week of March 2013. The first person I called, one of the organizers, confirmed it. My questions seemed to reignite some frustration about the night. "It felt disrespectful to the event," the organizer said. "Several high-level military officials were quite upset."

According to this individual, the mayor already looked "hammered" when he arrived. No one could smell alcohol, but he was definitely "out of it." Paul Ainslie was reasonably close with both Rob and Doug Ford. He was a member of the mayor's executive committee, but I was pretty sure he wouldn't lie to me if I asked him directly about it. I decided to call him next.

"I'm really sorry," I said. "I know this puts you in a difficult position …"

"Oh, no," Ainslie chuckled nervously.

"… I know that you asked the mayor to leave the Garrison Ball two weeks ago. I hear some of the military guests were really offended."

Silence.

"… And I know that you were the one who lobbied for him to come and you felt guilty. So I have to ask, why did you ask him to leave?"

"I really can't comment on that."

"Are you saying you didn't ask him to leave?"

"… No."

"No, what?"

Silence.

"I'm told the mayor seemed impaired."

We went back and forth a few more times, over a couple days. After some soul-searching, Ainslie called.

"You can say I urged the mayor's chief of staff, Mark Towhey, to have the mayor leave the event. I'm not going to comment on why."

Meanwhile, the *Star*'s Kevin Donovan worked his contacts and brought in two other sources on the ball's organizing committee, as well as a military reservist. Said one organizer, "He seemed either drunk, high, or had a medical condition." A prominent Ottawa conservative confirmed that the mayor seemed impaired.

In a front-page story on March 26, 2013—under the headline "'Intoxicated' Ford Asked to Leave Gala: Inner Circle Repeatedly Urged Mayor to Enter Rehab"—the *Toronto Star* made public something already widely known in political, media, and law enforcement circles: Rob Ford appeared to have a drinking problem, and it was impacting his mayoralty.

Five sources confirmed the mayor's struggle with alcohol and attempts to get him help. Three organizers and a few other guests confirmed the mayor's erratic state at the Garrison Ball. Our story included details about the Bier Markt (minus the alleged cocaine use), the LCBO sightings on Twitter, a brief mention of Sarah Thomson's allegation, and a rundown of earlier hints of trouble: the domestic calls, the 1999 drunk driving charge, and the hockey game incident. None of our main sources could be named. Some were affiliated with the police and military and were thereby constrained from taking a stance on such a controversial issue. Others were working in politics, where sharing dirty laundry about your boss, even to save his life, isn't a wise career move.

Paul Ainslie was the only primary source named in the investigation. For telling the truth, he was vilified. And so was the *Toronto Star.*

TEN

PATHOLOGICAL LIARS

I spent the night trapped on the edge of sleep, my restless brain refusing to be quiet. Every conversation I'd had over the past year, every story I'd written, everything I'd seen—it was all cycling through my mind at high speed on repeat. Now and again, exhaustion would take over and I'd start to drift off, but then the memories would become so vivid I'd jolt awake to ask a question. At 5:45 A.M., I figured I had been in bed long enough and put on a pot of coffee. The story would be online soon. Sitting at my computer, I heard the paper hit the carpet in the hallway outside my condo. A gentle bump—the culmination of a year's work. I ran to the door. The smell of ink made it real.

I spread the paper out on my dining room table and stared at the story, letting reality sink in. "'Intoxicated' Ford Asked to Leave Gala," by Robyn Doolittle and Kevin Donovan.

We had published a story saying the mayor of Toronto needed to go to rehab, according to his own staff. We had revealed that he'd been booted from a military charity ball for showing up impaired, and that those closest to him thought his drinking was affecting his job. Our story was explosive. Things were going to be different—for the mayor, for the city, for the *Star*, and for me.

Rob Ford's time as mayor could now be divided into two periods: before the Garrison Ball story and after. Until that morning, a huge piece of background had been missing from City Hall coverage. Why had the Ford administration lost control of council? Because the mayor was not around to steer the ship. So where was Ford? Struggling with alcohol, according to his own staff. Clues that something was wrong had been out there for a year, through sightings of Ford posted on Twitter, rumblings in the police community, and whispers in the corridors of City Hall. But before the Garrison Ball story, the public had never been let in on the secret. It was a tricky situation. Something like the bachelorette party run-in would come up, but reporters hadn't been able to write the story. Doing so would have required raising serious questions about the mayor's personal life, questions too sensitive to hinge on one unflattering photo.

As I sat sipping my coffee, I thought about how our investigation could pave the way for a more honest conversation on what was happening in our municipal government. As a journalist, it's always a difficult decision to report on an elected official's personal life. There has to be an overriding public interest—if someone's ability to do their job properly has been compromised, for example. This clearly seemed to be the case with Rob Ford, and until that Tuesday morning, no one outside the City Hall bubble was talking about it. It was a conversation Toronto deserved to be in on.

Kevin Donovan and I had interviews booked all day. When newspapers print a controversial story, reporters and publishers have to defend it, answer questions, and be accountable to the public. We knew we were going to take heat for the number of anonymous sources in the piece. But the key detail in our story—that the mayor was asked to leave a military ball—had a very credible name attached to it, Councillor Paul Ainslie. We had a pattern we could point to: the drunken tirade at the Maple Leafs game, the domestic incidents involving calls to the police, the photos on social media, a named woman who saw the mayor "inebriated" before entering the Bier Markt, as well as our five well-vetted confidential sources. And Ford's staff believed he needed to be in rehab. This was a matter of huge public interest.

With minutes to spare, I arrived at the CityNews studio for what would be my second TV interview ever and bumbled my way through it. I'm a fidgeter, and I say "like" and "you know" more times than I should. Donovan is the pro. Just as he was finishing up a radio interview with the CBC, I got a text from a former Ford staffer: "Let's hope he gets help."

The city was awake now, and news was getting around. Twitter was, predictably, having a news-junkie meltdown. Ford's office hadn't responded, but Doug Ford was on the attack. As I headed into City Hall, Doug was being interviewed by AM640 talk radio host John Oakley.

Oakley: "Do you plan to sue, Doug? ... If you feel he's been maligned unfairly and he's been slandered, will you launch a lawsuit?"

Ford: "Johnny, that's their plan, they want to drag us into another lawsuit and then it's going to be about Rob Ford suing the *Star* for the next two years...."

Oakley: "But don't you feel that a lawsuit, the severity of a lawsuit, if you're confident you would win that, wouldn't that finally put to rest any kind of question marks hanging around the mayor or his behaviour? ..."

Ford: "... That's their game.... Make no mistake about it, the *Star* all is part of the same little group that's going after Rob, the Clayton Rubys of the world, they are all working together.... I've never seen Rob drink at any event. Ever."

About 9:15 A.M., the mayor left his Etobicoke home, ignoring the reporters camped out front. At 11 A.M. he was scheduled to give heavyweight boxing legend George Chuvalo a key to the city. Chuvalo, who had twice taken on Muhammad Ali, now spent his days as an anti-drugs activist. Chuvalo had lost three sons to heroin addiction. After his second son died of an overdose, his wife committed suicide. The famed boxer, who in 1998 was awarded the Order of Canada, now travelled the country sharing his heartbreaking story with student and parent groups. He was also an old family friend of the Fords.

The press gallery was hoping Ford would address the *Star* story before the ceremony. But if precedent was any indication, the mayor was going to make the media ask him about it in front of Chuvalo.

At City Hall, a small army of reporters, photographers, and television crew had assembled outside the mayor's office. The first few floors of the building are arranged in a big circle. Visitors walk through the front doors, head past the welcome desk, and then the space opens up into a cavernous rotunda. The second and third floors are stacked in rings around this opening. The mayor's office is at the south end of the second floor, looking out over Nathan Phillips Square, with the councillors' offices spread out around the rest of the loop. The set-up means you can always get a good idea of what's happening in the main building. I stood on the ground floor and watched the press mob every passing councillor, asking for comment. Deputy Mayor Doug Holyday told reporters he had never seen Ford drink.

The mayor's black Escalade pulled up to City Hall about 10 A.M. Dozens of reporters crowded around the elevator in front of his office. When the doors slid open, an aide rushed forward to clear the way. Ford stepped out wearing a fixed smile, his eyes trained on the floor.

"Mayor!"

"Mayor Ford, were you kicked out of the Garrison event?"

"Do you have an alcohol problem?"

"Any comment on these allegations?"

Ford shook his head. "It's nonsense," he said, before disappearing behind his office door.

Ford's press secretary, George Christopoulos, finally gave a statement: "For the record, the mayor was not asked to leave the gala."

Come 11 A.M., the throng of reporters moved to the members' lounge behind the council chamber for the Chuvalo ceremony. To one side, black-and-white photos of the boxer in his heyday flashed across a screen. Rows of chairs were in front of the podium. Chuvalo was looking handsome in a dark suit, his grey hair slicked back at the sides James Dean style. He looked much younger than seventy-five. Some of Chuvalo's family, including his second wife, Joanne, were in the crowd. The occasion was feeling awkward. Chuvalo deserved the huge turnout, but with Ford still not properly addressing the *Star*'s story, most reporters were there for the mayor, not the boxer.

When Ford emerged from behind a blue curtain, his forehead

was dripping with sweat, as it often is. He walked to the podium as if it were any other day.

"George, I want to thank you for being a friend to our family," he said. "I know my dad's up there, wishing he could be here. I know you've helped out many of us. And it's my pleasure now to present you with a key to the City of Toronto."

He handed Chuvalo a long flat box with a gold key inside. They posed for a photo, shook hands, and briefly embraced. Chuvalo said a few words.

Then it was time for questions. The *Star*'s City Hall bureau chief, David Rider, asked the question no one else wanted to: "Mayor Ford, can you address the story in the *Star* this morning?"

Predictably, Ford looked furious.

"You know what, guys, this is about George Chuvalo," he said. "If you wanna address this, number one it's an outright lie. It's the *Toronto Star* going after me, again, and again, and again. They're relentless. That's fine. I'll go head to head with the *Toronto Star* any time."

He was not going to address any of the specifics. He was not going to talk about the Bier Markt, or his staff's concerns, or the photos on Twitter. Ford retreated to his comfort zone—campaigning—framing the *Star* as a political opponent rather than a newspaper.

"Just let's wait, let's just wait until the election ... and then we'll see what happens," he fumed, getting more and more worked up with each passing sentence. "I'm sick of— It's patho— It's just lies after lies and lies! And I've called you pathological liars and you are! So why don't you take me to court?" Ford paused as if to consider his own suggestion, then, apparently deciding it was in fact a good idea, puffed out his chest and added, "Let the courts decide. You guys are liars. It's about George Chuvalo today, guys. Have some respect."

The Fords were always being asked why they didn't sue for libel if the *Star* was lying. Now the mayor was flipping it around. If he was wrong in calling the *Star* liars, why didn't they sue *him*? It seemed like a clever strategy. Ford Nation was going to eat that up, I thought. And at the end of the day, winning over the public was what mattered.

Later that day at City Hall, two councillors broke their silence on the long-held concerns about the mayor's health.

Councillor Joe Mihevc, who despite leaning to the left had a friendly relationship with the Ford administration, told 680News, "I think many of us have witnessed things that the *Toronto Star* has reported." Mihevc said he was worried about the city and about the mayor himself. "There is clearly some work that he needs to do. It is simply not accurate that the whole world is lying."

Well-liked rookie councillor Sarah Doucette—a progressive whom Doug Ford had described as one of his favourite councillors—told the *Star*, "It has been known at City Hall for quite a while that he may have a drinking problem." Doucette clarified that she had personally never seen anything, but that some of her colleagues had witnessed the mayor appearing impaired at "festivals, galas and other events" during the past year. "In some respects, I wish this had gotten out earlier, because if he needs help, please do it now," she said.

After the *Star* posted Doucette's comments online, the *National Post* tried to talk to her. "Ms. Doucette confirmed making the statement," it reported, "but refused to repeat it to the *Post* and other media outlets later in the day, after members of the mayor's staff left her City Hall office." She had been advised to keep quiet.

The usual suspects were slamming the *Star* on talk radio and Twitter, but otherwise reaction seemed fair. The CBC confirmed a big component of the *Star*'s story—that staff in Ford's office wanted the mayor to go to rehab.

Paul Ainslie was having a harder time. *The Globe and Mail* quoted a Ford ally questioning Ainslie's motives for saying what he had. Councillor Mike Del Grande called it "sour grapes" because the administration had not made Ainslie chair of the budget committee. The *Toronto Sun* printed something similar. Ford's chief of staff, Mark Towhey, told the *Globe*, "No one asked the mayor to leave and no one asked me to ask the mayor to leave." Ainslie stuck by his comments.

With all the interviews and press scrums that day, around the time I should have been eating dinner I realized I had missed lunch. It was getting late, and the editors still weren't sure what the main Ford story would be the next day. Then Garrison Ball co-chair Mark McQueen decided for us.

Six members of the thirteen-person Garrison Ball committee—not including Ainslie or the military personnel—signed a letter stating, "As a civilian member of the volunteer organizing committee of the 2013 Toronto Garrison Ball, I can confirm that I did not ask Rob Ford, Mayor of Toronto, to leave the event on February 23, 2013, for any reason. To my knowledge, no member of the event's organizing committee, including Councillor Paul Ainslie, directed the Mayor to leave the event that night."

One of the signatories later told me it felt like an attempt to smoke out the *Star*'s sources by seeing if anyone refused to sign. Except the wording of the letter missed the point; no one had directly asked Ford to leave. It was Towhey whom Ainslie had spoken with, and everyone knew that. Ainslie had publicly said so in the *Star* that morning. Given that, the wording of the letter seemed duplicitous. Organizers signed it feeling that technically it wasn't a lie. That nuance seemed to escape the public. On Twitter—an unscientific real-time gauge of public opinion—people seemed to be taking the committee's letter as some sort of proof that the *Star* story was off-base. Even some mainstream print and TV outlets were reporting on the letter in a way that suggested our story had been refuted. The facts were on our side, but the perception seemed to be that we'd gotten it wrong.

With deadline fast approaching, Donovan and I went back to our sources. It turned out Ainslie had sent out a statement of his own to the committee after our investigation. At the last possible moment, the *Star* got its hands on the email.

I think it's safe to say I was the only person who spoke with Mayor's Chief of Staff Mark Towhey. This was after being approached by @ least 8 people who were concerned about the Mayor's state.

I spoke briefly with the Mayor to see if there were any issues. He seemed to be somewhat incoherent. I told Mark Towhey, "I think it would be a good idea for the Mayor to leave."

I'm not aware of anyone else speaking to Mark Towhey.

I know it was me who pushed to have the Mayor attend the Ball. I'm very embarrassed about the media attention which the event has received.

With Ainslie's unequivocal admission that he'd asked the mayor's staff to get Ford to leave the Garrison Ball because people felt he was impaired, the *Star* was able to push the story forward again on Wednesday's front page.

Ford showed up at City Hall at noon and refused to answer any questions.

ELEVEN

FOR
SALE

Last call had come and gone when twenty-one-year-old
Anthony Smith and a nineteen-year-old friend left Loki
Lounge in downtown Toronto on March 28, 2013. The popular
nightclub in the King Street West bar district was the kind of
place where men wore sunglasses inside, women teetered on
heels they couldn't walk in, and most of the furniture was uphol-
stered in velvet.

Smith and his friend had known each other since they were
about ten years old. They used to play on the same basketball
team. Now, according to police, they were both members of the
Dixon City Bloods street gang.

At 2:30 A.M., they crossed to the north side of the street. The
gunshots came out of nowhere.

A bullet went through the back of Smith's head. His friend
was hit in the arm and back. When the sun came up, two
crimson pools of blood were still on the sidewalk. Smith was
pronounced dead before the morning was over. The friend
barely survived.

Four days later, my cell phone rang just after 9 A.M. It was a
man named Mohamed Farah. He wanted to meet.

"I have some information I think you'd like to see," he said. "It's about a prominent Toronto politician."

IT WAS AROUND NOON on Easter Monday. I was standing on a soccer field in a west-end Toronto park, talking on the phone to the *Star*'s editor-in-chief, Michael Cooke. Farah was waiting out of earshot on a nearby bench, holding his iPad.

"He says they want a hundred thousand dollars," I told Cooke. "I tried to explain that's a completely crazy number, but he seems set on it."

"Can you bring him to the newsroom?" Cooke asked.

Farah offered to drive. He was parked in an alley behind a Starbucks. I had three seconds to weigh the pros and cons of going with him or taking a cab. Pro: I could see his licence plate, run a check, and get his name and address. Con: I was alone, and any idiot knew not to get in a car with a stranger. Pro: It would build trust, provided he wasn't a rapist. Con: He might be a rapist.

"Sure, that'd be great if you could drive," I said.

The moment I spotted Farah's black sedan, I sent Cooke an email with a description of the vehicle and the plate number—just in case. I climbed into the passenger side. The car was clean and obviously quite new. I didn't see a scrap of trash.

The *Star* was fifteen minutes of city driving away. I used the time to get to know Farah a little better. I asked him about his job, his friends and hobbies. He seemed like a decent person. Smart and thoughtful, although he was definitely misrepresenting his altruism.

"It's not right what's happening," Farah told me. "I just really want the story out there. It has to get out there. People need to know about this."

"If you really want the story out there, why not just give us the video?" I asked.

He told me he was acting on behalf of a dealer, a young man he'd met through his work in the community. (Occasionally he would refer to two people. Maybe there was another dealer—maybe a girlfriend. It was hard to know.) Farah told me that this dealer was a good kid but had gotten messed up in the drug culture. He wanted out. Anthony Smith's recent murder had been a wake-up call. Smith had been a good friend. But the kid needed money to build a new life. The video was his ticket. Farah told me he had offered to help because he knew people in the media. One of them, he said, worked in New York—he would not tell me who it was, where they worked, or what they did—and that their organization was considering buying the footage.

"But I'd like for you guys to have it. The *Star* deserves to get the story. You've done the work."

"One hundred thousand dollars is way too much," I said.

"It's worth a million. They wanted a million. I told them that was too much."

"Mohamed, this sort of thing doesn't happen in Canada. We buy videos and photos from freelancers, yes, but that's like five hundred dollars. Maybe a thousand. I don't know if you follow this stuff, but it's not exactly a great time financially for the newspaper industry."

"The video will make you guys a lot of money. People would have to come to your site to see it. You could charge people to watch it."

I tried to explain that it didn't work like that. Someone would just make a copy and post it online.

"It's not just the cost. There are ethical issues here," I said. "Anyway, I'm at the bottom of the totem pole. It's not going to be my call. I'm just warning you—I don't think a hundred thousand dollars is going to happen."

We turned onto Yonge Street and followed it down to the lake, stopping outside the *Toronto Star* office tower. I phoned security to raise the gate so that we could park in the front lot, then sent Cooke a two-minute warning. He, along with city editor Irene Gentle, would be in the northwest conference room. Farah collected his iPad, cell phone, and keys. Everything was shut down because of the holiday. I had to swipe my security pass to get inside, then again to activate the elevator. We got off on the fifth floor and turned left at the wall where photos of the *Star*'s publishers, past and present, are displayed. Only a skeleton staff was in the newsroom. I doubt anyone even noticed us. We went straight to the conference room.

I introduced Cooke and Gentle to Farah. Everyone shook hands, and then we got to it.

Farah gave them the same spiel he had given me in the park. Using his iPad, he showed them the photo of Rob Ford with Anthony Smith and two others in front of the yellow-brick bungalow—a crack house, he said. Smith was dead, shot to death just four days earlier. Another of the men had been seriously wounded in the same incident. Next, he described the video. Farah claimed that it clearly showed Mayor Rob Ford smoking crack cocaine while uttering racist and homophobic slurs.

Then came the price tag: one hundred thousand dollars. Non-negotiable.

"Well, let's get one thing straight right now," Cooke said. "You're not going to get a hundred thousand dollars. Not even close. Now, there might be some price, but before we even talk about what it's worth, we need to see the video."

Farah said he needed time. He did not have a copy. The guy he was helping did not trust him with it, but he would let the dealer know we were interested.

Gentle and Cooke quizzed Farah about the video's contents.

How was the photo connected to the video?

It wasn't. Except that the dealer was friends with Anthony Smith.

When was the video shot?

Within the last six months.

Where?

Farah wouldn't say.

Was Ford alone in the footage?

Yes.

After twenty minutes of grilling, I walked Farah to his car and made plans to touch base later that day to set up our next meeting.

TUESDAY MORNING, APRIL 2, 2013, I was back in the conference room with Cooke and Gentle as well as the *Star*'s long-time newsroom lawyer, Bert Bruser, and its managing editor, Jane Davenport. Kevin Donovan was on vacation. Everyone had been briefed on Farah's astonishing claim, but Cooke asked me to recount the story in detail, from the first phone call to our last text message, once more for the group. When I got to the part

about a hundred thousand dollars, everyone seemed to collect-
ively cringe.

"Now he's supposed to go back to his guy and sort out how
we can see the video," I said. "He texted me last night and we're
going to meet around six o'clock today up in Etobicoke."

There was silence for a few moments as the editors looked
around the room, weighing the gravity of what we were dealing
with. Bruser rubbed his bearded chin and shook his head.
His face is always impossible to read. I couldn't tell if he was
taking in the magnitude of the allegations or trying to figure
out a damage-control strategy for this hoax I had gotten us
involved in.

"So," Davenport said, "are we considering paying a hundred
thousand dollars for this video?"

Davenport was just thirty-six when in June 2012 the *Star*
named her managing editor, Michael Cooke's second-in-
command. Together, they were the perfect pair. Davenport
was the calculated and cautious yin to Cooke's aggressive and
spontaneous yang. When Davenport spoke, she gave the impression that every word had been chosen deliberately.

"We're not going to pay that," Cooke replied. "But, if it's
real, and that's a big if, and if we can confirm that it's real, we
might pay something."

The *Toronto Star* does not pay for stories. It is explicitly
stated in the newspaper's code of conduct: "The *Star* does not
pay for information." But it does pay for commodities such as
photos and video. If Farah had come to the *Star* asking for five
hundred dollars, my guess is we would have paid him on the
spot. The issue here was the size of the ransom and the people we
would be giving it to. What would a self-described drug dealer

do with that kind of money? Did we believe he wanted to turn his life around? On the other hand, if this video did exist, if it proved that the mayor of Toronto was smoking crack cocaine, the implications for the city were enormous. Given the immense public interest of a story like that, maybe it *was* worth paying a hundred thousand dollars to drug dealers.

But there were other problems. How would we be able to tell if Ford was smoking *drugs*? How could we even be sure it was him? Could the video be doctored? Everyone agreed we needed to see the thing before we could assess its value. Besides, there was another, more pressing question to deal with: What if this was a set-up?

The day before Farah had called, Doug Ford devoted the first part of the brothers' weekly radio show to the *Star* and its supposed vendetta, suggesting the paper would go to any length to "politically kill Rob Ford." He targeted Cooke specifically, talking about his days as editor-in-chief of the *New York Daily News*, and in particular his role in the reality TV show *Tabloid Wars*. He had found and quoted Cooke's colourful statement about pressing one's foot on the competition's throat "till their eyes bulge and leak blood."

Was it possible someone was trying to embarrass us with a fake story, baiting the hook with the kind of over-the-top yarn they thought Cooke would do anything to get?

"It's possible," I told my editors. "It would be a pretty elaborate hoax, but it's certainly possible. I'm just assuming everything I say is being recorded."

I'd try to get a better feel for the situation when I saw Farah that night. Lawyer Bert Bruser said I should have someone with me for physical and journalistic protection. With Donovan still gone, the group selected Jesse McLean, a young and talented reporter on Donovan's investigative team. McLean and I had known each other for years, having worked together at our campus newspaper.

Before I left, Cooke looked me in the eye. "I know you know this, but I'm going to say it anyway. No one can know about this. Not anyone outside this room—even your friends in the newsroom."

"Got it."

It was the start of a lonely six weeks.

JESSE MCLEAN AND I pulled onto the highway just in time for rush-hour traffic. We were going to meet Farah at a Country Style doughnut shop in a north Etobicoke plaza on Dixon Road near the airport. The neighbourhood was sometimes called Little Mogadishu, sometimes Rexdale. By the mid-1990s, half the population in the area was Somali. In fact, according to some of the people who lived there, Canada was known simply as "Dixon" in Somali refugee camps across East Africa. It was a lower-income part of town, as communities with large immigrant populations tend to be.

The community centred on six high-rises on the north side of Dixon, which stood like fortresses around two courtyards. These grey towers were actually condos, although they looked a lot more like subsidized housing, especially on the inside. The stairwells reeked of urine. Walls were etched with gang graffiti, carpets were old and stained, and there were signs of disrepair on every floor. One tower had a serious rodent infestation. The average price of a condo in Toronto was more than three hundred thousand dollars. In Dixon, you could find two-bedrooms for under sixty thousand—half of what they used to be worth. Crime was a problem, especially of late. A gang known as the Dixon City Bloods had a foothold in the complex, especially the 320 building. Shootings and robberies were frequent in Rexdale. Frustrated community leaders were constantly fighting to get media coverage for all the good things happening in the otherwise vibrant neighbourhood.

We pulled into the plaza parking lot across from the towers at about 6 P.M. There were hardly any free tables at the doughnut shop, which was the case all day most every day. The people who hung around were usually middle-aged to elderly men from the neighbourhood. They sat in clusters, chatting with friends, reading the paper, and watching the CP24 news channel on a big flat-screen TV.

McLean and I slid into a booth. I texted Farah a few minutes before he was supposed to arrive: "Hey you want a coffee?" He wrote back, "Tea please—medium sugar 2 milk." A few minutes later, he phoned from somewhere in the parking lot. He didn't want to sit or be seen with us. We could go for a drive, but not in his car. So we took ours.

He got in the front with me, McLean sat in the back, and we went on a little tour for the next hour. We drove along Dixon Road, through the tower parking lots, to the high school and the surrounding neighbourhood. We asked Farah a lot of the same questions I had asked him on that first ride to the *Star*. His answers were all the same, which was a good sign. We went to a community basketball game and met some of Farah's friends. We covertly fact-checked what he'd been telling us. Everything matched up. Back in the car, we asked Farah more about the video and the circumstances in which it had been taken. And what about the photo? Where was that house?

"It's around here. That's all I'm going to say. You've got to be patient," Farah said. "This is about building trust."

Trust seemed to mean our willingness to pay. The conversation always curled back to money.

"This is about protection," Farah said. Could we help the dealer's family if the government tried to deport them after the story ran? Would we protect Farah's and the dealer's identity?

McLean and I explained how confidential sources worked, that we would never reveal their identities even if compelled to do so by a court. If we made a promise of anonymity, we would keep it. This seemed to satisfy him. We said if someone was being unlawfully deported, that would certainly be a story the *Star* would cover, and the press had great influence. We could also try to hook the dealer up with our lawyer to answer any questions. Farah nodded approvingly. (In the end, the *Star* agreed to keep Farah's name secret, until he revealed himself as "the broker" to two media outlets in November 2013. As for the dealer, the *Star* never granted him anonymity. We learned his name—Mohamed Siad—only after reporter Jayme Poisson spent months uncovering it.)

We dropped Farah off about 7:30 P.M. We were no closer to the video, but more convinced that there was one. I told him I would get in touch after we'd had a chance to relay some of his concerns to the editors.

THE NEXT DAY AT THE *Toronto Star* offices, the same group plus Jesse McLean was back in the northwest boardroom.

"Farah told me he turned down twenty thousand dollars from another outlet," I said. "Although he's likely just bargaining; I guess that was an indication of what he won't accept."

We debated whether there was a way to set up some sort of scholarship fund. If they actually just wanted to start over, maybe we could help without handing over cash? But how would that work? Would we pay their rent? Their food? Would they give status reports? It seemed complicated. We got back to the idea of just buying it.

Jane Davenport spoke up.

"I'm very uncomfortable with the idea of paying for it," she said. "How do we know what they'll do with the money? What if they buy a gun and kill someone?"

It was a sobering thought.

Then again, if the mayor really was smoking crack cocaine, the city needed to know. Nothing like this had ever happened in Canada, but there were precedents in the US and the UK of news outlets paying big money for exclusive footage. We were unanimous that, no matter what we decided, we would disclose what we did and why.

From where I was sitting, it felt like the editors' problem with the dollar amount was not so much about the *Star*'s bottom line as the ethical concerns. (Contrary to what some critics have suggested, the *Star* actually lost several hundred thousand dollars' worth of subscriptions from people who believed the Fords. It would have been far cheaper to have bought the video.) Yes, there was an awareness that breaking this story would be huge for the *Toronto Star*, a big win in a crowded newspaper town. But no one was willing to compromise the integrity of the paper—even for the scoop of the century.

McLean and I headed back to Etobicoke that afternoon to look for the house in the photo before meeting again with Farah. It had been a few days since I'd seen the picture, and Farah was more and more reluctant to let us see it again. He didn't want us finding the place. All we had to go on was my memory and his claim that it was a place where people smoked crack. The brick was light, and the house was somewhere near Don Bosco Catholic Secondary School, which was about five minutes from the Dixon towers. We drove up and down each street, looking for unkempt lawns, broken windows, and chipped paint, jotting down a few licence plate numbers to check later.

Then we met Farah for another long conversation that ended up the same place it began.

Such was the dance for the next twenty days. We'd talk to Farah, then meet in the northwest conference room. The *Star's* executive editor, Murdoch Davis, the man who watched the newsroom's money, was added to the roster. Donovan got back from vacation and was extremely apprehensive. "I'm not saying it's impossible, but I can't believe that the mayor would let himself be videotaped doing this. I just have a hard time believing these guys."

Farah wasn't helping the skepticism. One weekend, he promised to let us see the video but then never responded to any messages when the time came close. Another time, we showed up thinking we could see the footage, only to have the same conversation over again. Farah was also becoming frustrated. We were not budging on the cash issue. He stopped talking to me for ten days in mid-April.

McLean and I kept up the search for the house in the photo. We talked to a few locals who had also heard about the video and the crack house, but they wouldn't share anything more than that. Meanwhile, Donovan worked his sources for information about Ford's activities in the area.

On April 22, I sent Farah a text message: "Hey dude. Whether there's video or not I still want to do this story. I thought you did too."

He finally wrote back: "I'm trying my best, I will reach out when I have something or when I'm done. All the best."

Shortly after, I approached senior editors at the paper. "They're never going to let us see it if we don't at least say we might buy it," I said.

It was a sentence we had been avoiding, but it seemed like the only way. I got the go-ahead to tell Farah we would be open to negotiating a price—if we could see it.

I called him that night. We could see the video by the end of the week.

IT'S ABOUT 11 P.M. on May 3, 2013. Donovan and I are sitting in a parked car near the Dixon towers, not speaking, just writing; writing down everything we can remember.

"Mo took us 320 Dixon lot. Left car to get dealer. Man returned. Lanky. Somali? Scabs on arms. Bulging eyes. Looked nervous. Black T-shirt. Short hair. Big forehead. Didn't want to talk. Pulled out iPhone—black. Hit play. Definitely Ford. White button-up T-shirt. Buttons open at neck. Holding glass pipe— dark at the end."

And so on.

At first the dealer had wanted to play the video with no volume. "Sound's extra," he told us. But we convinced him we needed to hear what was being said in order to assess the value. He eventually relented.

The video was about a minute and a half long. Rob Ford was sitting on a chair beside a small table. To me, there was no question it was him. He was sitting against a white wall in sunshine, no more than seven feet from the camera. It looked like it had been shot on an iPhone in high definition. Ford had his eyes closed the way he does when he's answering questions in a press conference. He was bobbing around on his chair, slurring, swaying, and rambling. At points, he lifted up his arms, bent at the elbow like a chicken, and then he sort of squirmed all over. He was talking, but it was hard to remember any of the words, because they didn't connect. At one point, someone off-camera says something like, "You love football. That's what you should be doing."

In my notes, I wrote that Ford responds, "Yeah, I take these kids … (something) minorities," maybe "fucking minorities."

After that, Ford starts to talk politics. He says something like, "Everyone expects me to be right-wing, I'm supposed to be this great …" but then he loses his train of thought. Off-camera, the person says something like, "I wanna shove my foot up Justin Trudeau's ass so far it comes out the other end." Both the voice and Ford are yelling, although the person off-screen doesn't seem impaired. Ford seems to chuckle at the comment. "Justin Trudeau's a fag," he says. Shortly after, a cell phone rings. Ford looks directly at the camera filming him and says, "That phone better not be on." Then the screen goes dark.

We watched the footage three times, committing the details to memory. Remember, we'd been instructed to leave all our stuff back in our car, including my purse with my notebook.

During one pass, I kept the phone four inches from my face to look at the clear stem of the glass pipe. It was definitely black at the end, as crack pipes tend to be. I checked to see if smoke came out of Ford's mouth. It did. I wanted to see if he held the lighter below the tube rather than curl the flame above, the way you would with a tobacco or marijuana pipe. It was definitely being lit underneath.

"It's crack," the dealer said. He was becoming more and more agitated the longer he sat in the car. Of course, there was no way to know for sure what Ford was smoking. All we could tell was that it looked like a crack pipe. And he looked impaired.

"Are you worried, if this comes out, about your safety? Will the mayor know it's you?" I asked the dealer.

"Money is safety."

Farah drove us back to our car. I told him I'd call the next day, after we had a chance to speak with our editors.

Donovan and I didn't say anything as we pulled out of the plaza. We parked in a lot one block west and pulled out our notebooks. Once we had written down everything we could remember, we compared notes. They were more or less the same, although Donovan had more detail in some parts and I had more in others. About the person off-camera, we were split. My impression was that it was a woman with a really gruff, masculine voice. Donovan thought it was a man. Donovan had also heard "fucking minorities," while I remembered more about the comment "I wanna shove my foot up Justin Trudeau's ass." We both picked up on the "fag" reference. We had both seen a clear tube with black at the end and smoke. And we were both positive it was Ford.

Donovan phoned Cooke, Davenport, and Bruser and put

them on speakerphone. The trio was at the National Newspaper Awards in Ottawa, where Jesse McLean had just won the top prize for investigations with another *Star* reporter.

"It's real," Donovan said.

MONDAY MORNING WE WERE BACK in the conference room for a conversation that was no longer hypothetical. Were we going to pay for this? Some people in the room wanted to buy it. Others did not.

As the head of the *Star*'s investigative unit, Donovan took the lead on the story.

We met with Farah in the same west-end park I had taken him to a month earlier.

"We're not going to pay a hundred thousand," Donovan said.

"This is worth a million. It's gotta be a hundred thousand," Farah said.

"You need to come back with something more reasonable," Donovan said.

Farah said the dealer wasn't going to accept anything lower than the asking price.

Now that Donovan and I had seen the footage, there was going to be a story at some point, whether we got the video or not. Maybe it made sense to pay their price just for the legal protection alone, in case Ford sued the *Star*. My opinion changed numerous times. On the one hand, I desperately wanted Toronto to see what Donovan and I had seen. On the other, I shared the concerns about where the money was going. More selfishly, I didn't want my whole career to be defined by a story for which the *Star* had paid one hundred thousand dollars to make happen.

The only thing I knew for sure was that if we wanted that tape, we should be prepared to pay the six figures. I had the sense that these guys were doing something that their friends either did not know about or did not approve of. It didn't seem inconceivable that if the video came out it could put them—and maybe their families—at serious risk. I didn't know how many ways the money was being split. I suspected Farah was going to get a cut, although he denied it. At the very least, he'd made reference to two other people. So, assuming the total payment was going to at least be split in half, I sort of understood the large price tag. If they did intend to completely uproot their lives and move, that wasn't something that could easily be done for a share of twenty thousand dollars.

In a final big meeting at the *Star*, we decided the paper would not pay for the video.

"I have confidence that Kevin and Robyn can get this story through old-fashioned reporting," Davenport said. Cooke agreed.

Part of me was relieved. Part of me felt nauseated at the prospect of another year on this investigation. But it was the right call.

Donovan and I met that afternoon. He drew up a battle plan and gave me a list of people he had been pursuing with ties to Ford and drugs. The rest of the investigative team would be getting involved. This was going to be a long slog. But it would be worth it. And in the meantime we would leave Farah to think things over.

KEEPING A SECRET IS TOUGH. Keeping a secret that I'd seen the mayor of Toronto smoking from what looked like a crack pipe was exhausting. My *Star* friends knew not to ask what I was working on. My mom called to see if everything was okay—she'd noticed I hadn't been writing much. "Oh, you know, just taking some time off after the big Garrison story," I said, lying to my own mother.

Donovan was never a fan of concentrating on just one thing. "You should spend some days at City Hall. Let people see you there," he told me. So I went back to the beat.

The day before my life changed forever, I covered a story about some activist foodies who had decided to protest Toronto's perplexing street-food bylaws. A group called Food Forward had set up a "guerrilla food cart" in front of City Hall, handing out apples to passersby, I wrote. The next morning, one of the organizers called to complain that I had used the word *guerilla*. I had apparently insinuated that they were gun-wielding rebel fighters. "I was just trying to use an interesting word to describe your fruit protest," I sighed. "I don't think anyone would read that and actually think you were holding AK-47s." She wanted a correction. I referred her to the *Star*'s public editor, then put my head down on my desk. I'd seen video of the mayor maybe smoking crack cocaine, and I was spending my morning dealing with aggravated food cart protestors.

At 12:02 P.M., my cell phone rang again. I didn't recognize the number. Not more Food Forward people, I thought.

"Hey, Robyn!" It was a TV news producer I knew. "I have to ask you something, but please keep it confidential.... We just got a call from CNN. Have you heard anything about a video of the mayor smoking crack?"

I almost hit the floor. I managed to chuckle nonchalantly, "Nope, but if you hear anything more about that, I'd certainly like to know."

"Yeah, I know it sounds crazy. I just figured, if somebody knew it would be you."

"Okay, talk soon," I said, while typing out an email to the editors, subject line: "ALERT!—CNN may have our video."

I left City Hall and headed to the *Star*, texting Farah on the way. He told me he had shown the video to an editor at the American gossip website Gawker, and that Gawker was trying to broker a deal with CNN to buy the video. By 4:30 P.M., we learned that CNN had called the mayor's office to see if they knew about it. I called Farah again to warn him. He was panicking.

Back in the conference room, we discussed our options. If CNN and Gawker were going to buy the video, that was not such a bad thing. At least the story would get out.

"Do we think Gawker isn't just going to write a story?" I asked.

"They might," Cooke said.

That night, Cooke and I were at a third-floor dim sum restaurant in Chinatown for a *Star* food writer's book launch. I noticed Cooke sneak out about 8:25 P.M. Seconds later, my friend Jonathan Goldsbie ran over to me with his cell phone. Suddenly, everyone seemed to be looking at their phones.

"Robyn, did you see this?" he said. Gawker had posted the photo of Ford with Anthony Smith and two other men in front of the yellow-brick house. The headline: "For Sale: A Video of Toronto Mayor Rob Ford Smoking Crack Cocaine."

I'm pretty sure I yelled "Fuck!"

I dove under a table where I had been hiding my purse. I tried Cooke's cell. No answer. In my four-inch heels, I sprinted to the stairwell, hoping I hadn't missed him. I rounded the steps to the second floor. I could see him hailing a cab. I started banging like a crazy person on the full-length Plexiglas window. He spotted me. "Stay there!" I gestured. Six seconds later, I was on the street.

"Gawker just published the story," I heaved.

A taxi pulled up.

We got in the cab.

"One Yonge Street, please," Cooke said.

TWELVE

ANYTHING ELSE?

Michael Cooke and I arrived at the *Star* building about fifteen minutes after the Gawker story went online. In the taxi ride back to the office, Cooke had called in the troops. Kevin Donovan was coaching a girls' soccer practice. Cooke texted him a simple "Get in." It was 8:45 P.M., May 16, 2013.

"Just start to write," Cooke said as we entered the newsroom. I headed to my desk and pulled out my notes from the night in the car.

Sometimes, I spend hours on the first few lines of my articles, tinkering and fiddling until the lead is just right. There was no time for that now. We had less than three hours to get a response from Ford, write the story, edit it, lawyer it, and get it on the page. I tuned out everything and started to type. I had only a vague notion of the conversations happening around me. The senior editors and our lawyer, huddling around the newsroom, sometimes in Cooke's office, sometimes at the big table near the front, were trying to nail down what we could legally print and how best to do it.

In 2009, the Supreme Court of Canada created a new defence for libel in this country that would prove to be very important for the *Star* that night. In a nutshell, it allowed journalists to tackle contentious stories of public interest where hard evidence, like a video, might not be available—provided the reporters could prove they acted professionally, did their best to verify the information, and attempted to get both sides of the story. It is known as the responsible journalism defence.

In the decision, Chief Justice Beverley McLachlin wrote that if journalists were only able to publish stories where hold-it-in-your-hand evidence existed, "information that is reliable and in the public's interest to know may never see the light of day." She said that a "standard of perfection" would lead to the "inevitable silencing of critical comment."

Because the *Star* did not have a copy of the video, that Supreme Court decision provided a crucial defence for the paper. Our story—that drug dealers were trying to sell a video of the mayor appearing to smoke crack cocaine—was clearly in the public interest. Donovan and I had done our best to verify the accuracy by viewing the video and meeting the sellers. Now we needed to give the mayor a chance to respond.

At 9:04 P.M., I sent text messages to Ford's chief of staff, Mark Towhey, and to his press secretary, George Christopoulos. "Hi George and Mark. The Toronto Star would like to speak with you both regarding the allegations about mayor Rob Ford smoking crack on a video and the Gawker story." Neither responded. I phoned. No answer. The allegation wouldn't have come as a surprise to either. CNN had asked the same thing earlier in the day.

Between 9:15 and 10 P.M., Kevin Donovan repeatedly tried the mayor at his office and home line. No answer. He left messages. He also tried Christopoulos. City Hall reporter

Paul Moloney and photographer Tara Walton went to the mayor's house in Etobicoke. Moloney knocked several times at the front door and put a note in the mail slot. They were told to "move along" by a man who seemed to be acting as security. Next, Moloney and Walton went to Doug Ford's home, which was close by. No answer. They left another note and then returned to the mayor's home. Still nothing.

At 9:45 P.M., I got in touch with Ford's lawyer, Dennis Morris, and explained what we had seen. He asked me, "How can you know what he's smoking?" He said the story was "false and defamatory." Morris and Donovan spoke as well, and Ford's lawyer repeated the eyebrow-raising quote. My bureau chief, David Rider, got Towhey on the phone before 10 P.M. After Rider explained the story, Towhey hung up.

We emailed and tweeted and texted and phoned other members of the mayor's staff throughout the evening.

I wrote for about an hour, then sent what I had to Donovan, who stitched it together with what he'd written. A version went online about 11 P.M.

Throughout the evening, I had been talking to Farah. We still did not have a copy of the photo of Ford with Anthony Smith. "Please, it's out there already," I said. "Just send us the photo. Gawker already has the thing online."

At truly the eleventh hour, 10:57 P.M., Farah sent me the picture. Our drop-dead deadline was closing in. Senior editors crowded around a big computer monitor to examine the photo, running various tests to see if it had been tampered with. We decided to blur the faces of the two men we didn't know, in case they were juveniles. Finally, the front page was sent to the printing plant. There is a reason the process of printing a newspaper every day is sometimes called "the daily miracle."

At 12:30 A.M., I unlocked the door to my condo. I had thirty text messages and missed phone calls. There was a half-angry voice mail from my parents. "You got in a car with drug dealers!?" They'd apparently read the online version of the story. I'd call them later. Sleep, I told myself. I had to go to sleep. Instead, I lay in bed and read reaction on Twitter for longer than I care to admit. The backlash was already starting.

A NICE WOMAN handed me a glass of a water. We'd be on air in a few minutes, she warned. I thanked her, downed the contents, then made sure there wasn't mascara all over my face before heading to the glass console in the centre of the studio. The CBC afternoon news host Reshmi Nair was standing on the other side with her laptop. A photo of Rob Ford, his lips pursed, looking off into the distance, was on a giant screen behind us. Hours earlier, our story—"Ford in 'Crack Video' Scandal"—had been splashed over most of the *Star*'s front page.

"Okay," Nair began, "so how do you know that it's actually Rob Ford in that video you saw?"

"You know, I think when it came to us, all we knew was that there was this supposed video that showed the mayor smoking crack cocaine," I said. "We had no expectations. The video stunned us. It shocked us. It is about ninety seconds long. It is crystal clear.... We were confident that it was Mayor Rob Ford in the video."

Next, Nair chose her words carefully, so as to avoid being sued. The CBC had not seen the footage and could not verify its contents, she said, before asking why I couldn't prove what my paper was alleging. Why didn't we have the video? I explained that the *Star* was not prepared to pay one hundred thousand dollars for the footage.

"Deputy Mayor Doug Holyday is saying you can't trust drug dealers," Nair said.

"I'm not trusting drug dealers. I'm trusting my eyes. So, I saw this video—with my own eyes," I said. "Who these guys are, [what] their motivations are, they've told us some stories: believe them, don't believe them. I believe my own eyes. Kevin Donovan believes his own eyes."

THAT FRIDAY MORNING, my streetcar slid to a stop in front of City Hall just as the old courthouse clock next door chimed 8 A.M. Reporters and camera crews were everywhere. I could see from Twitter that another pack was outside the mayor's home.

When Ford left his house that day, he walked past the press smiling. "Absolutely not true," he said. "It's ridiculous. It's another *Toronto Star* ..." He trailed off. Reporters continued to shout questions as he climbed into his black Escalade. "All right, I'll see you guys down at City Hall."

The story was picked up around the globe. *The Guardian, The New York Times, The Washington Post,* NPR, MSNBC, CNN, and *The Sydney Morning Herald* all reported on the mayor of Toronto's crack cocaine scandal.

"I have bad news for you, Canada," Josh Barro wrote on Bloomberg's economic and politics blog, *The Ticker.* "Americans have learned about Rob Ford, and we'll have no more of your smug superiority."

A Washington, DC, alternative weekly asked their city's former mayor Marion Barry for his thoughts on the scandal. (In 1990, Barry was convicted for drug possession after he was video-taped as part of an FBI sting operation smoking crack cocaine in a hotel room.) "Unless he was entrapped by the government, it's not similar," Barry said.

When Ford pulled up to City Hall, camera crews were waiting. Councillors from across the political spectrum called on the mayor to address the crack story in detail, but Ford ignored questions as he walked into his office without a word. Later, he emerged only briefly to say, "Anyways, like I said this morning, these allegations are ridiculous, another story with respect to the *Toronto Star* going after me, and that's all I have to say."

The day came and went without any of Ford's usual fiery denunciations. The mayor's press secretary and chief of staff were silent. Even the mayor's staunchest defender, his brother Doug, said nothing. The brothers cancelled their weekly radio show that Sunday. A spokesperson for the Toronto police said the service was "monitoring the situation closely."

In fact, unbeknownst to us at the time, Chief Bill Blair was taking much more aggressive steps. On May 18, 2013, he contacted one of his most trusted investigators, Detective Sergeant Gary Giroux. Giroux was a seasoned homicide detec-tive who had handled some of the city's most high-profile cases. Now, he would be asked to take on one of the most controversial investigations in Toronto Police Service history: to find out if the mayor was smoking crack with gangsters. He wouldn't be alone. A small and very secret taskforce was assembled. There was Detective Joyce Schertzer, who was handling the Anthony Smith murder case, as well as Detective Constable Amy Davey,

Detective Constable David Lavallee, and Detective Sergeant Domenic Sinopoli. The elaborate probe would become known as Project Brazen 2. It would last six months and would enlist the help of a Cessna spy plane, wiretaps, and extensive ground surveillance. And luck was on Giroux's side. The gang peddling the crack video was already being watched, and listened to, by Toronto police as part of the massive guns and drug investigation called Project Traveller. Wiretaps captured some of those targets discussing the crack video. Police pulled Sandro Lisi's phone records. The story they would tell was troubling.

At 8:18 P.M., ten minutes before the crack video story was posted on Gawker, Ford had phoned his friend Lisi, suspected drug dealer and occasional driver. The call lasted forty seconds. Lisi then began sending a flurry of text messages. At 9:25 P.M.— as the *Star* sent out a breaking-news alert that the video was real and that both Donovan and I had seen it—Lisi was phoning Fabio Basso, Ford's "stoner" friend since high school. We didn't know it at the time, but Basso lived at 15 Windsor Road, the yellow-brick bungalow in the infamous Ford photo.

Through the night and into the next day, as Mayor Ford dodged reporters, Lisi talked to Basso six more times.

Then at 1:17 P.M. on May 17—minutes after talking to Basso—Lisi called Mohamed Siad, the dealer who was trying to sell us the video. The call lasted three seconds. A second call lasted eight seconds. Then Lisi called Basso back. Throughout the day, Lisi phoned and texted a variety of people living in or near the Dixon towers. He also spoke numerous times with Dave Price, the mayor's old friend and recently hired staff member. At 5:26 P.M., Mayor Ford called Lisi. There would be five more calls between the two of them before midnight. At 11:24 P.M. and

11:44 P.M., Lisi phoned Siad again. On the Saturday—two days into the scandal—Lisi and Ford spoke six times. That morning, Lisi and Siad connected once for a few seconds. Around this time, two men came knocking on Fabio Basso's front door, demanding he get the video back. According to a friend of the Basso family, Fabio told them to "fuck off." He was more worried about repercussions from the Dixon City Bloods than from the Fords. Basso would pay for his defiance.

Ford showed up at City Hall on Tuesday, May 21, for a special council debate on a proposed casino, a wildly unpopular scheme that his administration had been pushing. He lost the vote and ducked out about 2 P.M. without answering questions. We would later learn that around 11 P.M. that night, a man wielding a metal pipe forced his way into Fabio Basso's home. The assailant tossed Basso's elderly mother to the ground before striking Basso repeatedly. He then turned on Basso's girlfriend when she tried to defend him. The attack itself was fast. Fabio "said it happened real quick: bop, bop, bop," a friend of the Basso family later told me. Even more troubling, the same night that Basso was beaten, a twenty-seven-year-old man was shot in the leg on the seventeenth floor of 320 Dixon, the same building where I'd watched the crack video. The man had been shot outside unit 1701 after partying with friends in unit 1703, a known drug hotspot.

Details about the phone calls and the attack at Windsor Road weren't known at the time, but the mayor's silence was telling. Reporters kept the pressure on.

The *National Post*'s Christie Blatchford wrote, "Reporters have asked him directly if the video is a fake, and got his broad back in reply.... I can tell you how I would react if someone ever claimed to have a video of me doing the same thing—I would be spitting, incoherently mad; I would be screaming my utter innocence from the rooftops, and I could do this and would do it because I know I have never smoked crack or hung around this group. Therefore, there could be no video of me doing it."

By the middle of week one, #Crackgate hit American late-night TV. *The Daily Show, Jimmy Kimmel Live,* and *The Tonight Show* all went after Toronto's mayor. With the increased attention, the dealer decided to raise the price for the video to two hundred thousand dollars. Gawker launched a crowd-sourcing campaign—"Crackstarter"—to buy the footage. "It seems like a form of extortion.... I mean is any of this legal?" Doug Ford asked the *Toronto Sun.* He did not explain why, if there was no video, it would matter.

On day six, Doug Ford held a press conference outside the mayor's office. As he had done so many times before, Doug had prepared a fiery denunciation of the *Star* that ignored the issues at hand. This time, the horde of reporters weren't taking it.

"I'm not speaking for the mayor," Doug said. "The mayor is my brother. I love him and he'll speak for himself—"

A reporter interrupted: "When?"

"… My brother is an honest and hard-working man with integrity, a man who has dedicated his—"

A citizen who happened to be nearby started to heckle him. Doug Ford looked rattled, but he kept going.

"… He is the people's mayor …"

The rumbling of questions grew louder.

"We have come a long way in the past two years. We are turning the corner. And we are now on the right path."

Why was he here today?

"All of this of course is overshadowed by the constant stream of accusations coming forward against this mayor."

Was the mayor done hiding?

"Never, never has a Canadian politician or his family … been targeted, targeted by the media this way. They zealously, and I say zealously, stalk my mother, my children. The media hides in the bushes at our cottage as they did this weekend. That my kids couldn't even enjoy the weekend, 'cause they were in the bushes, taking videos of them, and harasses our family at home."

When was the mayor going to talk?

"To the folks at Gawker, what you are doing is disgusting and morally wrong. Giving away prizes to try to raise money for drug dealers and extortionists is disgraceful. When the mayor faces serious accusations by no means will we be pressured by the *Toronto Star* to answer their questions on their time frame."

It wasn't just the *Star*! Why wouldn't the mayor talk?

"I want to thank the thousands of supporters out there who believe in the job Mayor Ford and this administration is doing."

Shaken, Doug Ford retreated into his office as reporters shouted after him.

ON MAY 23, in the first of what would become a flood of departures from his office, the mayor fired his chief of staff, Mark Towhey. Sources told every major newspaper in town that Towhey had told Ford he needed to get treatment for his issues.

But still there was no word from the mayor.

Finally, eight days after the *Star* and Gawker broke the video story, and with the media crush outside his office not abating, the mayor made a statement.

"I'd like to take this opportunity to address a number of issues that have circulated in the media over the last few days," Ford said, with Doug at his side. "There's been a serious accusation from the *Toronto Star* that I use crack cocaine. I do not use crack cocaine nor am I an addict of crack cocaine. As for a video, I cannot comment on a video that I have never seen or does not exist...."

"I would like to assure everyone that we are continuing to fight for the taxpayers every day and it's business as usual at City Hall."

Ford took no questions—and there were many. Had he *ever* smoked crack cocaine? How did he know Anthony Smith? What was he doing at that house? And so on.

I obviously knew Ford was lying. He knew there was a video. He'd looked directly at the camera and said "That phone better not be on." But what I didn't know at the time was that before Mohamed Farah had contacted me, Ford may have already been trying to get the footage back. Wiretap conversations, captured by police as part of Project Traveller, suggested that Ford had offered five thousand dollars and a car to the dealer, Mohamed Siad, in exchange for the recording. On March 27 police were listening as Siad told his friend, Siyadin Abdi, that he planned to meet the mayor and ask for "one hundred and fifty," which police took to mean a hundred and fifty thousand dollars. Abdi suggested that that wouldn't be safe. Siad didn't want to listen. It's impossible to know whether they're telling the truth. But months later, when all of this came out—the attack at Windsor Road, the numerous calls between Ford and Lisi, the attempts to track down Siad after the video story broke—it was hard to look at the evidence and not feel as if you were living in an episode of *The Wire*.

Police records show that in the two days leading up to Ford's denial, the mayor and Lisi spoke fifteen times. On May 24—the day Ford finally addressed the allegations, smirking to reporters as he declared that the video "does not exist"—the mayor touched base with Lisi three times. Apparently no one had any idea they were being watched.

Shortly after the press conference, the exodus from the mayor's office picked up. Ford's press secretary and another long-time aide left. (Eight would leave by the fall.)

A few dozen reporters set up camp outside the mayor's glass-walled office. They sat there all day—through lunch, past dinner, and into the night—until the senior staff went home, then were back first thing the next morning. Even councillors, both friends and foes of the mayor, joined in to watch the circus. TV journalists reported live from the hallway all day long.

Things heated up again on May 25, when *The Globe and Mail* published its story alleging that Doug Ford had sold hashish for a number of years in the 1980s. The investigation also touched on Randy Ford's involvement in the drug trade. It accused Dave Price, who had recently been hired as the mayor's director of logistics and operations, of being a "former participant in Doug Ford's hashish enterprise."

A few days later, the *Star* dropped another bombshell. According to numerous sources, the morning after the video story went online the mayor told his senior staff not to worry, because he knew where the video was. Ford mentioned two apartment units on the seventeenth floor of 320 Dixon: 1701 and 1703. (Four days after the mayor said this to his staff, the shooting took place outside 1701.) The story, written by the *Star*'s Queen's Park bureau chief, Robert Benzie, as well as

Kevin Donovan, detailed a conversation between Price and Mark Towhey.

> "Hypothetically," Price asked Towhey, if someone had told him where the video was, "what would we do?"
>
> The straitlaced former military man told Price that nobody should do anything other than contact police.
>
> At one point, according to an account of the conversation, Towhey was heard to remark, "We're not getting the f---ing thing!"

After two more long-time staffers quit, Ford held a press conference to stress that "things are fine" in his office. As soon as he finished his speech, Ford was asked about the *Star* story. The exchange gave birth to a new catchphrase at City Hall.

Q: "Have you done any illegal drugs since you've been mayor?"

A: "Anything else?"

Q: "Have you tried to obtain the video, sir?"

A: "Anything else?"

Q: "Are you upset that the deputy mayor says he believes there's a tape? Does that upset you?"

A: "Anything else?"

Q: "The premier suggests she's ready to step in if needed."

A: "I think the premier should take care of the problems that she has at Queen's Park right now."

Q: "Did you mention an address to David Price?"

A: "Anything else?"

Q: "How did you know Anthony Smith, sir?"

A: "Anything else?"

Q: "Why are people leaving? What's going on in your office?"

A: "There's nothing going on in my office, obviously. I'm bringing in new staff, and if people have a better opportunity, I encourage them to move on."

Video or no video, as I watched the story develop from inside my little journalism bubble, I thought we were faring well. The evidence was on our side: Ford's staff was leaving in droves, the mayor was still refusing to answer any questions or talk about the allegations in any detail. He was refusing to discuss the photo with Anthony Smith or answer questions about the mysterious shooting in one of the Dixon towers. The *Globe's* investigation had laid out a pattern of drug involvement. Other news outlets—organizations that had been sympathetic to Ford through the Garrison Ball controversy—were hammering the mayor every day for not coming clean. People had to believe us, I thought.

My bubble was about to burst.

THIRTEEN

VIDEO, SCHMIDEO

It was hard to accept. On June 1, Ipsos Reid released a poll showing that almost half the city said they believed the mayor's claim that he did not smoke crack cocaine. People living in Etobicoke were more likely to believe him (61 percent) than those in the downtown (40 percent). And a third of those polled said they would re-elect Ford if a vote were held the next day. That was down just 9 points from his 2010 numbers.

But here was the kicker: of those surveyed, 45 percent—practically half the population of Canada's largest city—said they thought the video was "a hoax and part of a conspiracy to discredit the mayor."

THE ROB FORD CRACK COCAINE scandal didn't just set off a firestorm of public debate. The fallout prompted a serious discussion, even some soul-searching, in the journalism community. Several high-profile media critics and commentators criticized the *Star* for publishing the story without possessing the video and/or for "trusting" drug dealers.

When the chatter was at its peak, the chair of Ryerson

University's journalism program, Ivor Shapiro, waded in with an article for J-Source, the Canadian Journalism Project's website.

> When did the accepted standard for reporters' verification become that raw evidence must be seen by the audience to be believed?
>
> If a reporter sees with her own eyes a document, witnesses with his eyes an event taking place, or hears with her own ears a statement being made, is this not good enough as the basis for reporting?
>
> Must I now record every interview and hyperlink to the tape when I write a damaging story?
>
> If I don't have a camera rolling when I witness a cop beating a citizen, must I then hold my tongue, at least until I find another (named) witness? Nope. I came. I saw. I report. No verification required.

In September, the *National Post*'s Christie Blatchford said something similar at an Empire Club of Canada panel discussion with Kevin Donovan. She said she absolutely believed the *Star*, but following the story had been difficult. Yes, journalists had always gone out, seen things, and reported back. She talked about being in Afghanistan and witnessing a firefight, then writing about it. She was essentially asking her readers to take her word for it, based on her record. With the crack video story, she was "asking my readers to trust me, because I trust [the *Star*]."

And that's asking a lot when nearly half the public doesn't believe the original source.

Tom Rosenstiel, the executive director of the American Press Institute, is an author, journalist, and one of the leading media critics in North America. Rosenstiel says that public trust in journalists has been eroding for decades. And it's not just the media that people have a problem with. Faith in all institutions, government, hospitals, the court system, is on the decline. But Rosenstiel believes that in the case of journalism a number of special circumstances are driving that growing skepticism.

"People have more sources of information. The minute the press shifted from being a homogenized group of gatekeepers, who all had similar standards, to a more diverse group of information providers, they began distinguishing themselves by dumping on each other," he says.

This was the norm before the Second World War, when every city had several different dailies. Newspapers attacked their rivals, often on the front page, Rosenstiel says. With the advent of TV, the number of newspapers shrank. And everyone started to be more polite to each other. That changed again in the 1990s, most notably with the arrival of Fox News.

"They decided to distinguish themselves by saying, 'We'll do what talk radio did. [We'll say,] We don't have the bias that other media has.'" A few years later, this continued with the blogs, says Rosenstiel. "The ideological wars that we see in politics are playing out in these new media spaces."

Moaning about how it was better in the old days won't do much good, he says. Through Twitter and YouTube, readers have become used to seeing news with their own eyes. Whether it's a mass shooting or a natural disaster, live images and video are circulating online well before the mainstream press has written a word. In this climate, when that proof is not available, journalists need to be more transparent about what they do and how they do it.

"The old era of media, when we were the only source, was the 'trust me' media era," he says. The media could say, "'I saw it. Take my word for it.' Now we live in the 'show me' era of media. Show me why I should believe you. That does not mean that you have to have courtroom-worthy evidence. But it does mean that you have to show what evidence you've got and explain why you believe it."

In 1964, *The New York Times*'s David Halberstam won a Pulitzer Prize for his work on the Vietnam War. Halberstam's reporting called into question whether the United States would be able to defeat the Communist guerrilla forces and the North Vietnamese Army. President John F. Kennedy famously called the *Times* and urged the publisher to pull Halberstam out of Vietnam. "If you go back and look at that reporting, it's all anonymous sources," says Rosenstiel. "It's all filtered through him. What he's seen. You couldn't write it that way today."

Today, journalists need to take great pains to lay out the evidence for readers. Quoting an anonymous source isn't good enough. News outlets need to explain why that person can be trusted, what efforts it took to verify their information, and why they can't be named. Reporters need to say what they know and what they don't know.

"This is the world we live in," says Rosenstiel. "There's no point in looking back. The question is: Is it better or worse? Yes, there are some things about this that are much better, and some things about this that are much more difficult."

IN 1985, THE PEW RESEARCH CENTER, a non-partisan think tank based in Washington, DC, began measuring how Americans feel about the country's news outlets. In the inaugural poll, 55 percent trusted the media to get the facts right, and 34 percent thought journalists were fair to all sides. Those numbers have been in steady decline ever since. As of July 2013, just 26 percent of Americans believe news reports are accurate, and only 19 percent think reporters treat both sides fairly.

Drill further into the numbers and the news gets even more disheartening for journalists. According to Pew's 2013 data, 71 percent of Americans think the press tries to hide its mistakes, and 58 percent think news outlets are politically biased. Conservatives tend to have a harsher view of the media. Three-quarters of Democrats feel news organizations are highly professional. Only half of Republicans feel the same. Republicans are also more likely to think news stories are inaccurate.

It's a similar story north of the border. A 2013 survey from Ipsos Reid revealed that only 29 percent of Canadians trust journalists. (Local municipal politicians come in at 17 percent.)

In the United Kingdom, an ongoing poll by market research firm YouGov has shown that public trust in journalists has plummeted in every medium, from TV to broadsheet newspapers to tabloids. Between 2003 and November 2012, confidence in the BBC has fallen from 81 percent to 44 percent, and confidence in "upmarket" newspapers such as *The Guardian* and *The Telegraph* dropped from 65 percent to 38 percent.

So what gives?

Carroll Doherty is the associate director of Pew Research. He points out that even in the mid-1980s, a supposed golden age of journalism, nearly half of the public had misgivings about the media. Confidence in the press has been steadily eroding since the 1990s, and partway through the George W. Bush presidency it fell into a full-blown tailspin.

"There was a growing sense in that period that news organizations were biased and not being fair to the president.... In the Obama era it's just continued," he says.

Doherty's assessment seems to be supported by Gallup, a global research consulting firm. Gallup has been tracking public trust in mass media since 1997. Its figures indicate significant declines in 2004, a year after the invasion of Iraq.

At least in the United States, polls show a correlation between declining trust in media and growing partisanship. A major study from Pew in 2012 found that American values were more divided along partisan lines than at any other time in the twenty-five years they had been keeping score. The gap first widened in 2002, then remained steady until Barack Obama's election in 2008, when it started to widen again.

The New York Times—one of the most respected newspapers in the world—has taken one of the biggest hits. According to a 2012 poll from Pew, only 49 percent of Americans trust the newspaper—down 9 points from two years earlier. The *Times* is tied with Fox News and *USA Today* as the least trustworthy of America's major news organizations. And the partisan divide is stark. Two-thirds of liberals believe the paper, compared to little more than one-third of conservatives.

Doherty suspects the numbers are fuelled by perception rather than by any editorial change. "Most of these people probably don't regularly read *The New York Times*, but it's reputational. I think there's a sense that *The New York Times* is seen as somewhat liberal," he says.

In Canada, partisanship is actually on the decline, but it

could still be playing a role in how Canadians feel about their news, says Nelson Wiseman, a politics professor at the University of Toronto who has followed the Ford phenomenon closely.

Wiseman blames television. Specifically, American television.

"We are awash in American coverage," he says. "I think there are significant differences between the US and Canada, but I'll add that the United States shows Canada its future in so many ways."

This influence is especially apparent in federal politics, he says. Just look at how the New Democratic Party has mimicked—with some success—Obama's campaign model. Or how the Conservatives have adopted a Karl Rove political strategy of running down their opponents with negative ads to keep the attention off themselves.

"Now you're seeing that American influence with the media," he says.

In April 2011, the Sun Media chain launched a cable news channel that some have dubbed "Fox News North." Sun News Network styles itself as "Canada's Home for Hard News and Straight Talk." It broadcasts twenty-four hours a day, seven days a week. Its flashy graphics, good-looking hosts, controversial personalities, and conservative slant screams USA.

But they weren't the first.

Talk radio stations have been targeting this ultra-right niche market for years. And while Canadian networks aren't nearly as outlandish as some of the stations south of the border, at least in Toronto talk radio has increasingly veered in that direction since Rob Ford became mayor.

The best example came in February 2010, when Newstalk 1010 launched *The Jerry Agar Show*. Agar is a Canadian-born radio personality who rose to prominence on US airwaves in Kansas City, New York, and Chicago. Agar is a Tea Party defender. He opposes same-sex marriage, has questions about the science of global warming, and believes Canada should move to a privatized health care system. His hiring signalled a significant, and obviously conscious, shuffle to the right for this already conservative-leaning station. The swing right continued in February 2012, when Newstalk decided to axe their Sunday afternoon host Josh Matlow, a mild-mannered city councillor who liked to talk about upcoming city events and getting along. They gave the slot to the Ford brothers.

In October 2012, I met Agar for dinner at a restaurant across the street from the Sun News studio, where he's often an on-air guest. We talked about the impact talk radio was having on the Toronto electorate. An Ipsos Reid poll for the Canadian Journalism Foundation released that month found that nearly half of Canadians consulted talk radio stations for their news. Only 43 percent looked to a daily newspaper. This scared me. Talk radio is entertaining, but not always careful with the facts. By its nature, these programs are conversations happening on the fly. Hosts don't have the luxury of time, unlike newspaper reporters, to look up every fact. This means incorrect statements are rarely corrected—whether it's Rob Ford claiming to have saved taxpayers "a billion dollars" or a random caller talking about how a *Star* reporter was caught sneaking around the mayor's backyard. I wanted to know how Agar felt about his industry's role in shaping public opinion.

Agar looks exactly like how you would picture an outspoken talk radio host. He keeps a few shirt buttons open at the collar and his white hair is swept straight back like

Michael Douglas's. When he talks, his dark eyebrows move around just as much as his lips.

Was talk radio news or entertainment? I asked him.

"I'm not a journalist. I'm a guy with an opinion. I have to make my show entertaining, the same way you have to make your articles interesting to read," the fifty-seven-year-old said.

That's fine, I said, except studies showed that a good chunk of Torontonians get their news from talk radio—a source that to me does not seem overly concerned about accuracy. He cut me off.

"We're no different in that regard than you guys. Mistakes are constant [in newspapers]," he said. If a guest or a caller says something that isn't true, Agar said he'd correct the record if he noticed the mistake—but there isn't time to fact-check everything. In other cases, he might just not care.

As for talk radio bias, he said, at least they're more honest about it. "Look, you can try as hard as you want to be an objective reporter, and I'm sure you do try real hard, but good, honest, decent people who are doing the best job they can as a reporter still have their view of how the world works."

THE ATRIUM AT RYERSON UNIVERSITY, my alma mater, was set up like a courtroom, with rows of folding chairs arranged for the audience and three tables at the front—one for the accused, another for the accuser, and a third for the panel of judges.

Each table was outfitted with a set of cordless microphones and glasses of water. The room itself felt like an outdoor courtyard, with beige and white walls that looked like stone and a soaring glass ceiling that flooded the space with natural light. At least one hundred people—not including the TV crews—had shown up for the hearing.

I was in the front row behind the *Toronto Star*'s table, at which Michael Cooke and Kevin Donovan prepared to argue our case. They sat shoulder to shoulder in dark suits and white shirts, a stack of notes in front of them. On the other side of the room was a middle-aged woman named Darylle Donley. Donley seemed overwhelmed by the attention. She sat stone still, hands clasped, and looked straight ahead at the three adjudicators. Her thick shoulder-length red hair was held in place by chunky sunglasses she had pushed on top of her head. Donley was one of the reasons we were all here.

It was September 9, 2013, nearly four months since we had printed our story about the Ford video. Donley was a Ford supporter living downtown on the east side. After reading our story, she had written to the Ontario Press Council to accuse the *Star* of shoddy ethics and fabrication. "I would be curious to know just how far a TV or radio reporter or newspaper person has to go before they are sanctioned and curtailed? The Ford brothers are being lied about, innuendos and allegations are being made against them," she wrote.

Hers was one of forty-one similar grievances received by the press council. A dozen had arrived right after the *Star*'s "crack video" story appeared. A few dozen more arrived a week later, when *The Globe and Mail* ran its investigation about Doug Ford's years as an alleged high school drug dealer. Now, both papers had been hauled in front of the province's media ethics watchdog to explain themselves.

It was a remarkable moment. The press council, an independent agency established in 1972 and funded by newspapers, was created to investigate accusations of unsavoury journalistic practices and ethics. About one hundred complaints are received each year, and only a handful make it to the public hearing stage. The threshold is supposed to be high. Cases that get adjudicated typically involve allegations of plagiarism, established factual errors, or contentious editorial positions—such as the 2001 case in which a national newspaper, according to the ruling, "appeared to suggest every person living in Germany during the Second World War was an active agent in Hitler's genocide."

The story Donovan and I had written, while a huge news event in Toronto, was actually quite basic: two journalists had seen something and then written about it. That was the job stripped down to its simplest form. We went out, observed, asked questions, tried to get answers, and reported back. That the press council had decided to adjudicate Donley's complaint seemed to lend credence to the notion that this was no longer good enough.

The stakes were high. Despite the amount of evidence in our favour, the *Star* was suffering in the court of public opinion. The attacks came from every angle—letters, email, phone, Twitter, texts, Facebook, talk radio, and conservative columnists. Four months later, and they were still coming. Donovan and I were getting death threats and harassing calls at all hours of the night. The paper was under siege with complaints.

But for me the most upsetting thing was the June poll that showed nearly half of the city thought we were lying. Seeing those numbers knocked the wind out of me. On more than one occasion that summer, I had been out at a bar or restaurant around the city and heard people talking. Many just couldn't believe Rob Ford might be smoking crack. Which meant that nothing the *Star* said about it could be true.

Had journalists made things up before? Yes. We've all heard about *The New York Times*'s Jayson Blair, *USA Today*'s Jack Kelley, and *The New Republic*'s Stephen Glass. Canadian publications, including the *National Post*, *The Globe and Mail*, and, yes, the *Toronto Star*, have also dealt with fabrication and plagiarism scandals. But these were cases of lone individuals bent on deceiving their colleagues, not an entire newsroom conspiring to deceive the public. Because if Kevin Donovan and I had made up the story, a dozen senior people in the newsroom—including the publisher, the editor-in-chief, the managing editor, the city editor, and our lawyer—had to have been in on it. We'd told our editors about the video footage two weeks before Gawker's story ran. Were all those people at the *Toronto Star*, Canada's largest newspaper, lying?

Half of Toronto seemed to think this was possible. It was very clear that many did not understand what we do, how we do it, and the rigorous checks in place to keep us accountable. This press council hearing was our chance to enlighten.

Shortly after 10 A.M., panel chair George Thomson—a former provincial court judge, law professor, and provincial deputy minister—called the meeting to order. The press council, Thomson explained, was an independent agency with fifteen council members, the majority of whom were professionals not affiliated with news media. On this day, the council would be looking at three questions concerning the *Star*'s story. Did the *Star* article deal with a matter that was in the public interest? Were adequate efforts made to verify allegations? And was the mayor given a reasonable opportunity to respond and had the paper printed that response? Thomson turned to the complainant first to see if she had an opening statement. Darylle Donley softly shook her head.

Now it was our turn. Michael Cooke leaned in to the microphone.

"The *Toronto Star* is glad to be sitting in front of you today and to be given the opportunity to talk about the front page of Friday, the seventeenth of May," he began. "The press council has said in a letter to us that we at the *Star* are not to concern ourselves this morning on whether that story is true or not. I'm going to tell you now, with great emphasis, that that story is true. Every word of it.

"I ask for your indulgence here as I read just a little in the story. This is how it began: 'A cellphone video that appears to show Mayor Ford smoking crack cocaine is being shopped around Toronto by a group of Somali men involved in the drug trade. Two *Toronto Star* reporters have viewed the video three times. It appears to show Ford in a room, sitting in a chair, wearing a white shirt, top buttons open, inhaling from what appears to be a glass crack pipe. Ford is incoherent, trading jibes with an off-camera speaker who goads the clearly impaired mayor by raising topics including Liberal leader Justin Trudeau and the Don Bosco high school football team that Ford coaches.'

"Those are the opening paragraphs, which were true then, they're true now, and every word in that story is true this morning," Cooke said.

ON OCTOBER 16, 2013, the Ontario Press Council dismissed the complaints against the *Star* and the *Globe*. The panel found that both papers had acted responsibly while reporting on a matter of significant public interest.

In the case of the *Star*, the panel concluded, "Council does not agree with the position that the story could not be written unless the newspaper had the video in its possession or that it could not publish without naming its sources."

Before most people even had a chance to read the full decision, Doug Ford was on AM640.

"Who is the press council?" he complained to host John Oakley. "They are a bunch of cronies, all of the insiders trying to make judgments on the *Toronto Star* and *Globe and Mail* and a lot of them probably worked for the *Toronto Star* at some point."

In fact, in addition to George Thomson, the cases were heard by Joanne De Laurentiis, the chief executive officer of the Investment Funds Institute of Canada, and the deputy editor of the *Ottawa Citizen*, Drew Gragg.

FOURTEEN

PROJECT TRAVELLER

Thirteen-year-old Connor Stevenson was looking for Nikes that day in the mall. His older sister, Taylor, wanted a pair of Toms.

It was Saturday, June 2, 2012, and the Toronto Eaton Centre was packed. Thousands of people were wandering around the six-storey shopping centre that day, as bright summer sun streamed in through the vaulted glass ceiling. The Eaton Centre takes up two city blocks on the west side of Yonge Street, smack in the centre of downtown, bordered by City Hall, the financial district, Ryerson University, and a crowded public square.

Around 6:20 P.M., Connor and Taylor's mother, Jo-Anne Finney, suggested they grab a bite to eat before the long drive back to Port Hope, Ontario.

The trio headed to the Eaton Centre's lower-level food court, then managed to scope out an empty table in the bustling eatery. They'd barely been sitting a minute when the shots started. It sounded like fireworks.

Pop! Pop! Pop! Pop! Pop!

A man collapsed. He'd soon be dead. People were screaming,

diving under tables, knocking over chairs as they bolted for the escalators, leaving cell phones and purses and clothing behind. A twenty-eight-year-old pregnant woman was knocked over. She went into labour.

Pop! Pop! Pop!

Taylor looked over at her brother. His face was frozen. Blood was pooling around his hairline. It started to drip down his face. "Call 911!" Taylor started to scream. She grabbed her little brother and dragged him to the wall as the shots continued.

"Oh, I love you so much, Connor!" she said as he slipped out of consciousness.

After what felt like hours but was really just minutes, two paramedics were at the teen's side.

"Save my boy!" Jo-Anne Finney wailed as police, with guns drawn, sprinted throughout the mall, searching for the shooter.

In the end, two men, both alleged gang members, were dead. And five innocent people were wounded.

After numerous harrowing surgeries, Connor Stevenson survived, though doctors weren't able to remove all of the shrapnel from his head.

It was one of the worst mass shootings in Canada's history. Compared to other major cities, Toronto is remarkably safe. By the end of 2012, there would be just fifty-four homicides. Chicago, a city of similar size, recorded 506 over the same period. But the brazenness of the Eaton Centre attack—that it had happened in a popular indoor mall and tourist destination—left people shaken and afraid.

On June 5, the day the food court reopened, Mayor Rob Ford toured the area with members of his staff and the media, reassuring Toronto residents that the city was still safe.

In truth, there was cause for concern. By May 2012, the Toronto Police Service's 23 Division in north Etobicoke—an area that included the six Dixon high-rise towers—was recording a 133 percent increase in gun violence. And then in July, more tragedy. Across town in Scarborough, a gunfight broke out at a community barbecue on Danzig Street. Two innocent people were killed and twenty-three injured, including a toddler.

The mayor released a statement declaring "war on these violent gangs."

The next day he told CP24 news host Stephen LeDrew, "I want something to be done. I want these people out of the city. And I'm not going to stop. Not put 'em in jail, then come back and you can live in the city. No. I want 'em out of the city. Go somewhere else. I don't want 'em living in the city anymore."

What Ford didn't know was that the chief of police was already doing something. In June 2012, the service launched what would become Project Traveller, a massive investigation into a north Etobicoke gang that police suspected was smuggling guns into the city from the United States. The group called itself the Dixon City Bloods, a.k.a. Dixon Goonies, and its members were operating primarily out of the six towers at the corner of Dixon Road and Kipling Avenue. Project Traveller would last a year and involve extensive ground surveillance, wiretaps, and use of police informants. It would culminate in a dramatic pre-dawn raid in June 2013. Dozens of people in Ontario, Alberta, and Michigan would be arrested. A total of twenty-eight search warrants would be executed in Toronto, with police seizing any electronic devices—cell phones, computer equipment, and hard drives—connected to the suspects.

Of all the gangs, in all the city, Rob Ford had to walk into theirs.

Mayor Ford had at some point gotten mixed up with one of the most closely watched group of drug dealers in Toronto. What were the odds that police would be wiretapping the cell phone of a man who had covertly filmed Ford smoking crack? Or that police would happen to be watching the brick bungalow at 15 Windsor Road where Ford would party with Fabio Basso and members of the Dixon City Bloods?

Toronto police knew about the crack video long before it hit the papers. But once the *Star* and Gawker reported on the footage, the second, spin-off probe was created: Project Brazen 2. It was launched two days after the crack video story went live. Detectives started with Project Traveller intelligence, of which there was an abundance. They began going through *Toronto Star* stories, and they tracked down Leo Navarro at the Bier Markt to talk about St. Patrick's Day 2012. Police interviewed numerous former and current staff members in the mayor's office about Ford's alleged drug use. They monitored the phone activity of the mayor, his associates, and his staff. And—in what would become most damaging to Ford—police began following Ford's driver, Sandro Lisi, the man who had driven the mayor to the Garrison Ball.

For the next six months, the *Toronto Star* and the Toronto Police Service were doing more or less the same job: investigating the mayor of Toronto.

IN THE FIRST FEW DAYS after the crack story broke, the public was divided on what to believe.

For many, the possibility that Ford might be using drugs was too bizarre to accept, given that he'd called the *Star* news team "pathological liars" for suggesting he had problems with alcohol.

People wanted to see the video. And the *Star* couldn't give it to them. We had to push the story forward the old-fashioned way, with on-the-ground reporting. The photo was the best place to start.

The *Star* had to find that house.

THERE IT WAS … Or at least, there it might be, Tim Alamenciak thought. He stopped the car and held up the photo, looked at the house, then back to the photo, then back at the house again.

It was like one of those spot-the-difference games that children play. The light fixture matched. Both had white glass, black edges, and the same unusual boxy shape, like upside-down pyramids with the pointed part cut off. Both houses had the same dark garage doors, the same white trim, and the same yellow brick.

Yes, the search was over. Finally.

Alamenciak was about to grab his camera to send a shot back to the *Star* newsroom. But then he spotted the difference. The garage was on the wrong side. In the Ford photo, the edge of the house wasn't visible, but a utility meter was poking out on the far left. Presumably, it was attached to a wall of the house. That would put the garage on the right, and at this house it was on the left.

Damn, he thought.

Alamenciak shifted the car into gear and kept going.

For days, the *Star* had been searching for the mysterious house behind Rob Ford and three young men in the photograph given to me by Mohamed Farah, the broker of the crack video. If we could locate the house, then perhaps we could start to learn why the mayor had been there with Anthony Smith, the young man later shot to death.

On May 21, it was Alamenciak, a twenty-eight-year-old intern reporter, who had printed off an enlarged copy of the photo and set out for north Etobicoke. There wasn't much to go on. We believed the house was somewhere in the residential neighbourhood just behind the six Dixon towers, but not much of it was visible in the photo, and Farah had refused to help us. We also didn't know how long ago the photo had been taken, although there was snow on the ground. It was dark outside, and Ford and the other three occupied most of the frame. Behind them you could see the black garage door with white trim, the light-yellow brick. Garbage, or maybe yard equipment, had been dumped at the top of the driveway.

Alamenciak started on a road running parallel to Dixon Road just north of the towers. He kept the car moving fast enough to avoid suspicion, although anyone looking closely would have wondered why the same Ford Fusion was looping up and down every street on the block. On each street he saw similar houses, but the brick would be too dark, the garage light too round, or the door the wrong colour. And when he thought he had a match, it turned out the garage was on the wrong side. An hour went by.

And then Alamenciak turned onto Windsor Road. As soon as he spotted number 15, he hit the brakes. It was identical to the one in the photo in every way. The wire, the junk on the driveway, the utility meter. The Dixon towers were less than two hundred feet away, separated from the house by a grassy walkway at the foot of the road and a chain-link fence.

Alamenciak needed to get photos to take back to the newsroom, but a man was mowing the lawn. He parked the car a few doors down and waited. Forty-five minutes went by before the man went inside. Alamenciak pulled up out front, fired off a dozen shots with his long lens, and drove off.

Back at the *Star*, reporter Jesse McLean and Alamenciak put the new shot beside the old one. They looked at the pattern of the bricks along the trim. They examined the gap between the top of the garage and the light. In the Ford photo, there seemed to be little grooves along the very top where the roof soffit seemed to start. These were obvious in the new photo.

It was a match.

FIFTEEN WINDSOR ROAD belonged to a woman named Lina Basso, property records showed. She and her husband, Elio, had lived on the street since at least the 1970s. Elio, a bricklayer, had died in 2009, and according to his obituary the couple had four children—a daughter, Elena, and three sons, Mario, Enzo, and Fabio, the quiet stoner who had befriended Rob Ford back in high school—as well as two grandchildren. Lina Basso was elderly, and we believed she was living in the house. It was perplexing. There was no obvious link between her and three men with connections to a violent street gang. Maybe there was a basement apartment she was renting out. Could the men be friends of her grandchildren? We started to watch the house.

During the previous week, a group of *Star* reporters, including Amy Dempsey, Arshy Mann, and Tim Alamenciak, had been sifting through social media sites looking for clues to why the three men in the photo were hanging out with Ford.

Anthony Smith was a good jumping-off point. Smith had been fatally shot on March 28. A friend of his was hit in the same incident but survived. We believed that the friend was one of the two unidentified people in the Ford photo. Now we needed a name. Since Smith's death, his friends had been regularly posting tributes on Facebook, Twitter, and Instagram. There were dozens of messages, such as "RIP Rondo"—Smith's alias—and references to the Dixon City Bloods. The *Star* reporters were going through each and tracing the author.

Arshy Mann, an intern, had been working on the *Star's* police scanner desk, which we call the radio room, the day before Tim Alamenciak found the house. With an ear on the crackling cop chatter, Mann spent his shift digging around Facebook for links to Smith. He came across an account for someone who called himself Sosa Grindhard and saw that the Facebook address for this person was facebook.com/RealDixon. Sosa looked fresh out of high school. His face still carried some baby fat in the cheeks, and his beard was patchy. He looked exactly like the bearded figure on the far right of the Ford photo. The more Mann searched, the more evidence piled up. The page included photos of Anthony Smith that had never been made public. "RIP Big Bro," said one caption. "Forever In My Heart Mourn Till We Join You General ..." There was also a Twitter account for SosaDoubleUp, and this was the most interesting lead. Shortly after the March 28 shooting, people were tweeting at Sosa to get better. "Inshallah You Get A Fast Recovery Blood @SosaDoubleUp" and "Good seeing my brother @SosaDoubleUp insha'Allah speedy recovery ahh" were among the well wishes.

This looked like our guy, but what was Sosa's real name?

After another week of mining social media sites, we strongly believed Sosa was a nineteen-year-old living in north Etobicoke named Muhammad Khattak. We ran a property search in the area and located what we believed to be his home. It was a ten-minute drive north of Dixon.

On May 27, I knocked on the front door. A woman answered who identified herself as Zen, Khattak's mother. Her eyes were pink and puffy. She was clearly going through a rough time. I held up the photo and told her that we knew the man in the hooded sweatshirt was her son. I asked why he was with the mayor. At first, Zen tried to lie, but she eventually broke down. She told me she had recognized her son as soon as the photo was published—even though his face had been blurred. She said she had confronted Khattak.

"Was I drinking? Was I smoking? Did you see anything with me?," had been his response, she said.

She also confirmed that Khattak had been shot twice the night Smith was killed and that he remained disabled. "I'm still in shock. I'm still dead. Brain is dead. Because my son, he is traumatized." Zen said that Khattak's arm was basically useless and that he limped.

Smith and Khattak had been friends since they were young, she said. They played on the same basketball team and both were good kids. "My son, I know him, he's a very innocent kid. They're friends. They're having fun, whatever they're doing outside. But I know them—they are nice kids. They are very nice."

I could not speak with Khattak, she said, because he wasn't home. He had left Toronto as soon as the video story ran, in case the media came knocking.

Amy Dempsey and I wrote Khattak's story the next day. We now had confirmation that two of the three young men pictured with Ford had ties to gun violence.

Meanwhile, Gawker was still trying to raise two hundred thousand dollars for the video through crowdsourcing. In such a circuslike atmosphere, there was little we could do to get the video. Astonishingly, it looked like the Crackstarter campaign was going to hit its goal. But not long after Gawker launched it, the dealer seemed to get cold feet. He was telling kids in Dixon that the video was gone. According to Farah, they were worried about moving that kind of money across the border. They thought the police were watching. Farah wanted me to give him advice. I explained that it was not my place to get involved. He was getting irritated. At one point Farah tried to tell me that the *Star* should give him some money for all the work he had done.

It had been nearly two weeks since Toronto had learned about the video, and the police were still keeping quiet. I had met with a few police sources and was told something was coming, but no one would give me details.

Star reporter Jayme Poisson was also going through her contacts—and she hit the motherlode.

Poisson, along with reporter David Bruser, had recently finished an investigative series about the illegal gun pipeline between the United States and Canada. Their stories tracked how cheaply purchased handguns were moving up Interstate 75 into the border city of Windsor, Ontario, and eventually landing on Toronto streets, where a hundred-and-fifty-dollar firearm could be sold for more than two thousand. It turned out that investigators believed a north Etobicoke gang played a big role in the network.

The gang? The Dixon City Bloods. The very gang Anthony Smith and maybe Muhammad Khattak belonged to.

Poisson learned that Toronto police were part of a sweeping gun- and drug-smuggling probe called Project Traveller, which included police services from across Canada.

On June 13, at 5 A.M., police across the province and as far away as Alberta would move in. Were the *Star*'s contacts involved? Would police get the crack video? Would Ford be implicated?

It was possible. Poisson learned that the Bloods were being wiretapped and investigators knew all about the crack video.

GAWKER'S CRACKSTARTER CAMPAIGN reached the two-hundred-thousand-dollar goal on May 27. The week before, Gawker editor John Cook revealed that their contact had lost touch with the dealer. "Our confidence that we can consummate this transaction has diminished," he announced. Gawker decided to give the dealer a few weeks to come forward; otherwise the money would be donated to a Canadian charity dealing with drug addiction. This news emboldened our skeptics, who questioned why the dealer, who'd once agreed to sell the footage for one hundred thousand dollars, was now prepared to walk away from twice that.

The *Star* began regularly watching the house on Windsor Road. It looked like the old woman did in fact live there. Grown children, maybe in their forties, were often at the house—but no young men in their late teens or twenties.

On June 3, I tried the old-fashioned knock-on-the-door tactic. I'd sent Kevin Donovan an email so the newsroom would know where I was.

It was early afternoon, and there were no cars in the driveway. From the street, 15 Windsor Road looked like an average brick bungalow, a simple place with three front windows, a little walk-up front door, and some potted flowers by the steps. There were two big trees in the front yard and a well-groomed hedge around the perimeter. There were no broken windows, and apart from a little shopping trolley and two corn brooms, there was no clutter out front. My grandmother could have lived here, I thought. But then I noticed the cats. I counted seven, but there could have been more. They seemed to be living in the garage, and I noticed the big black door was raised half a foot off the ground. They were running in and out, watching me. I headed up the brown tiled steps to the front door. A little white kitten with brown spots was at the top. It got scared and ran away. As soon as I was on the doorstep, I smelled it. Thick and pungent. Something between cigarette smoke and unwashed bedsheets. This place was not as it seemed.

I rapped on the front door and turned on my recorder. There was a rustle inside. I thought I saw the white curtains move. A frail-looking woman, about five feet tall, slowly opened the door. Her grey hair was pulled back in a messy bun and she looked at me suspiciously.

I introduced myself, but I wasn't sure she spoke English. She looked confused. "What's your name?" I asked her.

"Lina Basso."

"Lina, do you recognize your driveway in this picture?" I said, holding up the Rob Ford photo, pointing to the yellow brick and garage door. "It looks like your house in the background."

She studied the photo for a few moments, then turned to look back inside.

"Fabio!" she called down the hallway behind her.

"Do you have a grandson?" I asked.

"I have my son. He's over forty."

"Is he here?"

"Yes."

"Can I talk to him?"

Lina nodded and turned around. She walked as if every step was a struggle. With the door open, the stench was even stronger.

"Fabio?" Lina said, turning around a corner at the end of the short hallway. I could hear a man whispering. He sounded agitated, but I couldn't make out any words. A few seconds later, Lina returned.

"He's in the shower. I talked to him in the shower," she said in a thick accent.

"Okay. I will come back, then? Or what's a good way to get in touch with Fabio? I'll just wait?"

Lina reached for the photo again. "This is all together, they were?"

I didn't quite understand what she meant, but I let her talk. She told me she had three sons and one was at work. What that had to do with the photo she was staring at, I didn't know. Before I could ask, someone started yelling from inside the house.

There was a commotion, and a woman with wild curly brown hair and tanned leathery skin came storming down the hallway. She was in a long dark skirt and looked rail thin. She grabbed Lina's shoulders and shoved her down the hallway, slamming the front door.

"Don't you ever come back!" she screamed at me through a closed window, although I could hear her fine. Her voice was deep and raspy. It was hard to know how old she was. She could have been forty or sixty.

"Are you hurting her?" I yelled at the glass.

"You fucking— You scavengers!"

"Why was the mayor here?" I yelled back.

"You come back to my house, I'll call the police!"

Kevin Donovan reached the woman on the phone later that night.

"Rob Ford's the greatest mayor ever. You guys are scavengers," she said. "You come back to my house, I'll call the police."

That was Elena.

THE NEXT MORNING, a team of *Star* reporters spread out across various Toronto courthouses to check whether any of the Bassos had ever been charged. Ontario records are not kept in a central database. The paperwork is almost always stored at the court where the case was handled. It turned out that both Fabio and Elena had spent time in front of a judge. Jayme Poisson was downtown at the Old City Hall courthouse. I was up at 2201 Finch Avenue West, the north Etobicoke courthouse. I didn't have any dates or the exact charges, but fortunately the court clerk was feeling generous. I filled out some incomplete forms and he said he would be in touch. It could take a few days or, if the documents were in storage, maybe weeks.

That afternoon, Kevin Donovan and Poisson went back to Windsor Road to talk to neighbours. Four residents on the street said the house was known for drug activity. People were always going in and out, they said. Some visitors seemed to come from the Dixon towers. This unwanted traffic had been a sore point in the community for years. In 2011, the city installed the chain-link fence between the Windsor Road cul-de-sac and the apartments after residents repeatedly complained to the local councillor about the drug and gun problems. The councillor? Doug Ford.

On June 5, I went back to Windsor Road and was watching the house from down the street. A slate-blue truck was out front, and a black SUV I didn't recognize was in the driveway. I jotted down the licence plates and sent them to the *Star*'s library research staff so they could run a check. I decided it was probably better to try to catch the visitors on their way out. Maybe more people would arrive. About twenty minutes later, a tall man in sunglasses headed down the driveway. At that same moment, an orange taxi pulled into the driveway, then back out, then parked by the curb in front of the truck. A young woman with a notepad got out and walked up to the man. (I later learned she was a *Globe* reporter.)

This stakeout was over. I walked over with tape recorder in hand.

The man's name was David Profitt. He was forty-five and he'd known both Ford and Fabio Basso for years.

"I know all these guys. I grew up in Etobicoke," Profitt said. According to him, Ford and Fabio had met in high school. Fabio went to Don Bosco, which was just around the corner from Windsor Road, but had spent a semester at Scarlett Heights.

Profitt said he didn't want to get involved in the story. He'd just stopped in on his way to the airport and he was late for his flight.

The conversation lasted only about two minutes, but it was an important one. Other sources had told us that Rob Ford and

Fabio Basso had been friends since they were teenagers. And now we had someone we could name linking the two.

POISSON, DONOVAN, AND I PUBLISHED our story about the house on June 5. Two days later, when our court documents came back, we were able to shed more light on the people Ford was spending time with.

Elena Basso Johnson—nickname Princess—was fifty-one and had been found guilty of trafficking cocaine. Her brother Fabio, forty-five, had been convicted of possessing a prohibited weapon—a spring-activated knife—in 2005. Both had been found guilty of theft, Fabio for shoplifting "blue-ray DVDs and TV wall mounts" from Walmart, and Johnson for stealing lipstick from the Bay. Johnson's cocaine charge was in February 2006. She pleaded guilty in 2011. After our story ran, we learned that Johnson in particular had been cycling in and out of the court system for years, including convictions for "communicate for the purpose of prostitution" (1998 and 2002), multiple drug offences (1994, 1996, and 2004), and obstruction of a peace officer (1998 and 2000). In 2002, Johnson was convicted of performing an indecent act—"fellatio in a public place"—and received a suspended sentence. Fabio Basso had been convicted of drug offences in 1990 and 2002, as well as impaired driving in 1993.

We'd also been able to confirm that Toronto police had been called to 15 Windsor for a break-and-enter and assault the same night the man was shot on the seventeenth floor of 320 Dixon. (By this point, we were pretty sure 15 Windsor was also where the crack video had been filmed.)

Most damningly, the *Star*'s Queen's Park bureau chief, Robert Benzie, and Kevin Donovan learned about the meeting Ford had with his staff about the two units at Dixon where he believed the video might be. This was the video that supposedly did not exist. Their story ran on the front page.

With each new development the link between the mayor and drug activity was growing stronger, but the public still wasn't sure what to believe. We did win over one skeptic. On June 10, the mayor fired Councillor Jaye Robinson from the executive committee after Robinson called for Ford to take time off and get help for his "personal issues." When I interviewed Robinson for this book, she made a confession. "I'm embarrassed, but actually I didn't believe you guys after the Garrison Ball story," she said. "I guess I was wearing rose-coloured glasses. I kinda was buying the story that you were after him and he really wasn't doing these things. I thought the *Star* was picking on the mayor, and the mayor's office perpetuated that idea." Robinson had come to realize that wasn't true. "There obviously is a problem."

Until that point, the Toronto police had been able to watch our investigation unfold with each new story. We were about to learn what they'd been up to.

AT 4 A.M. ON JUNE 13, 2013, six police officers on motorcycles blocked off the intersection beside the six Dixon towers. Cruisers with darkened headlights sped silently towards the condo complex. The buildings are arranged in two clusters of three. There's the 320-330-340 group and the 370-380-390 group. Both encircle grassy courtyards. A curving laneway connects each building for pick-up and drop-off, and a giant parking lot runs along the north end of each cluster.

On the morning of the Project Traveller raids, because of Jayme Poisson's excellent information, a dozen *Star* reporters and photographers left for Etobicoke around 2 A.M., hours before forty-two tactical teams in riot gear would descend on the neighbourhood. Two groups of us were stationed at the towers. Another was in front of the mayor's home—just in case. And two more roved the area, keeping an eye on the local police detachment, Muhammad Khattak's home, and 15 Windsor.

I was sitting in a parked car in front of 320 Dixon, not far from where I'd watched the video a month earlier. A group of kids, probably in their late teens or early twenties, were partying on a twelfth-floor balcony, smoking, drinking, and taking photos of themselves with their cell phones. Their laughter echoed between the towers. They had no idea what was coming. I'd later learn that the unit they were in was one of the apartments to get raided.

I, on the other hand, did know what was coming, but the scope of it still caught me off guard. At 5 A.M., to the minute, a convoy of white cube vans rolled into the Dixon lot. Before the vans even stopped, the rear doors were sliding open revealing what looked like well over one hundred police officers in riot gear, with black vests, helmets, and knee pads. Some were wearing black masks. They marched silently into the buildings, carrying guns and battering rams. The parking lot changed from being nearly empty to a war zone in less than fifteen seconds.

Once the officers were inside, my colleagues and I got out of the car for a better look, keeping a safe distance so as not to interfere. Suddenly, there was a blast and a flicker of light from inside the 320 tower. A woman screamed. Lights in the dark towers started coming on as people went to their windows to investigate. Another crack split the air. The police were using percussion grenades, otherwise known as "flashbangs." After smashing in a door, officers use them to disorient the people inside. They're mostly safe, although they will leave a black scorch mark on the floor. For the next hour, police led half a dozen people out of the towers in handcuffs. Investigators seized various electronics from many of the units.

Anthony Smith's friend Muhammad Khattak was among those arrested. So was a man named Monir Kassim, who we soon learned was the remaining man in the Ford photo. Kassim, twenty, was charged with trafficking in weapons and drugs—cocaine and marijuana, specifically—for the benefit of a criminal organization and a firearm offence. Khattak was also charged with trafficking cocaine for the gang, as well as dealing marijuana. This was a key development in the story. People said they didn't believe us because we couldn't produce a video. Yet here we had a photo that showed the mayor with a dead man and two men arrested for dealing cocaine. (Mohamed Farah, the broker, was also swept up in the raid on charges of possessing the proceeds of crime and several gun-related offences.)

At a noon press conference, Toronto police announced that they'd made nineteen arrests in Toronto and that dozens of others had taken place across the country. The year-long probe, which had involved seventeen police agencies, had netted drugs worth three million dollars, forty firearms, and hundreds of thousands of dollars in cash.

The *Star* played the story huge. We had live coverage on our website, a live blog, videos, photos, and frequently updated stories. As for the connection to the mayor, we decided to let readers connect the dots. That morning, we reported that Toronto police were executing raids in an Etobicoke neighbourhood that was "ground zero for the alleged Rob Ford crack cocaine video scandal." CTV News took it further. By lunch, they were reporting that a "highly placed source" had confirmed to the network that individuals being targeted in Project Traveller had been heard discussing the crack video on wiretaps.

"CTV News has learned that Toronto police were investigating the existence of an alleged video involving Mayor Rob Ford, several weeks before the story first appeared in the *Toronto Star*. As part of the investigation leading to the raids on Thursday, officers obtained telephone wire-tap evidence," the story said. In Canada, it is illegal to write about an active wiretap. It is not unusual for police to leave wiretaps in place for several days after arrests take place to capture reaction from people of interest.

At a press conference at Police Headquarters that afternoon, Deputy Chief Mark Saunders said investigators were targeting the Dixon City Bloods. "This gang has been networking with associates from Windsor to Edmonton since 2006, where members have been responsible and involved in shootings, robberies, possession, and trafficking of drugs and firearms." Chief Bill Blair said investigators believed the gang was part of a network of gun smugglers moving weapons across the border through Windsor. "I think we've cut off that pipeline, that supply of guns, and that's going to make the city of Toronto a safer place."

But when it came time for questions, the media wanted to know about the mayor. The chief was asked if the investigation into the Dixon City Bloods had extended to the mayor's office. "I'm not in a position to disclose that," he said. Neither would he say whether officers had come across Ford's name during the year-long probe. When asked about the photo in front of 15 Windsor Road, he confirmed that it was real and that "there are aspects of those individuals who form part of this investigation." Again and again, Blair was asked about whether Ford had connections to Project Traveller, and every time the chief was interestingly vague. "All of the evidence has been secured and it will come out in court, where it belongs," Blair said. "We will not jeopardize this case."

His silence was remarkable.

As *Star* columnist Rosie DiManno wrote afterwards, "Given the intense speculation since Crackgate exploded, the questions flung daily at the mayor—which he has largely refused to answer, apart from saying that he is not a crack addict and insisting no videotape exists—Blair could have easily removed Ford from the equation by clearly stating what the investigation is not pursuing, the angles that have no merit or traction, which wouldn't compromise the case when it's prosecuted. This Blair painstakingly avoided doing."

At City Hall, the mayor played dumb. "I understand there were some raids done on Dixon Road. Some houses that are, I think, they're on Windsor ... that's all I know," Ford said. Reporters tried to question him again later in the day. "I've answered so many questions, I don't know if you guys can't get it through your thick skulls. Seriously? ... I've already answered all these questions. I have nothing to do with this."

Ford was asked if he believed he was under investigation.

"They can investigate me all they want. I haven't done anything wrong," he said. "I have nothing to hide."

FIFTEEN

OUTRIGHT WAR

When Alexander "Sandro" Lisi left his Etobicoke home on July 11, 2013, a Toronto police surveillance team was following him. Officers watched as Lisi gassed up his Range Rover, visited with friends, and made a stop at Richview Cleaners.

Then the officers tailed Lisi to another gas station, an Esso, which happened to be located at the end of Rob Ford's street. When Lisi arrived at 5:40 P.M., the mayor's black Escalade was already there. Ford had shown up two minutes earlier and headed straight to the bathroom, despite the fact that his house was less than a minute away.

Lisi parked his Range Rover on the far side of the gas pumps and climbed out carrying a large manila envelope. He walked to the back of his car, put something inside, then headed into the kiosk while text messaging. Ford was still in the bathroom. Lisi grabbed a few bottles of Gatorade and a bag of chips, then headed to the cash register. At 5:42 P.M. he went back outside, looked around, walked to the mayor's Escalade, and slipped the manila envelope into the passenger side. A few minutes later, Ford left the washroom, bought some Gatorade and chewing gum, then went back to his Escalade and drove off.

Ford's approval rating had climbed 5 points since the crack story broke. Those close to him say he felt emboldened, having once again survived a scandal where others had written him off. Perhaps he thought he was being careful. Perhaps he felt invincible. Or maybe he couldn't stop himself. Whatever the explanation, Ford's drinking and drug use didn't slow down that summer. If anything, he became reckless.

The police investigation into Rob Ford had begun on May 18, two days after the story of the crack video broke. Between June 26 and September 7, 2013, investigators involved in Project Brazen 2 documented nearly a dozen covert handoffs between Lisi and Ford: at his child's soccer game, at the Esso station, at Ford's home, in a small park that in 2010 the city had renamed Douglas Ford Park in honour of the mayor's late father.

The pair's preferred meeting spot seemed to be the parking lot of Scarlett Heights high school, which is about the length of three football fields away from his mother's home. The scenario was usually the same: Ford would drive up in his Escalade, Lisi in his Range Rover. Lisi would get out of his car carrying something—a plastic bag, an oversized computer case, dry cleaning, a gift bag—and get into Ford's SUV. They'd sit for a while, sometimes an hour, then part ways.

There was a meeting on Monday, August 26, two days before the mayor casually confessed to reporters he had "smoked a lot" of marijuana. And two more in early September, around the time the Ontario Press Council held hearings into the *Toronto Star*'s and *The Globe and Mail*'s reporting on the Fords.

On one occasion, Ford met another individual in the lot— someone in a white stretch limousine. At least one of Ford's Scarlett visits was photographed by a Cessna spy plane. It was

Sunday, July 28, and Ford had spent his early afternoon on Newstalk 1010, explaining to listeners why Toronto desperately needed a proper football stadium. At 4:15 P.M., he was followed to a liquor store in Etobicoke. With the sun still high in the sky, the mayor drove over to Scarlett Heights and parked in the empty rear lot. He tossed something in the garbage and then waited, reading something on his lap. A little while later, Lisi arrived. He parked about twenty feet away and then walked over to the Escalade carrying some McDonald's takeout and a white plastic bag. Ford and Lisi sat for thirty minutes, eating and talking. At one point, the mayor got out to urinate under some trees. Before they went their separate ways, Lisi also tossed something in the garbage.

Later, police went to investigate. Lisi had thrown out a submarine sandwich bag. Ford had gotten rid of two empty liquor bottles—Iceberg Vodka and Russian Prince Vodka—as well as a McDonald's receipt.

On one occasion, one of Ford's staff members met Lisi at a grocery store near the mayor's house. Court records would show that Ford sometimes asked his young special assistants to set up meetings with Lisi.

It wasn't just the mayor's behaviour that was troubling for investigators, it was the company he was keeping. Lisi had an extensive criminal record, including criminal harassment, assaulting an ex-girlfriend, and threatening another woman. And he wasn't the only dodgy person the mayor of Toronto was hanging out with.

There was also Bruno Bellissimo, whom Ford had known since high school. Bellissimo, an admitted crack user with a fraud and theft convictions, had been with the mayor and Lisi at the Garrison Ball. On March 25—the night before the *Star*'s story about that event was published—Ford had gone to visit Bellissimo at the Toronto West Detention Centre after visiting hours. Bellissimo had been arrested for assaulting his parents and threatening to kill his mother. Ford had initially asked if he could have a tour of the facility, since he was the mayor. When the guards refused, Ford revealed that he wanted to see Bellissimo. He was again denied. On August 12, the day before one of Ford's clandestine meetings with Lisi, *The Globe and Mail* wrote about the mayor's mysterious jailhouse visit. Ford has never explained what he was doing there.

A few days before the *Globe* story appeared, Ford had shown up drunk at Toronto's Taste of the Danforth street festival. Someone there filmed him slurring and swaying, telling people on the street he wanted to go "party." When the footage landed on YouTube, it caused a firestorm. It was the first time Toronto residents were presented with indisputable evidence of Ford being impaired. On his Sunday radio show, Ford admitted to having had a few beers, a significant confession, considering his reaction to the Garrison Ball story.

In the middle of August, the *Toronto Star* published a front-page story exposing Ford's connections to Etobicoke's drug scene, the nefarious company he was keeping, and the fact that Toronto police were investigating attempts by the mayor's friends to get back the crack video—a video Ford still claimed did not exist. Even with the spotlight again drawn to his substance use, Ford continued to live recklessly. He didn't stop meeting with Lisi, partying with friends, and drinking to excess. On August 27, police were yet again called to Ford's home for a domestic assault. No charges were laid.

By now, Project Brazen 2 was hardly a covert operation. Even the Fords knew they were being watched. (Doug Ford would later tell the *Toronto Sun* he'd seen a surveillance plane circling overhead at his mother's home. He told the paper, "I stood there and gave them the finger.") But the billion-dollar question was, What would come of it? Were police going to charge the mayor? Or just his friends? If so, what was on the table? Drug use? Something to do with the video?

The answer came at 8 P.M. on October 1. Word came down that Toronto police were raiding numerous addresses in north Etobicoke. Sandro Lisi, as well as an associate of his, forty-seven-year-old Jamshid Bahrami, the owner of Richview Cleaners dry-cleaning shop, had been taken into custody. Lisi was charged with marijuana trafficking, possession of the proceeds of crime, possession of marijuana, and conspiracy to commit an indictable offence. Bahrami was charged with possession of cocaine, three counts of trafficking in marijuana, and conspiracy to commit an indictable offence. That night, I waited in a car near Ford's house with *Star* reporter Jayme Poisson. We watched a chubby raccoon wander up and down the sidewalk for a few hours. It was quiet.

The next morning, the mayor invited reporters to a press conference at his local Etobicoke Esso station, the same gas station where police had watched many of those mysterious package handoffs between Ford and Lisi. Ford looked calm and confident. "He's a good guy," Ford said of Lisi. "I don't throw my friends under the bus."

Numerous sources say that behind the scenes both Rob and Doug Ford were nervous. And with good reason. If police had been following Lisi, the mayor knew he was likely caught up in that investigation somehow. Doug Ford had his own political career to think about. He had his sights set on being premier of Ontario within the next two years. If Rob went down, the whole Ford brand might go with him.

Within days of Lisi's arrest, word got around that police had compiled nearly five hundred pages of intelligence to request a search warrant in connection with the arrest—which is unheard of, considering the relatively minor charges that were laid. There was obviously more to it. I, along with every other journalist in Toronto covering the Ford story, had heard that police were investigating the mayor, but we had no idea how elaborate that probe was until details of those documents began to leak out. The Cessna. Tracking devices. A secret video camera. The surveillance teams. The wiretaps. The information gathered apparently contained details about the crack cocaine video and Ford's drug use, and included interviews with former staff members that would be devastating to the mayor.

Media lawyers—including some from the *Star*—applied to have those documents made public. On October 30, Superior Court Justice Ian Nordheimer became a hero to every journalist in the city when he agreed to release a redacted version of the five-hundred-page document, allowing reporters to see the part that formed the core case against Lisi—a part in which the mayor played a starring role. In November, Nordheimer would consider releasing the rest.

Nordheimer saw no reason to delay. A PDF of the Project Brazen 2 documents would be emailed to reporters the next morning.

ON THE MORNING OF OCTOBER 31, *Star* reporter Jayme Poisson picked me up outside the same Starbucks where I'd met Mohamed Farah seven months earlier. We got to the *Star* around 8:30 A.M., and already the whole place was buzzing. It felt a lot like an election night. Every desk was filled. Reporters were jogging around the newsroom while editors were shouting at one another to figure out where so-and-so was stationed or which reporter would be chasing which councillor for reaction. Since I'm usually stationed at City Hall, I grabbed a desk with Kevin Donovan's investigative team. Every reporter in the city was going to be chasing the same story with the same information. Our job, as soon as the Project Brazen 2 documents came in, was to plow through those nearly five hundred pages the fastest, pull out the highlights, and present them in the best way possible. Donovan divided the document up into five sections. I was given pages 100 to 180. Another reporter on the team was assigned to go through surveillance photos. Each of us would write up relevant bits for a quick-hit web story while also recording any names, addresses, and anecdotes that needed following up.

The search warrant application was due any time after 9 A.M. We had an idea of what the full document included, but it wasn't clear how much Ford would be implicated in this first partial release. Would it show photos of Ford buying? Would it link the mayor to the Dixon City Bloods? What about his relationship with the Basso family at 15 Windsor Road, or the attempts to retrieve the crack video?

The mayor was clearly on edge. When he left his home that morning at 9:30 A.M., he lost his temper at a group of reporters who swarmed him near his car.

"Are you a focus of the police probe?"

"Guys, can you get off my driveway, please?" He began repeating the sentence over and over.

"What can you tell the people of Toronto about your involvement?"

"Can you get off my property, please! Okay don't— Get off my property!" he started to scream as the crush of reporters and photographers retreated to the sidewalk.

When a *Sun* photographer stepped back onto the driveway to take Ford's photo, the mayor angrily approached him. "What don't you understand? Get off the property, partner!" he hollered, shoving the camera lens aside.

Around the time the mayor pulled into City Hall, the photos connected to Project Brazen 2 were released. Many looked like something out of the *Cops* reality show. Grainy nighttime photos of the mayor and Sandro Lisi walking near his SUV. Aerial photos of Ford's Escalade in an empty parking lot. Gas station surveillance footage. Mug shots of Ford's friends.

Then the document itself came in ten minutes later. It was worse than I thought it would be.

I started reading a police interview with former Ford staff member Chris Fickel.

In November, December 2012 and into January 2013, FICKEL noticed that LISI was driving the Mayor around a lot of the time.

FICKEL does not know where the Mayor got marihuana [*sic*] from but has heard that "Sandro" may be the person who provides the Mayor with marihuana and possibly cocaine....

FICKEL does not know what LISI does for a living but believes he is a drug dealer.

FICKEL bases this information on rumors but it seems to be common knowledge.

I read about the mysterious envelope handoff at the Etobicoke Esso station on July 11. The timing was shocking to me. This would have been just a few days after Toronto was hit with a massive rainstorm that in a matter of minutes had turned highways into rivers, commuter trains into sinking ships, and basements into swimming pools. The July 8 flood was the most costly natural disaster in Ontario's history. And there was Ford, in the middle of this crisis, engaged in suspicious behaviour.

The revelations kept coming with each new page.

The mayor's recently fired chief of staff, Mark Towhey, told detectives he suspected Lisi was a drug dealer. George Christopoulos told police that a young aide had "brought up concerns that Lisi was providing the mayor with illegal drugs" and that Lisi was driving the mayor to "hot spots." On June 15, police watched the mayor's executive assistant, Tom Beyer, meet with Lisi at a grocery store near Diane Ford's home. Lisi got in Beyer's car, they drove a short distance, and then parted ways. The documents also indicated that police believed 15 Windsor Road was a drug den and that Ford may have been paying the Bassos' water bills.

The most interesting details related to phone records. Ford and Lisi were in almost constant communication. Lisi was also in regular contact with people in Ford's office. But most damning was that the records suggested something nefarious had happened after the crack video story went live, with the mayor phoning Lisi, who phoned Basso, who phoned Mohamed Siad—the dealer selling the footage—then Basso and Lisi speaking again, then Lisi phoning the mayor. This continued throughout the week. And on day eight, the mayor announced there was no video.

About an hour after the documents arrived, my cell phone rang. It was a cop I'm friendly with.

"The chief is having a press conference in half an hour. You're gonna wanna watch it," he said.

"Can you give me a hint? Are you arresting him?"

"No. Just watch."

"If you're not arresting him, then what's the big deal?"

"Just trust me. You're going to love this."

AT 11:30 A.M., pretty well everyone in the *Star* newsroom put down their work and headed for one of the large TV screens in the newsroom, where local news was running Chief Bill Blair's press conference live. We were clustered into two groups, one near the editors' hub in the middle and one at the back, where most of the reporters working on the story were sitting.

Right on time, Chief Blair walked to the podium with a prepared speech. He spoke in his trademark choppy, cop-talk manner.

"Good morning, ladies and gentlemen," Blair began. "As you are aware, the Toronto Police Service undertook a very significant major investigation last year. It culminated on June 13 of this year with the arrest of several dozen suspects, the laying of over two hundred charges, and the execution of numerous search warrants...."

Where was he going with this? I thought.

"As a result of the evidence that was seized on June 13, at the conclusion of Project Traveller, a number of electronic devices, computers, telephones, and hard drives were seized...."

Hard drives? Seized? No. They couldn't have ...

"On October 29, on Tuesday of this week, we received information from our computer technology section that in the examination of a hard drive that had been seized on June 13, they were able to identify a number of files that had been deleted and that they were able to recover those files...."

There were gasps in the newsroom. I covered my mouth. I think I grabbed some nearby person's wrist, but I can't quite remember.

"As a result, I have been advised [it was so like Blair to draw this out] that we are now in possession of a recovered digital video file—"

The newsroom exploded. People cheered and clapped and punched their arms in the air. It was hard to hear the rest of the chief's speech.

"—relevant to the investigations that have been conducted. That file contains video images, which appear to be those images which were previously reported in the press."

He couldn't quite conceal a smirk as he delivered his last line to the room of stunned reporters: "I'll be happy to take your questions now."

My eyes welled with tears. Numerous others reacted the same way. It wasn't about being vindicated. We'd always known we were reporting honestly. It was about the truth coming out to the public. It was about loving the job we do, and knowing how important it was. I felt proud to be working at the *Star*, to be working at a newspaper that had the guts to pursue this kind of story, for having the fortitude to stand by it, and to keep the pressure on despite intense criticism from both Fords. We'd all been in this together. We'd all been called liars. We'd all watched the erosion of trust in our profession, courtesy the Ford brothers' attacks on the media. Every reporter, photographer, and editor had spent the last six months fielding the same questions from family, friends, and strangers: "So ... is the video real?" The truth had come out. Toronto was going to get to see the video. I will never forget that moment as long as I live. A few minutes later, the *Star's* publisher, John Cruickshank, called everyone to the centre of the newsroom.

"This was a victory for journalism," he said.

For Rob Ford, it was the beginning of the worst week of his life.

ON THAT THURSDAY MORNING, Police Chief Bill Blair didn't just confirm that the video was real, he also announced that investigators had charged Alexander "Sandro" Lisi with extortion over alleged attempts to retrieve the video after the *Star's* and Gawker's stories ran. Blair also revealed that police had recovered "several" video files from the hard drive, and that one other was "relevant" to the Project Brazen 2 investigation. And while Blair refused to discuss the specific contents of the footage—other than to say that it was likely filmed at Windsor Road, that it showed Mayor Ford, and that his actions were "consistent" with what had been reported in the media—the chief did offer some personal reaction when a reporter asked if the video had shocked him.

"I'm disappointed," Blair said after a short pause. "I think, as a citizen of Toronto, I'm disappointed. I know this is a traumatic issue for the citizens of this city and for the reputation of this city, and that concerns me."

At City Hall, it was pandemonium. Councillors began calling for the mayor's resignation, but in what should have been a surprise to no one, Ford said he wasn't going anywhere. In fact, he suggested that the chief was wrong. "I think everybody has seen the allegations against me today," Ford said. "I wish I could come out and defend myself. Unfortunately, I can't, 'cause it's before the court, and that's all I can say right now."

But this time it wasn't working. Across the spectrum, city councillors were severing ties with the Ford administration. The next day, the *Toronto Star*, the *National Post*, and the *Toronto Sun* published editorials calling for Ford to step down. Four days after that, *The Globe and Mail* followed suit.

Council doesn't have impeachment procedures. Only the Ontario provincial government has the power to remove the mayor of Toronto, but that kind of intervention had never happened before. It seemed like a dangerous precedent to set. Mayor Ford may have become unfit for office because of his links to criminality, his drug issues, and his thuggish behaviour. But what if, in the future, city councillors who simply disagreed with a mayor decided to oust him or her? No one, from the governing Liberals to the opposition Conservatives to city councillors of every stripe, was eager to go down that road.

Councillors decided to go a different route. They began poring through the City of Toronto Act, trying to find ways to marginalize the disgraced mayor. Some of Ford's power was protected by provincial law, such as his role as the city's chief executive. That couldn't be changed. But some of his authority was non-statutory—it had been delegated by council. And what council giveth, council could taketh away.

The most obvious target was the mayor's ability to appoint committee chairs. Taking that away would essentially dismantle Ford's caucus, freeing up right-wing councillors to oppose the mayor openly. Ford had only one vote on council. The power of the office lay in the influence the mayor had. Without control of committees, Ford would have no whip. Next, council looked at the mayor's special authority during a crisis. The mayor's ability to declare, and end, a state of emergency was guaranteed by provincial legislation, but what happened in between wasn't covered. Council wanted to transfer that power to Deputy Mayor Norm Kelly.

The mayor switched to offence mode. The Fords' long-time lawyer, Dennis Morris, got involved. Together, they publicly called on Chief Blair to release the footage. It was a curious strategy. Given what I'd seen six months earlier, I couldn't imagine that the mayor actually wanted that made public. Perhaps they were gambling on the fact that Blair wouldn't make the video public because it would taint Lisi's extortion trial, and that Blair's refusal would create enough doubt for Ford Nation to stick with the mayor. Maybe they figured that if Lisi pleaded guilty, the video would never get entered into evidence, and therefore never be released. Or perhaps they were trying to run out the clock, to make it to the October 2014 election before a trial date. On all fronts, it was a weak plan. My police sources were insisting that there was no way the footage would be buried.

By Friday afternoon, it looked as if Ford was coming to his senses. The entire family—Doug, Randy, Rob, Kathy, and

Diane, as well as the mayor's chief of staff, Earl Provost—had a long meeting at the Ford family home in Etobicoke. When Ford came outside, reporters were waiting on the cul-de-sac. By now, Detective Sergeant Gary Giroux had confirmed that police wanted to interview the mayor but that he wasn't cooperating.

Saturday was quiet. There was rampant speculation that on the brothers' Sunday radio show, Rob Ford would announce plans to take some time off and get medical treatment. I was skeptical. It would be entirely out of character.

He didn't let me down.

Ford pulled up to Newstalk 1010's studio blaring the Bee Gees' "Stayin' Alive" from his black Escalade. As the show began, two of Ford's staff members brought the media coffee and Timbit doughnuts. The Brothers Ford marched into the studio holding prepared speeches, looking ready for battle.

"Chief, I'm asking you to release this video, now," Rob Ford said, his voice strong and direct. "Toronto residents deserve to see it. And people need to judge for themselves what they see on this video. Friends, I'm the first one to admit, I am not perfect. I have made mistakes. I have made mistakes, and all I can do right now is apologize for the mistakes. I sincerely, sincerely apologize."

Exactly what he was apologizing for wasn't clear. Ford mentioned the night he was "hammered" on the Danforth as something he regretted. He apologized for texting while driving. He said things had gotten "out of control" on St. Patrick's Day 2012. But when Toronto residents phoned in later in the show and asked the mayor point-blank about his drug use, Ford dodged the questions. He said he couldn't comment on the video. In the end, the mayor promised to cut back on his drinking, but he said it was unrealistic to think he'd never have a drink again. Brother Doug chimed in, "You're going to curb your drinking, especially in public…. You can stay in your basement, have a few pops."

Ford tried to avoid reporters on his way out of Newstalk, but we were waiting in the parking garage. At first, Ford relayed through a security guard that if we didn't leave, he'd call the police. Newstalk 1010 had invited us into the building to cover the show, so we weren't leaving. After a short standoff, Ford walked into the garage flanked by two staff members.

It was like a mob. I was blinded by camera flashes.

As he walked past, I shouted, "Mayor Ford, have you ever smoked crack cocaine?"

Then someone else said, "Mayor Ford, have you ever smoked crack cocaine?"

A third: "Mayor Ford, do you have an addiction problem?"

A fourth: "Mayor Ford, have you ever smoked crack cocaine?"

He peeled out of the driveway fast enough that several of us had to jump out of the way.

The pressure didn't let up the next week, and on Tuesday Doug Ford made it worse, essentially accusing Chief Bill Blair of being part of the *Toronto Star* conspiracy against his brother. The mayor wouldn't be resigning, but Doug Ford thought Blair should.

"[Blair] believes that he's the judge, the jury, and the executioner," he said on AM640's *John Oakley Show*. "He wanted to go out and put a political bullet right between the mayor's eyes, and thought that would be the final bullet to knock the mayor off, and he showed his cards—he thought he had a royal flush and … he has a couple of pairs of deuces," Doug said, "I think personally—this is just Doug Ford's opinion—he needs to step down until the probe is done, and there's obviously a bias right now, moving forward in this city, with a police chief against the mayor of this city."

Afterwards, Doug Ford headed to Ryerson University for a pre-scheduled talk with journalism students about how the media had it in for his family. He told the students how I'd stalked his elderly mother. How I and some of my other colleagues would hide in the bushes at the family's cottage, behind the mayor's house, sometimes in his backyard. He presented these allegations as fact.

Around the time Doug Ford's lecture got to the subject of the *Star* vendetta, Rob Ford drove his Escalade into the parking lot of City Hall and had a brainwave. He phoned his chief of staff.

"I'm going to blow their minds" was all he said.

As had been the case for the last week, dozens of reporters were waiting outside Ford's office. By chance, I happened to be there that morning. Ford walked off the elevator, a funny expression on his face. When someone asked him why Doug was doing all the talking, Ford stopped and turned to us, which was unusual.

"You guys have asked me a question. You asked me a question back in May, and you can repeat that question."

We looked around at each other. What was he talking about? Someone asked about the video.

"You asked me a couple questions," Ford said, "and what were those questions?"

Jackson Proskow from Global News asked, "Do you smoke crack cocaine?"

Ford looked right at him. "Exactly! Yes, I have smoked crack cocaine. But, no, do I? Am I an addict? No. Have I tried it? Probably in one of my drunken stupors, probably approximately about a year ago."

I nearly dropped my tape recorder. Did I just hallucinate? I looked around at my colleagues. We all had our mouths open.

"I answered your question," continued Ford. "You ask the question properly, I'll answer it…. So, I wasn't lying. You didn't ask the correct questions."

The mayor walked away shortly after.

Even Ford's confession was not wholly truthful. He had been asked dozens of times if he'd *ever* smoked crack. And the *Star* now knew that the video was filmed in February 2013. So unless he wasn't smoking crack out of that glass vial, that too did not add up. Again, Ford wanted to wipe the slate clean with an apology.

THE SPEED AT WHICH THINGS unravelled from there was stunning. Every day became more surreal than the previous one. With his admission, Ford lost every friend at city council. It wasn't just the hard drug use. It was the lying. The mayor could no longer be trusted. And worst of all: he was refusing to do the dignified thing and step aside.

"I think he's lost the moral authority to lead," said Councillor Denzil Minnan-Wong that same Tuesday. "We're in uncharted territory."

Minnan-Wong began investigating ways to censure the mayor. Left-wing councillor John Filion drew up a series of motions to strip the mayor of his power. A council that had been bitterly divided for the last three years suddenly found itself working towards a common goal. People put aside partisan differences and began talking about what was best for the city, how to protect its image and the integrity of its local government.

Meanwhile, reporters from around the world were booking plane tickets to Canada, the country with the crack-smoking mayor. CNN set up a live satellite truck behind City Hall. The BBC flew in a correspondent. Toronto's mayor was regularly being skewered on American late-night television.

On November 7, with the world documenting every crazy twist emerging from City Hall, the *Star* revealed it had obtained another video of the mayor.

The video showed the mayor raging, pacing, punching the air, and threatening to kill somebody. "I'm gonna kill that fucking guy. I'm telling you, it's first-degree murder," he says, talking rapidly. "I'll rip his fucking throat out. I'll poke his eyes out.... I'll make sure that motherfucker's dead.... I'm a sick motherfucker, dude."

Ford seemed to be ranting about someone who'd called the three Ford brothers "liars" and "thieves." The clip is seventy-seven seconds long and seems to have been shot in August 2013. Someone off-camera tells Ford to wait until "after ... the by-election," referring to a provincial election in Etobicoke. In the footage, it's obvious that the mayor is on something.

That afternoon, Ford was once again apologizing. "I just wanted to come out and tell you I saw a video. It's extremely embarrassing. The whole world's going to see it. You know what? I don't have a problem with that…. I hope none of you have ever or will ever be in that state. Obviously, I was extremely, extremely inebriated."

But that wasn't the last bit of breaking news.

That evening, I was in the City Hall press gallery, finishing a story about how recent events would likely shake up the mayoral candidate roster for 2014, when I heard Diane Ford talking. I whirled around in my chair and there was Ford's mother and his addict sister, Kathy, having a sit-down TV interview with CP24 anchor Stephen LeDrew.

"Oh, my god," I cried out, "Kathy Ford is on television!"

I couldn't believe it. Kathy Ford had never appeared publicly. The *Star* didn't even have a photo of her in its archives. Now, she was sitting with her mother on a big beige couch in what I recognized to be the Ford family home, volunteering for an interview. Kathy, wearing a red slouchy turtleneck with a black shawl, was the spitting image of her baby brother. She had the same pug nose, heavy brow, turned-down mouth, and blond hair.

It was a train wreck, and I couldn't look away. I wondered what addled strategy would involve bringing out a drug-addicted sister to defend a mayor accused of drug addiction. Why would one of the most powerful politicians in the country have his mother fight his battles? Kathy and Diane Ford had to have done this on their own. Somewhere, I imagined Doug Ford's head exploding.

"I was so angry," Kathy began. "I guess, before this, first of all, at Rob, my brother. I love him to death. I will support him to his dying day. As my dad always said, 'United we stand, divided we fall.' And we have lived by that as a family. And it's hard, sometimes, but to see the people jumping on the bandwagon. And the people that did not support him and just taking this for all it's worth."

Kathy spoke with the husky voice of someone who had lived a hard life. It was difficult to follow her scattered train of thought.

"Robbie is not a drug addict. I know, because I'm a former addict. Or an addict, if you would want to say. And as an alcoholic, if you want to consider binge drinking, once every three months and you get totally plastered, which he just makes a fool out of himself, and I've even asked him to leave my own— one time I saw him, fine—but he has done so much other things than this. And it seems— Nobody, I mean, unfortunately, yes, this has all come out. And it's horrible, and the first person that was upset was my mom."

We were all watching through our fingers by this point. It was so awkward, so telling, you almost felt guilty seeing it.

Now it was Diane Ford's turn. A grandmother eight times over, Diane was still a striking woman. She wore an all-black ensemble with a chunky belt and stylish black glasses. Her short blond hair was swept back and coiffed.

"It's not acceptable behaviour," she said. "He is the mayor of the city. But he knows that better than anyone. Now but, you know, to err is human, but to forgive is divine. And we all err ... but forgiveness isn't in the eyes of the media right now."

Both women said that Rob wouldn't be resigning. There was no need. They'd had a family meeting the previous Friday and talked everything through.

"It was a real outpouring of feelings. There was nothing put on. There were no lies. There was— I think it was just how we all felt about each other. What our expectations, what my expect-ations, are for my family," Diane said. "I didn't say shape up or ship out, but I did say, 'You know, Rob, this is— You've gotta maybe smarten up a little bit. Get back on line. I know you can do it. I know you are doing it. But now you have to—' He does have a problem ... he has a problem. He's got a weight problem."

Diane had come up with a five-point strategy to set things right. Get a driver. Lose some weight. Put an alcohol detector in the car. Get a new group of friends. See a counsellor, maybe a psychologist.

Stephen LeDrew clarified: So do they think Rob has not had a substance issue?

"No. Absolutely not," Kathy said. "He couldn't function if he was. He couldn't accomplish the things he has. Some people say you're an alcoholic if you binge drink ... other people say, if you have one every night before dinner, you're an alcoholic. It depends what you want to consider an alcoholic. And Robbie does not drink every night, and he does not drink one. When Robbie drinks, I think he just goes full tilt."

Then Diane addressed the question a lot of people were no doubt thinking, given that more than one of the Ford children had grown up with substance issues.

"They weren't raised that way at all."

This prompted Kathy to start on a subject that Diane clearly thought was a mistake.

"And [Rob] being the youngest, and watching all the rest of us grow up," she said. "And, you know, I'm not saying that we were bad or anything, but I'm just saying—"

Her mother shot her a look and they both chuckled. Kathy stopped talking and LeDrew changed the subject.

I re-watched the interview twice that night. To me, it was the clearest window ever provided into the Ford family. The spectre of Doug Ford Sr., the loyalty and tension between the siblings, the denial, the shifting of blame, the entitlement. And to say, after the stunning revelations of the previous week, that Rob Ford's problem was his weight, that if he'd just put a Breathalyzer in his car things would be better? It was flabbergasting—as if some combination of ambition, family allegiance, and denial had clouded their judgment.

I later learned that the whole interview had been a surprise to everyone in the family except Kathy. She'd personally phoned LeDrew and invited him to the Ford house. Diane had come home and found television crews in her living room. She'd thought she better sit in on it. Doug and Rob were apparently both furious.

The next Monday, November 11, Ford spoke at the city's Remembrance Day ceremony. A veteran refused to shake his hand, but most of the people who approached him were supportive. He vowed to stay the course. He spent all of Tuesday in the lobby of City Hall signing novelty Rob Ford bobble-head dolls for twenty dollars each to benefit the United Way charity. People lined up for hours to meet the mayor. The toys sold out that afternoon. Many landed on Kijiji and eBay, going for upwards of five hundred dollars.

By Wednesday's council meeting, City Hall had become a circus. Hundreds of raucous protestors marched on Nathan Phillips Square, demanding the embattled mayor resign, while inside the chamber, Doug Ford was screaming at Councillor Denzil Minnan-Wong to confess whether he'd ever used illegal drugs. Minnan-Wong, a trained lawyer, veteran councillor, and once one of the administration's most devoted soldiers, was now the author of a symbolic motion calling on Ford to step aside. It was high treason as far as the Ford brothers were concerned. At one point, Ford seemed to confront Minnan-Wong on the floor, standing nose-to-nose to him, blocking his path, while CNN and ABC livestreamed the meeting. That afternoon Minnan-Wong questioned the mayor directly: "Mr. Mayor, have you purchased illegal drugs in the last two years?" Ford froze. After eight seconds of silence, he replied, "Yes, I have." City council voted 37–5—including nay votes from Rob and Doug Ford—for the mayor to take a leave. Ford pledged to ignore the toothless edict.

And just when it seemed that Toronto City Hall couldn't become more dysfunctional, Justice Ian Nordheimer released another chunk of the Project Brazen 2 documents.

Police had interviewed half a dozen of Ford's former staff members. Their stories turned a drug scandal into something much more troubling. There were allegations of physical abuse against staff, marijuana use, drinking while driving, and sexual harassment. Ford's former deputy communications officer, Isaac Ransom, had told police that Ford was "totally out of it" the night of St. Patrick's Day and that his mood swung wildly. Staff said one minute he wanted to dance, the next he was breaking down and crying about his late father. Then later, according to Ransom, he made lewd comments to his policy adviser Olivia Gondek. According to Ransom, Ford had told Gondek that night, "I'm going to eat you out" and "I banged your pussy." Gondek categorically denies this occurred. Ransom also claimed Ford "told a female guard at City Hall that he 'was going to eat her box.'"

That same night, according to interviews with Ford's former staff members, the mayor popped an OxyContin pill and was partying at City Hall with a woman they believed was an escort. According to Ransom, that night Ford also used a racial slur to refer to a cab driver, calling him a "Paki" and making fun of his accent. Former chief of staff Mark Towhey had told detectives he believed Ford was an alcoholic. Young staff members described Ford handing down menial tasks like changing light bulbs at his home. That may not seem scandalous compared to hard drugs and prostitutes, but in Ford Nation abusing the public purse is an unforgivable sin. Former Ford aide Chris Fickel told police that he was once summoned to the mayor's home to fix the family computer. He brought his girlfriend, thinking it wouldn't take long. Detectives spoke with the girlfriend, Victoria Hills, about the incident.

Hills told police that sometime in January 2013, Fickel was picking her up for dinner around 6:30 P.M. when the mayor called about his computer. They drove to Etobicoke, and when the mayor learned that Hills was sitting outside, he insisted she come in. She was directed to the downstairs living room and took a seat next to Renata Ford. The Ford children were playing upstairs.

"The Mayor asked HILLS if she would like something to drink, like a beer. HILLS declined," the Project Brazen 2 document said. Ford then asked her if she smoked marijuana and if she'd like a joint. She declined. Ford lit up alone.

"HILLS became uncomfortable after the Mayor began smoking the joint. He was the only one smoking it and he only offered it to her. She was uncomfortable because the Mayor of her city was offering her 'weed' in his house," the document said.

The day after this second release of documents, nine days after Ford had admitted to smoking crack, the mayor announced he would be suing some of his former staff members who had spoken to police. He said they were lying. "I have no other choice. I'm the last one to take legal action. I can't put up with it anymore."

Speaking to reporters outside his office, Ford denied using prostitutes, cocaine, and OxyContin, but conceded he may have driven while impaired. "I might have had some drinks and ... driven, which is absolutely wrong," he said. (In a subsequent interview, Ford clarified that he didn't mean to suggest he'd driven drunk. In fact, Ford said he'd never been impaired behind the wheel—despite having been convicted of drunk driving in 1999.)

Then Ford cheerfully turned the conversation to an upcoming Canadian Football League playoff game between the Toronto Argonauts and the Hamilton Tiger-Cats.

"I want to call Mayor [Bob Bratina] in Hamilton and tell him that we're going to have to spank their little Tiger-Cats.... Oh!" he added, apparently remembering one more issue he had with the Brazen 2 documents. "And the last thing was, Olivia Gondek. It says that I wanted to eat her pussy.... I've never said that in my life to her. I would never do that. I'm happily married. I've got more than enough to eat at home."

The mayor then left to attend a regularly scheduled council meeting.

On *The Daily Show* that night, Jon Stewart played the clip, then pushed his chair back and screamed, "What? What?! What?!! WHAT?!! WHAT?!!!," which seemed to sum up everyone's reaction.

The mayor held another press conference that afternoon to apologize for using "unforgivable language." And this time he did so with his little-seen wife, Renata, by his side. He asked for privacy for his family. The mayor said he was consulting a "team of health-care professionals," but he wouldn't elaborate. He then asked the media to respect his family's privacy. He made the request just before dragging Renata through a wall of reporters and television crews rather than take the side-door exit he typically used.

With the threats against staff members who cooperated with police, the free use of vulgar language, and the spectacle Ford created with Renata, it felt like a new low. The mayor had been exposed as a hard-drinking crack user and a liar, but now he was coming across as a bully beyond redemption.

After weeks of watching from the sidelines, Ontario premier Kathleen Wynne was finally forced to do something. "The things we are seeing and hearing about Mayor Rob Ford are truly disturbing," she said in a hastily called press conference. "The City of Toronto has a mayor and council that were elected by the residents of Toronto and must be accountable to them.... It is not the provincial government's role, nor its intention, to impose its preferences upon that government." But, she said, city council must be able to function. "If council were to clearly indicate that they lack the ability to function as a result of this matter, the province would respond to a request from council to be provided new tools, depending on what that request might be." There was one caveat. Because of the "extraordinary and unique nature of this type of intervention," Wynne would want all three provincial party leaders on board, which was unlikely, given the fact that Progressive Conservative leader Tim Hudak had closely aligned himself with the Ford brothers in the past.

While Wynne's threat was significant, in the end nothing had changed. City council was on its own. Councillors scheduled a series of special meetings, two on Friday and one on Monday, to strip Ford of much of his authority.

Keeping up with the developments over the next few days was dizzying work. Canadian Football League Commissioner Mark Cohon encouraged Ford to stay away from the Grey Cup playoff game. Iceberg Vodka officials released a statement distancing the brand from the mayor after Ford's comments on drinking and driving. Newstalk 1010 cancelled the brothers' radio show.

Meanwhile, in the United States, the scandal in Toronto had knocked Obamacare off the news cycle. Ford was the opening skit on *Saturday Night Live*. Friends of mine living or vacationing around the world—in Asia, Europe, and Australia—sent me text-message updates about the Ford coverage abroad.

The Ford brothers seemed increasingly unhinged by the attention. With Doug at his side, the mayor went on an American media blitz. He told Fox News he wanted to run for prime minister of Canada one day. He lost his temper with CNN's Bill Weir after the reporter pressed him on his behaviour. "I'm not an addict!" he said. "You guys can spin it every way you want." In the background, Doug Ford could be heard saying, "Okay, settle down." In an interview with *The Today Show*'s Matt Lauer, Ford seemed to contradict himself again about the video. This time, he said he could "barely even remember" when it was filmed—meaning he actually did remember.

On Monday, November 18, city council met once again to

make Rob Ford Toronto's mayor in name only. The previous Friday, council had taken away his control of the committees and his power during an emergency. Now it was time for the more contentious restrictions. After consulting with city lawyers, council felt it could legally transfer the mayor's staff to Deputy Mayor Norm Kelly as well as reduce Ford's office budget to a point where it couldn't function properly. The final blow was a motion to ban Ford from setting key matters of the legislative agenda. Kelly would run the executive committee. With a skeleton staff, minimal funding, and no power over policy, Rob Ford would be little more than a figurehead, and a disgraced one at that.

The Fords weren't going down without a fight. The meeting was the most bizarre in the chamber's history. The Ford brothers got into a shouting match with the audience. At one point, while charging to his brother's side, the mayor knocked over Councillor Pam McConnell, a grandmother. The brothers refused to follow the speaking rules. They heckled the crowd. It was vintage Rob Ford, but now there were two of them.

Before the vote, the mayor rose to speak. "This is nothing more than a coup d'état," he said angrily. "This, folks, reminds me of when—and I was watching with my brother—when Saddam attacked Kuwait and President Bush said, 'I warn you, I warn you, I warn you, do not.' Well, folks, if you think American-style politics is nasty, you guys have just attacked Kuwait.... Mark my words, friends. This is going to be outright war in the next election, and I'm going to do everything in my power—"

"Mayor Ford, your time's up," Speaker Nunziata interjected.

"—everything in my power to beat you guys."

"Thank you, Mayor Ford."

The mayor's mic was cut, but he continued to talk. "… What goes around comes around, friends. Remember what I'm saying."

The motions passed overwhelmingly.

SIXTEEN

FORD MORE YEARS

When Toronto voters chose Rob Ford to be their mayor on October 25, 2010, they knew full well they were electing a flawed man. Ford's temper and extensive catalogue of offensive speeches had been well documented. Voters knew he'd been embroiled in a high-profile domestic assault case, that he'd been convicted of drunk driving and charged with marijuana possession, and that security guards had had to drag him out of a professional hockey game after he drunkenly berated a couple from out of town. And voters also knew that when this loud, stranger-than-fiction character from Etobicoke got into trouble, his instinct was to try to lie his way out of it. He was elected anyway. Because, weighing the pros against the cons, Ford was the best candidate in the race. He ran the best campaign, he stayed on message, and he talked about issues people cared about.

When those same voters head to the polls on October 27, 2014, they will be evaluating a very different Rob Ford. Ford has now admitted to using crack cocaine while being mayor of Toronto, and then lying about it—vehemently—for months. He faces accusations of assaulting his staff members, using racial and homophobic slurs, being drunk at work, partying with prostitutes, sexually harassing female city employees, and driving while intoxicated. Questions about whether the mayor was being blackmailed continue to linger. Ford has been linked to a dangerous street gang that is alleged to have been part of a massive gun-smuggling ring. He seems to spend much of his free time socializing with criminals. And he may even be paying the bills at a known crack house. All that's just the stuff we know about at the time of publication. There will no doubt be more revelations, I suspect in the same vein.

A lot of people thought Rob Ford would step aside once the chief put an end to the debate about the video's existence. But those of us who have watched Ford closely over the last few years knew that would be entirely out of character. Now some pundits and politicos are speculating that he won't run for re-election, if something really damaging surfaces. If Toronto police directly link him to the extortion charges against Lisi, for example. I think the only thing that will prevent Rob Ford from putting his name on that ballot will be death or jail time. And if it were possible to run from prison, I think he would.

The question is: Can he win?

I believe it's possible, for a long list of reasons.

For one thing, it's hard to ignore the fact that after Ford admitted to smoking crack, an Ipsos Reid poll showed that while 76 percent of Torontonians wanted him to step down and get help, 40 percent still had a favourable view of his performance as mayor. Another survey by Forum Research taken the day Chief Bill Blair announced that police had the crack tape—but before Ford admitted to having used the drug—showed the mayor's approval rating at 44 percent. Up 5 points. Keep in mind, Ford was elected with 47 percent of the vote. Since February 2011, Forum Research has sampled Ford's approval rating more than thirty times. The average: 44 percent.

Crack didn't move the needle.

Now, approval rating is not the same thing as voting intention. But it's also not something to dismiss out of hand.

Polls suggest that Ford Nation—the mayor's rock-solid base, who would vote for him no matter what—makes up about 20 percent of Toronto's electorate. What the approval rating tells us is that another 20 percent, at the very least, support his political agenda. If Ford plays it straight until election day, if he can persuade voters that he has actually had a "come-to-Jesus moment," as he claimed to the CBC in November 2013, I believe he can bring these people on side. And maybe others too.

In the next election, Ford will once again be running as an underdog. And that could help him. A weakened Ford means more competition. In a crowded field, someone could win with less than 40 percent of the vote.

If Ford can convince voters that his personal problems don't change the fact that he's still the best person to be watching their money, I think it's entirely conceivable that he could win back enough support.

The reality is, the mayor's record boils down to a not-so-bad sound bite. In 2010 Ford talked a lot about general goals, such as slashing spending, cutting taxes, and making Toronto a better place to live. These are difficult things to measure in terms of success or failure. When it came to the quantifiable specifics, Ford kept it short and he's delivered on a lot of them.

He promised to cut office expense accounts. Contract out garbage collection. Make the TTC an essential service to prohibit strikes. And rescind two unpopular taxes for home buyers and car owners. Ford can claim "promise kept" on all of these, except for one of the taxes, which he'd vowed to partially reduce in the 2014 budget year. Now that his power has been taken away, Ford can reasonably claim he would have done this too, had it not been for an "undemocratic" coup by council, as the Ford brothers have described it.

Ford has not, as he claims, saved Toronto taxpayers "a billion dollars." But he can legitimately take credit for wrestling spending into submission. On Ford's watch, the city's gross operating budget has stayed more or less the same, increasing from $9.38 billion in 2011 to $9.43 billion in 2013. The non-partisan city manager, Joe Pennachetti, has said Ford has legitimately saved about four hundred million dollars.

Late in his mayoral campaign, Ford added "subways, subways, subways" to his platform. It was a gamble that he stood by throughout his term, and it paid off. In September 2013, the federal government agreed to contribute a portion of the cost to extend a subway line into Scarborough. With the added financial support, city council got behind the subway plan, despite having rejected it earlier on. Whether a subway gets built or not, highly populated Scarborough knows Ford championed the issue when no one else would. And as a bonus, now that Ford is marginalized at council, he can distance himself from any local tax increase needed to make the subway happen.

Finally, there is the mayor's crowning achievement, something even his critics concede was a major accomplishment: his administration's contract negotiations with the unions. The 2008–2009 recession tested public patience with public-sector unions in

Canada and abroad. Ford took on labour and won. City staff say the collective agreements negotiated with workers will save $139 million over four years.

If it hadn't been for the crack story and drinking allegations, it's hard to imagine a situation where Ford couldn't have won re-election on that record. And I still believe that there are many voters in Toronto whose primary concern when selecting a mayor is the impact that person will have on their property tax bill. As right-wing pundit Ezra Levant said on Sun News Network the night city council stripped Ford of his power, "He's run the city well despite his private life.... Ford is a deeply flawed man, but I'd take him drunk over his left-wing predecessor sober."

Levant said Ford offends the "fancy people," the folk who live downtown, enjoy the gay pride parade, and support bike lanes. Levant was stoking the urban–suburban rift that got Ford elected in the first place. That divide hasn't gotten any better since 2010.

In fact, little has changed since amalgamation. Back in 1997, when the provincial government led by Progressive Conservative premier Mike Harris decided to dissolve the six municipalities in and around Toronto and resurrect them as one giant city of 2.3 million, six mayors were left eyeing one job. In the end, it was North York's Mel Lastman, an outspoken populist right-winger, against old Toronto's Barbara Hall, a theatre-loving former lawyer and New Democrat. Lastman campaigned on a businesslike approach to government and a property tax freeze. Hall promised to protect the environment, promote business, and help neighbourhoods "flourish" after amalgamation. She won the core: Toronto, East York, York. He won the much more populous suburbs: Etobicoke, North York, Scarborough. So Lastman became mayor.

In the alternative weekly *NOW* magazine, former Toronto mayor John Sewell, a fervent progressive, wrote that Barbara Hall had done "well in the older cities of Toronto, York and East York where there is a strong democratic tradition that rewards those who respect the complexity of city life. But in the single-use suburbs which have been planned to emphasize blandness, Lastman's offer of stupid certainty—can you believe he actually suggested a 10-year tax freeze?—won the day."

Of the mood in the city after Lastman's victory, the *Toronto Star*'s Royson James wrote, "The air went out of Toronto's balloon last Monday night. The old Toronto, that is. The one dominated by left-leaning politicians, artists, journalists and the university-centred crowd. Their hip, theatre-loving mayor Barbara Hall was handily defeated by a brash millionaire from the suburbs and, oh no, the world will never be the same again."

Sound familiar?

That's not to say that an old City of Toronto candidate can't win the mayoralty. Certainly, David Miller was able to overcome the suburban hurdle. He did this, partly, by running as a populist, vowing to sweep out corruption in the wake of the MFP scandal, rather than as a hardcore progressive. But it's certainly more challenging for a left-winger in the current climate.

Darrell Bricker, the global CEO of Ipsos Public Affairs, would agree with me. In their book *The Big Shift*, Bricker and John Ibbitson, a political correspondent with *The Globe and Mail*, argue that Canada as a whole is poised for a lengthy period of conservative rule. The reason? New Canadians. Since 2006, Canada has had the fastest-growing population of all the G8 countries, and immigration is responsible for two-thirds of it.

And the majority of these people are moving into major metropolises, such as Toronto and Vancouver. *The Big Shift* argues that immigrants find they have more in common with those on the right in this country. They tend to be more religious, socially conservative, and averse to debt. These people are "strivers," who dream of working hard to own a home in a safe neighbourhood. On the other side there are the "creatives," who are more concerned about "community supports, the environment and international engagement."

The Big Shift concentrates on national politics, but Bricker believes the concept also applies to Toronto. "The way that I think the elites in Toronto have treated the likes of Rob Ford—as though it's almost an aberration, that it was a specific creation of a very unique political circumstance and it will never be replicated—I think that's wrong," he told me. "Leaving aside all the social pathologies of the Ford administration, the agenda of privatization, lower taxes, more questioning of unionization in terms of city staff—somebody running on that agenda will have a very good chance of winning."

So will that somebody be Ford, or a fiscal conservative like Karen Stintz, John Tory, or even Denzil Minnan-Wong? I think the polls show that Ford still has a shot.

Throughout his term, the mayor has enjoyed continuing strong support in the old boroughs. Even by November 2013, when the entire world was reporting on Toronto's "crack mayor," an Ipsos poll showed that 49 percent of people in Scarborough, 45 percent of people in Etobicoke, and 43 percent of people in North York approved of the job he was doing. Considering what he'd been through, those were pretty remarkable numbers. And they're only going to go up if he keeps his nose clean.

When it comes down to it, Rob Ford's political obituary has been rewritten countless times through the years. Yet, it's never run. The man has used up all nine lives and then some, and still he endures. Now, he's a global celebrity. A rock star who gets mobbed everywhere he goes. With his reputation in supposed tatters, he can haul out novelty bobble-heads of himself and people will line up for hours to pay for one. In normal times, admitting to smoking crack cocaine, being exposed as a compulsive liar, and getting caught up in two massive police investigations into guns, gangs, and drugs would spell the end of a political career. But these are Rob Ford times. They are not normal.

Despite everything, the mayor has, by and large, lived up to his election promises. If Ford does in fact follow through with his promise to sober up, lose weight, and get to work, how many voters could be won over by that kind of redemption story?

But suppose Rob Ford runs and loses in 2014. If history is any indication, that won't be the last of him or his family. For them, retreat is defeat, and the Fords won't quit. Their ambition may seem disconnected from reality—at the climax of Ford's fall from grace, he told Fox News, "Yes, one day I do want to run for prime minister," and on AM640 he said that Doug Ford "will be premier [of Ontario] one day"—but that does not appear to lessen its force. And if by chance something does happen that would remove Rob Ford from contention, the Ford family has in Doug another member ready and willing to pick up the torch. The notion that a Ford ought to lead, that another Ford will be ready to step in and assume the family's rightful place at the helm of government, seems obvious to them.

They are, after all—according to them—the Canadian Kennedys. Were the Kennedys not also dogged by drugs, drinking, and scandal? Why should the Fords not get a pass the same way they did? (Ezra Levant actually made this argument on Sun News.) But of course the Fords are no Kennedys. The Kennedys were flawed, yes, but they were also brilliant leaders who were instrumental in the civil rights movement, championing education reform and health care. The Kennedys' personal issues did not prevent them from accomplishing great things that made their country a better, more inclusive place to live.

The Fords' victories are neither grand nor inspiring. And after a term in power they have yet to produce a vision of what Toronto ought to be. Only what it shouldn't be. What the last mayoral election revealed is that, in Toronto's fractured political landscape, that's enough to get elected.

At 8:30 A.M. on January 2, 2014, Rob Ford filed his nomination papers. He'd arrived half an hour early to make sure he was first in line to see the city clerk. "Ford More Years," he said, debuting his campaign slogan while Doug looked on from the side. Doug Ford later told reporters he wouldn't be running for city council again, but that he was "eyeing" a provincial seat. In the meantime, he'd be running his brother's re-election bid.

To kick off his campaign, Rob Ford gave a short statement to reporters. "I've got the strongest track record, I've been the best mayor that this city's ever had. My record speaks for itself."

NOTES

In writing this book, I relied on close to two thousand hours of interviews that I conducted over the four years I've been covering City Hall. I interviewed hundreds of individuals: people in politics and law enforcement; friends and family of the Fords; opponents and critics of Rob and Doug Ford; former employees and political staff, including those who worked under Rob Ford as a councillor and others from his time as mayor; and business associates and former classmates. I have consulted thousands of pages of court documents, arrest paperwork, political debate transcripts, and Ford family records when possible, as well as thousands of news stories and television and radio broadcasts. In some cases, I have relied on information from sources who for a variety of reasons did not want their names printed, some because of their close relationship with the Ford family, others out of fear of professional repercussions, and still others who worried about legal implications. Most notably these individuals include two members of the extended Ford family, six former members of Rob Ford's mayoral staff, two former classmates of the Ford brothers, three members of the Garrison Ball organizing committee, and an associate of Renata Ford's. Neither the mayor nor his brother Doug agreed to be interviewed. To Doug Ford, I promised that if he sat down with me I would run an unedited transcript of our conversation. In writing this book—and preparing these notes—I have tried to be as open and transparent as possible about my reporting process and how I know the things I know. It's also worth noting that allegations contained in search warrant documents connected to Project Brazen 2 have not been proven in court.

PROLOGUE

pg. 5 **he didn't want to talk:** Months after the meeting in the car, the *Star* learned the alleged dealer's name: Mohamed Siad, aged twenty-seven. "Rob Ford Crack Scandal: Man Who Showed Rob Ford Crack Video Caught Up in Police Raids," *Toronto Star*, August 2, 2013.

CHAPTER 1: RESPECT THE TAXPAYER

pg. 7 **closing a twenty-five-point gap:** On September 19, 2010, Nanos Research released a poll that showed Rob Ford with 45.8 percent of the decided vote, George Smitherman with 21.3 percent, Joe Pantalone with 16.8 percent, Rocco Rossi with 9.7 percent, and Sarah Thomson with 6.4 percent. By the time voters went to the ballot box a month later, Rossi and Thomson had dropped out.

pg. 8 **"Tonight," he began:** This line was about a minute into the speech. The full speech is at www.youtube.com/watch?v=ALAQjRknPKM.

pg. 10 **In a profile interview for the *Toronto Star*:** Linda Diebel, "Adam Giambrone Has Bumpy Ride in Run for Mayor," *Toronto Star*, February 1, 2010.

pg. 11 **He cited the polarized political climate:** Vanessa Lu, "John Tory Won't Run for Mayor," *Toronto Star*, January 7, 2010.

pg. 14 **the return on every dollar could be leveraged:** Toronto Arts Foundation, January 2012, www.torontoartsfoundation.org/ Our-Programs/Advocacy.

pg. 14 **Unemployment was at 10.36 percent:** This is the three-month average, seasonally adjusted statistic for August–October, 2010. City of Toronto, Economic and Cultural Research Division.

pg. 14 **national average of 8 percent:** Statistics Canada, "Unemployment Rate, Canada, Provinces, Health Regions (2013 Boundaries) and Peer Groups."

pg. 14 **Bankruptcies in and around Toronto were nearly triple:** "Toronto's Economic Recovery Leaving Many Behind," TD Bank Financial Group, October 22, 2010, www.unitedwaytoronto.com/downloads/whatWeDo/reports/2010_TDEconomic_Recovery_Report.pdf.

pg. 15 **"Gino boy":** Ford denied using the slur, although numerous councillors said they heard it. Ford also apologized: "If Councillor Mammoliti thinks I offended him, I apologize." Bruce DeMara, "Councillors End Spat with Tepid Apologies: Ford Still Denies Making Ethnic Slur Against Italians," *Toronto Star*, March 7, 2002.

pg. 15 **"a waste of skin":** Paul Moloney and John Spears, "Councillors Square Off in a Verbal Slugfest," *Toronto Star*, July 19, 2005.

pg. 15 **"If you're not doing needles":** "Rob Ford on AIDS," *National Post*, June 28, 2006.

pg. 15–16 **"Who the fuck do you think you are?":** Dan and Rebecca Hope wrote a letter to city clerk Ulli Watkiss after the incident at the Maple Leafs game. It was entitled "A Rare Night Out."

pg. 16 **He coached her to say "no comment":** Jeff Gray and Timothy Appleby, "Ford Called Police Night Before Arrest," *The Globe and Mail*, March 27, 2008.

pg. 16 **"Rob Ford has reshuffled the deck":** David Rider, "Ford Surges into Second Place in Mayoral Poll," *Toronto Star*, April 16, 2010.

pg. 17 **claimed he'd forgotten about it:** Jonathan Jenkins and Rob Lamberti, "Ford Dodges Pot Bust in Florida," *Toronto Sun*, August 18, 2010.

pg. 17 **"The phone would not stop ringing that day":** Interview with Stefano Pileggi, August 23, 2013.

pg. 17 **close to twenty-five thousand dollars overnight in campaign donations:** Interview with two members of Rob Ford's campaign team, June and August 2013.

CHAPTER 2: DOUGIE LOVED POLITICS

pg. 20   **His daughter, Kathy, then aged thirty-seven, was a heroin user:** In an interview with CP24 on November 7, 2013, Kathy Ford told host Stephen LeDrew she was a former "addict." A high-placed police source, two members of the Fords' extended family, and a close associate of Kathy Ford who used to live with her have each told me directly that the mayor's sister is addicted to "drugs" or "heroin." Finally, when Kathy Ford's long-time lover Scott MacIntyre was arrested in 2012, his lawyer said the following in his submissions: "He has been in a relationship with her for several years. They are both involved in the use of drugs, they've gone through various periods of being clean and relapsing, and that's not an unusual situation." In rendering his decision, the judge banned MacIntyre and Ford from communicating while MacIntyre sought treatment for drug addiction. Kathy Ford, he said, "has her own issues. I think that her issues in combination with Mr. MacIntyre's issues are simply a prescription for disaster."

pg. 21   **Scharger, who ran his own polygraph company:** Nelson Scharger retired from the Toronto Police Service in 1995. Afterwards, he worked at his own company, N.S. Polygraph Services. Reached at his home in November 2013, Scharger declined to comment.

pg. 22   **The blast hit Kiklas in the chest:** Dieter A. Kiklas, letter to the editor, "Michael Kiklas Died a Hero Protecting Others," *Toronto Star*, August 21, 1998.

pg. 22   **News reports suggest he was dead:** Michelle Shephard, "Murder Suspect Eludes Police: Cottage Country Searched After Saturday Slaying," *Toronto Star*, July 26, 1998; and "Homicide Suspect Arrested," *The Globe and Mail*, July 27, 1998.

pg. 22   **Smoot-Hawley Tariff Act:** "The Battle of Smoot-Hawley," *The Economist*, December 18, 2008.

pg. 22   **The output of Canada's manufacturing sector:** Information in this paragraph was taken from an article by Joe Martin, director of Canadian business history at the Rotman School of Management, University of Toronto: "Great Depression Hit One Country Hardest of All,"

Bloomberg, March 26, 2013. See www.bloomberg.com/news/2013-03-26/great-depression-hit-one-country-hardest-of-all.html.

pg. 23 **By 1933, workers in Toronto were earning 60 percent:** James Lemon, *Toronto Since 1918* (Toronto: James Lorimer & Company, 1985), p. 60.

pg. 23 **Two years later, a quarter of the population:** James Lemon, *Toronto Since 1918* (Toronto: James Lorimer & Company, 1985), p. 59.

pg. 23 **By the early 1930s ... two largest ethnic groups, Jews and Italians:** Census of Canada 1931, "Population of Cities and Towns 10,000 and Over, Classified According to Racial Origin," p. 499.

pg. 23 **on public beaches:** Rosie DiManno, "Remembering the Christie Pits Riot," *Toronto Star*, August 10, 2013.

pg. 23 **Doug Sr. was raised in a rundown neighbourhood:** Information about Doug Ford Sr.'s early life was gathered through interviews with people who knew him, such as former MPP John Parker and his former business partner, Ted Herriott, as well as a former employee of Deco and two members of the Fords' extended family.

pg. 24 **"Marry me and you'll be marrying a millionaire":** Interview with member of the extended Ford family, May 2013.

pg. 24 **nearly enough brothers and sisters—nine:** In interviews about his father, Rob Ford has usually said Doug Sr. was one of nine children, although he has occasionally said he was one of ten. In the legislature, Doug Sr. said he was one of nine children.

pg. 25 **earning Salesman of the Month:** Interview with Councillor John Parker, July 29, 2013. Parker was an MPP with Doug Ford in the Ontario Legislature during the Mike Harris years.

pg. 25 **"My wife and I talked about it":** Interview with Ted Herriott, September 7, 2013.

pg. 26 **Ted Herriott was the president:** *Toronto City Directory, 1963*, Part 1 (Toronto Reference Library).

pg. 27 **"We thought Doug had two left feet":** Interview with Patricia Herriott, September 7, 2013.

pg. 28 **Doug Sr. became president, Clarence Campbell became vice-president:** *Toronto City Directory, 1967*, Part 1 (Toronto Reference Library).

pg. 28 **Kathy ran the administrative side:** Interview with Gary Moody, October 15, 2013.

pg. 29 **Deco employed about forty-five people:** Patrick McConnell, "Businessman Wins Humber Tory Nomination," *Etobicoke Life*, February 22, 1995.

pg. 29 **clearing millions of dollars in annual sales:** A 1994/1995 *Toronto City Directory* put estimated sales at between one million and ten million dollars and the number of employees at thirty-eight.

pg. 29 **a story told in the weekly *Etobicoke Life*:** Patrick McConnell, "Businessman Wins Humber Tory Nomination," *Etobicoke Life*, February 22, 1995.

pg. 30 **Robert Bruce, weighing in at nine pounds, one ounce:** Birth announcement, *Toronto Star*, May 31, 1969.

pg. 31 **By the early 1980s, they were appearing in the society pages:** Greg McArthur and Shannon Kari, "Globe Investigation: The Ford Family's History with Drug Dealing," *The Globe and Mail*, May 25, 2013.

pg. 31 **Doug Ford Sr. was a founding member of the Rexdale Rotary Club ... first CT scan machine:** Tamara Shephard, "Community Mourns Loss of Former MPP Doug Ford," *Toronto Star*, September 26, 2006.

pg. 32 **Between 1981 and 1987, he was twice found guilty of theft and assault:** Court documents showing charges and sentencing information from Toronto, Brampton, Cobourg, and Newmarket.

pg. 32 **the *Globe* ran a four-thousand-word investigation:** Greg McArthur and Shannon Kari, "Globe Investigation: The Ford Family's History with Drug Dealing," *The Globe and Mail*, May 25, 2013.

pg. 33 **"Three Etobicoke men have been charged":** "Charges Laid in $5,000 Extortion Bid After Man Held for 10 Hours," *Toronto Star*, December 12, 1986.

pg. 34 **"an outright lie":** Ann Hui and Amber Daugherty, "Doug Ford Disputes Globe Report on Family History with Drug Dealing," *The Globe and Mail,* May 25, 2013.

pg. 34 **"sleazy journalism … is that the best *The Globe and Mail* has?":** Jackson Proskow, "Doug Ford Denies Drug Trade Allegations," Global News, May 25, 2013. See http://globalnews.ca/news/589636/doug-ford-calls-drug-trade-allegations-sleazy-journalism.

pg. 35 **"If you want to go calling":** Bill Weir, "Reporter's Notebook: In the Heart of Ford Nation with Toronto's Embattled Mayor," CNN, November 18, 2013. See www.cnn.com/2013/11/18/world/weir-reporters-notebook.

pg. 35 **I reached out to hundreds of the Fords' former classmates:** The overwhelming majority of these calls were made by my research assistant, Simon Bredin. All quotes that appear in the book are a result of interviews I either conducted or fact-checked with the source. These include interviews with Mark Stenoff, Bill Gianakopoulos, Dave Miteff, David Profitt, and Laura Biernat, July–August 2013.

pg. 36 **The caption on the team photo that year:** Scarlett Heights Collegiate yearbook, 1985.

pg. 37 **"quiet stoner":** This is according to two former associates of Fabio Basso, interviewed June 7, 2013, and August 30, 2013. One of them attended Don Bosco Catholic Secondary School and the other attended Scarlett Heights Collegiate. The direct quote is from the June interview.

pg. 37 **"I know it might sound strange now … but Robbie was a little guy":** Marci McDonald, "The Weirdest Mayoralty Ever: The Inside Story of Rob Ford's City Hall," *Toronto Life,* May 15, 2012.

pg. 38 **but he dabbled in cocaine as well:** In an interview with Peter Mansbridge, the mayor said, "When I was younger, I experimented with drugs," after being asked whether he'd ever used cocaine, as opposed to crack cocaine, before. Peter Mansbridge, "Rob Ford Interview with Peter Mansbridge: 7 Key Points," CBC, November 19, 2013.

CHAPTER 3: THE CANADIAN KENNEDYS

pg. 45   **"Somehow or another he was jostled":** Michael Friscolanti, "Councillor's Sister Shot by Accident, Police Say," *National Post*, April 4, 2005.

pg. 45   **The shotgun wasn't Scott MacIntyre's:** Her Majesty the Queen v. Scott MacIntyre, Ontario Court of Justice, June 6, 2005. Official court transcript.

pg. 45   **It belonged to Doug Ford Sr., an avid collector:** Interview with member of the extended Ford family and a close associate of the Fords, May 2013.

pg. 46   **"The greatest economist I ever met in my whole life was my mother":** Legislative Debates (Hansard), Office of the Legislative Assembly of Ontario, March 4, 1997. See www.ontla.on.ca/web/house-proceedings/house_detail.do?Date=1997-03-04&Parl=36&Sess=1&locale=en#P46_10805.

pg. 47   **"It was 'Fords,' plural":** Interview with John Tory, August 23, 2013.

pg. 48   **Officer Timothy Marks:** Interview with Marks in Miami, July 17, 2013. Officer Marks does not remember arresting Rob Ford. I reconstructed the night's events based on detailed arrest paperwork, including the arrest affidavit; police department property receipt; operation procedures checklist; breath test result affidavit; Miranda warning waiver; traffic citation; affidavit of refusal to submit to breath, urine, or blood test; breath sample result; City of Miami Police Department DUI test report; and the police citation. What Marks said to Ford is not recorded in the documentation. Here, I rely on standard operating procedures, which Marks said he would have followed exactly, given that he was new to the force at the time of the arrest.

pg. 50   **"I admit maybe I had":** Amy Dempsey, "'Go Ahead Take Me to Jail,' Rob Ford Told Police," *Toronto Star*, August 19, 2010. For the "couple of bottles" quote I relied on Kelly Grant, "Ford's Drunk Driving Conviction Could Steer His Campaign Into the Ditch," *The Globe and Mail*, August 19, 2010.

pg. 51   **A February 2011 *Toronto Life* feature:** Jan Wong, "The Woman Behind the Mayor: Who Is Renata Ford?" *Toronto Life*, February 3, 2011.

pg. 52 **worked as a cabinetmaker:** According to Ontario divorce records for Renata Brejniak and Artur Kisicki, February 1996.

pg. 52 **In July 2005 ... Renata was arrested for impaired driving:** According to court documents.

pg. 53 **Conservative nominee in Etobicoke North, Sam Basra:** After Basra's failed federal campaign, he put his name on the ballot for a seat as a Toronto District School Board trustee in the 1997 fall municipal election. He withdrew before the election but ran again in 2000 and won. Following a string of legal problems involving his use of a series of different names—Sam Basran, Sam Basra, Sam Singh Basra, and Santokh Singh—an election rule violation, and his role as an immigration consultant, Basra served sixteen months of house arrest and paid a thirty-five-thousand-dollar fine. He resigned from the school board in 2002 before he could be removed.

pg. 53 **Things got bad in late 2003:** Information obtained from Ontario court documents.

pg. 53 **"pry bar and knife":** Information obtained from Ontario court documents.

pg. 53 **In 2008, Kathy was arrested for stealing toothbrushes:** Information obtained from Ontario court documents.

pg. 54 **It began at 7:30 A.M. on January 11, 2012:** All information and quotes about this incident comes from two official court transcripts: Her Majesty the Queen v. Scott MacIntyre, 2201 Finch Avenue West court, May 28, 2012, and June 13, 2012.

pg. 57 **his "best buddy ... steer it back on course ... Doug was never a soldier":** Cynthia Reason, "Remembering Douglas Ford as the Community Man," *Etobicoke Guardian*, October 3, 2006.

CHAPTER 4: COUNCILLOR FORD TO SPEAK

pg. 59 **The Harris government was making aggressive changes:** Thomas Walkom, "The Winds of Change: The Hard Part of Any Revolution, Including a Common Sense One, Is Following Through," *Toronto Star*, December 27, 1996.

pg. 59   **"If we are to fix the problems":** From introduction to "The Common Sense Revolution" platform booklet, May 3, 1994.

pg. 60   **opposition ranging from 65 to 81 percent:** Murray Campbell et al., "Metro Voters Reject Amalgamation: Harris Told to Leave Toronto Alone Amid Signs Opponents to Conservative Plan Smell Blood," *The Globe and Mail*, March 3, 1997.

pg. 60   **five of the six municipalities took the province to court:** Gail Swainson, "Megacity Hearings Were Held 'Too Late': Premier Also 'Trampled' on Rights, Court Told," *Toronto Star*, July 7, 1997.

pg. 60   **cut nearly in half to fifty-seven:** The first city council of the new megacity had fifty-six councillors plus a mayor. But during the first term, due to quorum problems, council ran a by-election for another seat in East York, making a total of fifty-eight positions on council. This information courtesy Wynna Brown, a manager in strategic communications with the City of Toronto, October 7, 2013.

pg. 60   **"I remember hearing [Ford] was really ticked off":** Interview with Gloria Lindsay Luby, August 2013.

pg. 61   **"We're both business people":** Interview with Mario Giansante, September 2013.

pg. 62   **Flynn came in third:** Dennis Flynn died in August 2003.

pg. 62   **"Oh, no, no, Robbie's a career politician":** Ted Herriott's recollection of a conversation he had with Diane Ford after the 1997 election, as told to me on September 7, 2013.

pg. 63   **If both of us ran, we knew we didn't have a good chance":** Interview with Mario Giansante, September 2013.

pg. 64   **The *Star* called Ford's bid "a bit of a long-shot":** Bruce DeMara, "Political Heavyweights Getting Ready to Rumble: City Election Promises Plenty of Exciting Duels," *Toronto Star*, October 13, 2000.

pg. 64   **"Rob Ford actually coached my son's football team":** Interview with Elizabeth Brown, August 2013.

pg. 64   **"strongest sign campaign in the city":** Bruce DeMara, "Time of the Signs Begins Busily: Candidates Rush Off the Mark as Lawn-Ad Ban Ends," *Toronto Star*, October 19, 2000.

pg. 65 **Those close to him say he is aware that he comes across as boorish, a clumsy speaker:** Interviews with two former mayoral staff members and a 2010 campaign strategist.

pg. 66 **"We don't have a revenue problem":** Royson James, "Budget Faces a Long and Whining Road," *Toronto Star*, January 28, 2001.

pg. 66 **"If Councillor Bussin ever wants to go out":** Don Wanagas, "Business Card Squabble Dwarfs Crisis: Councillors Bicker Over Minutiae While City Goes Broke," *National Post*, February 6, 2001.

pg. 66 **"We have to start today cutting back":** Royson James, "Tory Sales Pitch Guarantees Us a Budget Battle," *Toronto Star*, January 30, 2001.

pg. 67 **"What are the four words":** Don Wanagas, "The Odd Rantings of Young Rob Ford," *National Post*, March 9, 2001. Wanagas would go on to become director of communications for Mayor David Miller, who was staunchly progressive.

pg. 68 **"Homelessness is a cancer":** Vanessa Lu and Bruce DeMara, "Shelters to Be Distributed," *Toronto Star*, February 12, 2003.

pg. 68 **"You slithering snake":** Video of city council budget debate, February 2003. Currently available at www.youtube.com/watch?v=yOi2wIUCTnA.

pg. 68 **"waste of skin":** Paul Moloney and John Spears, "Councillors Square Off in Verbal Slugfest," *Toronto Star*, July 19, 2005.

pg. 68 **"Roads are built for buses":** "City Councillors on the Budget," *Toronto Star*, March 7, 2007.

pg. 69 **"You're not helping them, you're enabling them":** James Cowan, "Help Will Kill Addicts: Ford," *National Post*, October 17, 2005.

pg. 69 **"I don't understand: is it a guy dressed up like a girl":** "Transsexual or Transgender? Councillor Confused by Specifics," *The Globe and Mail*, June 17, 2005.

pg. 69 **"absolutely disgusting":** James Wallace, "$5,000 Grant for Gay Video Gets Councillors' Backs Up," *National Post*, June 12, 2001.

pg. 69 **"Gino boy":** Bruce DeMara, "Alleged Slur Sparks Latest Council Spat," *Toronto Star*, March 6, 2002.

pg. 69 **"I believe in Adam and Eve":** "Tete-A-Tete," *Toronto Star*, July 25, 2003.

pg. 69 **"If you're not doing needles"**: "Rob Ford on AIDS," *National Post,* June 28, 2006.

pg. 69 **"Those Oriental people work like dogs"**: Donovan Vincent, "City Hall Protesters Target Ford Remarks," *Toronto Star,* March 15, 2008; and Jeff Gray, "Ford Draws Rebuke, Saying 'Oriental' People Are 'Taking Over,'" *The Globe and Mail,* March 5, 2008.

pg. 70 **reprimanded half a dozen times:** In November 2007, Ford was rapped for refusing to disclose his office budget (he refused because he was paying out of his own pocket). In December 2007, Ford was told not to include the official Toronto logo on an invitation to his family's annual backyard barbecue. In February 2009, Ford erroneously accused Councillor Adam Vaughan of trying to get a campaign donor appointed to a city committee. In August 2009, Ford revealed that the city had spent $750,000 on a piece of property before the deal was finalized. In August 2010, Ford was warned against using city resources to solicit donations for his private football charity. At the same time, he was slammed for "improper use of influence" after asking active city lobbyists to donate to his charity.

pg. 70 **"I get criticized a lot, because from September and October"**: Ed Keenan, "Coach Ford's Absenteeism," *The Grid,* September 11, 2012.

pg. 71 **The chemistry on the team "wasn't great" to begin with:** Robert Cribb and Kristin Rushowy, "Teacher Asked Ford to Leave," *Toronto Star,* July 15, 2010.

pg. 71 **came "from gangs" and "broken homes"**: Daniel Dale, "Mayor Rob Ford Dismissed as Don Bosco Football Coach," *Toronto Star,* May 22, 2013.

pg. 72 **Ford was soliciting donations from eleven active lobbyist firms:** "Report on Violation of Code of Conduct, CC52.1," Toronto Integrity Commissioner Janet Leiper, August 12, 2010. See www.toronto.ca/legdocs/mmis/2010/cc/bgrd/CC52.1.pdf.

pg. 73 **"With Rob, they would call"**: Interview with former staffer in Ford's Ward 2 council office, September 8, 2013.

pg. 74 **"But it was like they wouldn't accept our answer"**: Interview with Councillor Karen Stintz, August 2013.

pg. 75 **"no compelling reason":** "Report on Involvement of Members in Matters Arising in Other Members' Wards," Toronto Integrity Commissioner David Mullan, September 12, 2005.

pg. 75 **"I don't understand how you can be communicating":** Paul Moloney, "Spend Big … Spend Little," *Toronto Star*, August 18, 2001. (Councillor David Shiner had spent $9,142 of his office budget by the six-month mark.)

pg. 76 **"The *Sun* and the *Star* made him … grandstanding about it":** Interview with Doug Holyday, August 14, 2013.

pg. 76 **"You know what?":** Jim Byers and Donovan Vincent, "Frugality Probe Goes Ahead," *Toronto Star*, May 25, 2007.

pg. 76 **"That's so a councillor can't spend a small fortune":** Paul Moloney, "Auditor Says Councillor Must Disclose Expenses," *Toronto Star*, November 20, 2007.

pg. 77 **"Even then, I thought that the general public would say":** Interview with Sandra Bussin, September 9, 2013.

pg. 77 **"torrent of verbal abuse":** Donovan Vincent and Robyn Doolittle, "Lawyer Defends Ford's Actions," *Toronto Star*, March 28, 2008.

pg. 78 **"Now that there is nothing funny":** John Barber, "It's So Awful You Can't Look Away," *The Globe and Mail*, March 31, 2008.

pg. 78 **Brejniak just said she was "okay":** Donovan Vincent and Robyn Doolittle, "Lawyer Defends Ford's Actions," *Toronto Star*, March 28, 2008.

pg. 78 **"no comment":** John Barber, "It's So Awful You Can't Look Away," *The Globe and Mail*, March 31, 2008. Also Jeff Gray and Timothy Appleby, "Ford Called Police Night Before Arrest," *The Globe and Mail*, March 27, 2008.

pg. 78 **"I'm just glad":** Dale Anne Freed, "Ford Cleared on Charges," *Toronto Star*, May 22, 2008.

pg. 79 **"rather large gentleman … asinine comments":** From Dan and Rebecca Hope's letter to Toronto's city clerk. The couple entitled it "A Rare Night Out."

pg. 80 **"This is unbelievable":** Paul Moloney and Vanessa Lu, "Arena Outburst Probed by City," *Toronto Star*, May 2, 2006.

pg. 80   **"Completely embarrassed":** Paul Moloney, "I'm Here Facing the Music Today," *Toronto Star*, May 3, 2006.

pg. 81   **"I was the laughingstock ... Hail Mary passes get caught":** Bill Dunphy, "Aspiring Mayor Hopes to Have the Last Laugh," *The Hamilton Spectator*, March 25, 2004.

pg. 82   **had been elected three years earlier:** At the time of amalgamation, elections were held every three years. After the 2006 race, the term was extended to four years.

CHAPTER 5: THE GRAVY TRAIN

pg. 84   **"Hey, buddy, nice to meet you":** Interview with Nick Kouvalis, August 2013.

pg. 88   **"Rob won for all sorts of reasons":** Interview with Stefano Pileggi, August 23, 2013.

pg. 90   **Ward 2 Etobicoke North, which had about 55,000 residents:** According to the 2006 census, the population of Ward 2 Etobicoke North was 54,780. See www.toronto.ca/wards2000/pdf/2006/ward2_2006 profiles.pdf.

pg. 91   **population of about 111,000:** According to the 2006 census. See www12.statcan.gc.ca/census-recensement/2006/dp-pd/prof/92-595/ P2C.cfm?TPL=RETR&LANG=E&GC=35022.

pg. 91   **"You're being ridiculous":** Interview with member of Ford's mayoral campaign team, July 2013.

pg. 93   **"troubled" by evidence:** "Tory Campaign Manager Acquitted of Threatening MP Jeff Watson," *The Windsor Star*, January 25, 2007.

pg. 94   **He trained his fire on business executive Rocco Rossi:** David Rider, "Would-Be Mayors in War of Words," *Toronto Star*, March 30, 2010.

pg. 94   **"You said, on the floor of council":** Video of Toronto Real Estate Board debate uploaded to George Smitherman's YouTube channel, May 7, 2010. See http://www.youtube.com/watch?v=6dTDFJUp86M.

pg. 95   **Ontario's auditor general, Jim McCarter, had released a damaging report:** "Special Report: Ontario's Electronic Health Records Initiative," Office of the Auditor General of Ontario, October 2009.

pg. 95 **Not enough of the right kind of information:** From "Special Report: Ontario's Electronic Health Records Initiative," Office of the Auditor General of Ontario, October 2009, p. 8: "There is no doubt that Ontario does not yet have an eHealth system that is meeting the needs of medical practitioners or the public ... our main concern is that the network remains significantly underutilized because as yet there is insufficient health-related information on it." The electronic records scandal dates back to 2002 with the creation of the Smart Systems for Health Agency. It was replaced in 2008—months after George Smitherman was moved out of the health minister position—by eHealth Ontario.

pg. 95 **It was a liability that according to insiders:** Robert Benzie and Rob Ferguson, "eHealth Scandal Dents Smitherman's Mayoral Run," *Toronto Star*, October 9, 2009.

pg. 96 **"I apologize if I offended you":** David Rider, "Rob Ford Apologizes for 2006 AIDS Comment," *Toronto Star*, May 11, 2010.

pg. 97 **"Nick, I know, I know":** Interview with Nick Kouvalis, August 2013.

pg. 97 **"It was very grassroots":** Interview with Roman Gawur, September 2013.

pg. 97 **Kouvalis was out jogging with Ford:** The story of the Dieter Doneit-Henderson incident was put together through interviews with Nick Kouvalis, Adrienne Batra, and Fraser Macdonald.

pg. 102 **She was one of Ford's biggest cheerleaders:** Rob Ford actually donated one thousand dollars to Sue-Ann Levy's political campaign when the columnist took a hiatus from her journalism gig to run for provincial office as a Conservative in 2009. When she lost, Levy picked up where she left off, ranting about socialists at "silly hall."

pg. 103 **"quietly [been] asked to stop coaching ... attack on his candidacy":** Robert Cribb and Kristin Rushowy, "Rob Ford Told He Was Unwelcome as a Football Coach at Toronto High School," *Toronto Star*, July 13, 2010.

pg. 104 **"outrageous, it's slanderous and patently incorrect":** Natalie Alcoba, "Rob Ford Denies He Was Pushed Out as High School Football Coach," *National Post*, July 14, 2010.

pg. 104   **"That's completely untrue":** Kelly Grant, "Former Student Football Player Says Rob Ford Never Hit Him," *The Globe and Mail*, July 28, 2010.

pg. 105   **"If Tory had got in, he would have won":** Interview with Nick Kouvalis, August 2013.

pg. 105   **"If you look at the campaigns I've been through":** Interview with John Tory, August 2013.

pg. 106   **"We're together. We have the same thoughts":** Don Peat, "Ford Weighs In on Same-Sex Marriage," *Toronto Sun*, August 4, 2010. Video of press conference at www.torontosun.com/videos/life/life/5828781001/ford-weighs-in-on-same-sex-marriage/407548958001/page/8.

pg. 107   **"corruption is a strong term":** Paul Moloney, "Ford's Corruption Charge Angers Miller," *Toronto Star*, August 12, 2010.

pg. 108   **"if I have to choose":** Robyn Doolittle, "Rob Ford Video Scandal: Don't Count the Mayor Out Yet, Political Strategists Say," *Toronto Star*, June 1, 2013. (I edited out "beats their wife" from the original, newspaper version.)

pg. 109   **"He's the best Christmas present":** Tamara Baluja, "Toronto City Hall Gallery Welcomes the New Mayor," *The Toronto Observer*, December 7, 2010.

CHAPTER 6: HE WON'T GIVE UP THE BLOW

pg. 111   **"Hey Renata," John says:** John (not his real name) secretly recorded this meeting. Confirming it was in fact Renata Ford's voice was a concern, since I don't know her voice well enough to make that judgment. After several months of work, I am confident it is her for the following reasons: John knew her cell phone number, which is not readily available (I obtained it from a staff member); the voice on her voice mail message sounds the same; when I played the recording for a member of Ford's extended family, that person confirmed it was her; John made other recordings. In another, Renata Ford talks about details of the couple's personal life and health history that I do not believe an impostor would easily know. The full recording I listened to is about twenty minutes long. John wanted to sell me the tape for two thousand dollars. I did not purchase the audio.

pg. 113 **"I figured, I'm not going to be a city councillor forever":** Interview with Councillor Jaye Robinson, August 12, 2013.

pg. 114 **Kouvalis had three questions:** Nick Kouvalis confirmed that this was how the meetings went.

pg. 115 **"If it's a strategy to sway votes":** Daniel Dale, "Ford's Hardball on Traffic Light Has Centrist Seeing Red," *Toronto Star*, July 26, 2011.

pg. 116 **"They talked about running it":** Interview with Paul Ainslie, July 2013.

pg. 116 **"I took a huge pay cut to take this job":** Interview with Councillor Jaye Robinson, August 12, 2013.

pg. 117 **"unanimous support":** Interview with Case Ootes, September 15, 2013.

pg. 118 **Rob Ford used his first press conference as mayor:** The financial figures included in this section are from Tess Kalinowski and David Rider, "'War on the Car Is Over': Ford Scraps Transit City," *Toronto Star*, December 2, 2010.

pg. 118 **"In my mind, we would kill Transit City":** Interview with Councillor Karen Stintz, August 2013.

pg. 119 **"This man can't even convince five people":** Robyn Doolittle, "Rob Ford Is Mr. Popular at City Hall," *Toronto Star*, August 26, 2010.

pg. 119 **"This is the beginning of a new era ... find new managers":** David Rider et al., "Ford's Budget: TTC, User Fees Increased," *Toronto Star*, January 10, 2011.

pg. 120 **"The mayor doesn't want a fare increase":** Raising transit fares by ten cents would have meant twenty-four million dollars in revenue. Because the call to Karen Stintz came the night before the budget launch, TTC staff didn't have time to find enough savings, so Stintz was forced to defend the increase while the mayor was saying he wasn't happy about it and planned to find a way to avoid it. Stintz said, "If there is a way to avoid this increase, we will find it." The next day, Stintz announced there would be no increase. City managers promised to find sixteen million dollars to help make the numbers work.

pg. 121 **"It's actually no one's business"**: Kenyon Wallace and Jayme Poisson, "Mayor Rob Ford Refuses to Discuss David Price's Future," *Toronto Star*, September 19, 2013. Video at www.thestar.com/news/city_hall/2013/09/19/mayor_rob_ford_refuses_to_discuss_david_prices_future.html.

pg. 122 **"My brother is not the mouthpiece"**: Paul Moloney, "Ford Vetoes a Veto," *Toronto Star*, February 18, 2011.

pg. 123 **his schedule said "DECO ALL DAY"**: Daniel Dale, "What Does Rob Ford Do All Day?" *Toronto Star*, March 24, 2011.

pg. 123 **"It's fair to say I didn't know where he was"**: Interview with Adrienne Batra, October 2013.

pg. 123 **"There was a lack of civility"**: Robyn Doolittle, "Top Toronto City Managers Report Culture of Fear, Bullying," *Toronto Star*, September 28, 2012.

pg. 124 **"Clearly, there is a lot of influence"**: Robyn Doolittle, "Top Toronto City Managers Report Culture of Fear, Bullying," *Toronto Star*, September 28, 2012.

pg. 124 **"political motivations"**: Robyn Doolittle, "Toronto City Council: Ombudsman Fiona Crean Under Attack for Scathing Report," *Toronto Star*, October 4, 2012.

pg. 124 **"The evidence certainly points"**: Paul Moloney, "Toronto Ombudsman Denied the Extra Full-Time Help She Asked For," *Toronto Star*, December 13, 2012.

pg. 125 **"Managers were coming to us proactively"**: Interview with Adrienne Batra, October 2013.

pg. 126 **"The Library Services could be reduced"**: KPMG, "City of Toronto Core Services Review, Executive Committee Governance," 2011. See www.toronto.ca/legdocs/mmis/2011/ex/bgrd/backgroundfile-39626.pdf.

pg. 126 **"I've got more libraries in my area"**: David Rider, "Fight Library Cuts, Maybe Get Margaret Atwood at Your Book Club," *Toronto Star*, July 24, 2011.

pg. 126 **"Twin Fordmayor seems to think those who eat Timbits"**: Margaret Atwood status on Twitter, https://twitter.com/MargaretAtwood/status/94483498701828097.

pg. 126 **"I value the Toronto Public Library"**: "My Thoughts on the Toronto Public Library," message on Karen Stintz's website, July 27, 2011, www.karenstintz.com/?p=1410.

pg. 127 **"That's Rob Ford!"**: Interview with Jason Hebert, summer 2012 and October 28, 2013.

pg. 127 **"This was the first time"**: Interview with former Ford staff member, August 2013.

pg. 129 **"ill-conceived" and "reckless"**: An open letter to Toronto councillors, signed by more than one hundred academics and experts, including Eric J. Miller, Paul Bedford, Richard Florida and Richard Sommer, September 15, 2011.

pg. 129 **"vote in the interests of protecting city services"**: Robyn Doolittle, "Massive Poll Shows Toronto Is United Against Ford's Proposed Cuts," *Toronto Star*, September 16, 2011.

pg. 130 **"You can take it. It can be your win"**: Interview with Councillor Josh Colle, July 2013.

pg. 131 **"Ford! It's me, Marg Delahunty!"**: "Marg Princess Warrior with Rob Ford," *This Hour Has 22 Minutes*, CBC, April 17, 2012.

pg. 132 **"You ... bitches!"**: "Rob Ford Denies Calling 911 Dispatcher Names," CBC, October 27, 2011.

pg. 134 **Canada ranked fifty-sixth:** Centre for Law and Democracy, "International RTI Ratings Results," September 13, 2013.

pg. 135 **"Canada is utterly behind"**: Interview with Toby Mendel, executive director of the Centre for Law and Democracy, October 7, 2013.

pg. 136 **at the mercy of whatever court clerk happens to be on duty:** Thankfully, change could be coming. In September 2013, after relentless hounding from *Star* reporter Jesse McLean, the ministry in charge of the provincial court system said it would review its policies on access to criminal court records. Attorney General John Gerretsen acknowledged that "in some courthouses, people are more likely to provide that information than in other courthouses." Gerretsen sent an edict to courthouse staff ordering them to be "consistently helpful." It is progress, but without legislative change Ontario's courts still seem to be operating on the honour system. Martin Regg Cohn, "John Gerretsen Lays Down Law on Sharing Public Information About Court Cases: Cohn," *Toronto Star*, October 3, 2013.

pg. 136 **"That offends me, because people hide behind privacy":** Information and Privacy Commissioner Ann Cavoukian, September 12, 2013.

pg. 136 **the way it works in "best practices" countries:** Interview with Toby Mendel, executive director of the Centre for Law and Democracy, October 7, 2013.

pg. 137 **"That doesn't quite make sense to me":** Interview with Camille Jobin-Davis, assistant director of New York State's Committee on Open Government, October 11, 2013.

pg. 138 **"Anyone, if it's you or I":** Robyn Doolittle, "Rob Ford 911 Calls Raise Questions, *Toronto Star*, December 30, 2011.

pg. 140 **"My first call was to a cellphone and the familiar voice":** Joe Warmington, "Ford Says Story Wrong on 911 Call," *Toronto Sun*, December 30, 2011.

CHAPTER 7: THE BIER MARKT

pg. 142 **"I think I just saw the mayor do blow":** Interview with Leo Navarro, March 2012, August 2013.

pg. 144 **"According to a server":** Jonathan Goldsbie, "The Rob Ford Agenda: March 12–18, 2012," *The Grid*, March 20, 2012.

pg. 146 **I agreed to keep his identity confidential:** Leo Navarro no longer works at the Bier Markt and has allowed me to use his name.

pg. 147 **Brooks Barnett:** I briefly spoke to Barnett on his cell phone in March 2012 and was told to go through media relations.

pg. 148 **"I'm trying to do my thing":** *Dean Blundell Show*, 102.1 The Edge, March 29, 2012.

pg. 149 **crouching like a football player:** This is according to two former staff members.

pg. 150 **"Paki" ... saw the mayor pop an OxyContin pill:** From Project Brazen 2's "Information to Obtain Search Warrant" court documents.

pg. 150 **start phoning constituents back ... "Fuck this":** Interview with two former Ford staff members, August 2013 and November 2013.

pg. 150 **At 2:30 A.M., Ford stumbled down to the City Hall security desk:** City Hall security incident report.

pg. 150 **"going to eat her box" ... "I banged your pussy":** From Project Brazen 2's "Information to Obtain Search Warrant" court documents.

pg. 151 **Provost jumped out of the cab:** Interviews with three former staff members and Project Brazen 2's "Information to Obtain Search Warrant" court documents.

pg. 151 **"We knew he drank":** Interview with former Ford staffer, August 2013.

pg. 152 **"That's the story you should be looking into":** Interview with former Ford staffer, April 2012.

pg. 153 **Ford's workload had been cut in half:** Robyn Doolittle, "Mayor Rob Ford Has Deeply Cut His Workload, Documents Show," *Toronto Star*, May 26, 2012.

pg. 153 **I spoke with a dozen prominent, non-partisan civic leaders:** These were individuals involved in large-scale city-building initiatives who work in the business community, academia, media, civic service, and activism.

pg. 156 **"Hey, buddy," he hollered:** Daniel Dale, "Daniel Dale on What Happened Near the Mayor's Home," *Toronto Star*, May 2, 2012.

pg. 157 **"My neighbour knocked on my door":** Rob Ford interview on the *Jerry Agar Show*, Newstalk 1010, May 3, 2012.

pg. 158 **"I want to start with the issue of private security":** Anne-Marie Mediwake interviewing Rob Ford, "*Star* Reporter Denies Peering into Rob Ford's Yard," CBC News Toronto, May 3, 2012. See www.cbc.ca/news/canada/toronto/star-reporter-denies-peering-into-rob-ford-s-yard-1.1197459.

pg. 158 **Global TV anchor Kris Reyes tweeted:** Tweet from Kris Reyes, @krisreyes, May 3, 2012. See http://liveblogs.globaltoronto.com/Event/Toronto_Morning_Show?Page=417.

pg. 158 **In December 2013, a year and a half after the fence incident:** Rob Ford appeared as a guest of one-time media baron Conrad Black on his new current affairs show, *The Zoomer*. In their thirty-five-minute discussion, Black asked Ford to describe some of the most "offensive events" he's experienced at the hands of the media. The mayor replied, "The worst one was Daniel Dale in my backyard taking pictures. I have little kids. When a guy's taking pictures of little kids, I don't want to say the word, but you start thinking, you know, what's this guy all about?" The insinuation to any reasonable person was clear. Ford was suggesting Dale was a pedophile. The next day, Ford boasted that he stood "by every word" of his interview with Black. After Ford repeated many of the erroneous claims to a Washington sports radio show Thursday morning—December 12, 2013—Dale served the mayor, ZoomerMedia, and its network, Vision TV, which broadcast the segment, with a libel notice. Ford issued a full retraction and apology.

CHAPTER 8: THE DIRTY DOZEN

pg. 160 **"Well, Rob," Doug said:** Episode of *The City*, Newstalk 1010, September 16, 2012.

pg. 162 **"that little prick":** Daniel Dale, "Integrity Commissioner Scolds Mayor Rob Ford and Councillor Doug Ford in Separate Reports," *Toronto Star*, February 1, 2012.

pg. 162 **"Adam Chaleff-Freudenthaler was not a typical twenty-six-year-old":** Interview with Chaleff-Freudenthaler, August 9, 2013. Additional reference material: Daniel Dale, "Meet Adam Chaleff-Freudenthaler: The 27-Year-Old Who Triggered Rob Ford's Downfall," *Toronto Star*, November 27, 2012; Rosie DiManno, "Adam Chaleff-Freudenthaler Is a Thorn in Mayor Rob Ford's Side," *Toronto Star*, February 6, 2013; Sarah Liss, "10 Teens Taking Over," *NOW*, www.nowtoronto.com/mobile/story.cfm?c=137555.

pg. 162 **By sixteen, he had been arrested:** Curtis Rush, "Police Apologize for Protestors' Strip-Search," *Toronto Star*, February 22, 2006.

pg. 164 **"Hey, you're the guy with the audits":** "Doug Ford Threat Complaint to Integrity Commissioner," affidavit of Adam Chaleff-Freudenthaler, July 15, 2011.

pg. 164 **"[Are you] threatening me?":** "Report on Violation of Code of Conduct," Integrity Commissioner Janet Leiper, January 30, 2012. See

www.toronto.ca/legdocs/mmis/2012/cc/bgrd/backgroundfile-44900.
pdf.

pg. 165 **Six months later:** "Report on Violation of Code of Conduct," Integrity Commissioner Janet Leiper, January 30, 2012. See www.toronto.ca/legdocs/mmis/2012/cc/bgrd/backgroundfile-44900.pdf.

pg. 165 **she released a separate report reprimanding the mayor:** "Report on Compliance with Council Decision CC 52.1," Integrity Commissioner Janet Leiper, January 30, 2012. See www.toronto.ca/legdocs/mmis/2012/cc/bgrd/backgroundfile-44902.pdf.

pg. 166 **"I want to explain how my charity works":** Rob Ford's Speech to Council February 7, 2010. See www.youtube.com/watch?v=vJW9bxPT2wQ.

pg. 169 **Magder filed a complaint with Toronto's lobbyist registrar:** John Lorinc, "Doug Ford's Tourist-Friendly Plan for Port Lands Faces Big Challenges," *The Globe and Mail*, September 5, 2011.

pg. 169 **"You can't, as a city councillor, speak to a motion":** Don Peat, "Judge Asked to Remove Ford from Office," *Toronto Sun*, March 12, 2012. Video at www.torontosun.com/2012/03/12/application-filed-to-remove-ford-from-office. And Natalie Alcoba, "Legal Action Puts Mayoralty On Line," *National Post*, March 12, 2012.

pg. 170 **"I'm fed up with all the stuff":** Kelly Grant, "Toronto Man Seeks Court Ouster of Mayor Rob Ford: Claims Conflict of Interest," *The Globe and Mail*, March 12, 2012.

pg. 174 **he announced that "Twittering" would be allowed:** All quotes relating to the hearing are taken from the official court transcript, Paul Magder v. Robert Ford, Ontario Superior Court of Justice, 361 University Avenue, Room 6-1, Toronto, September 5, 2012.

pg. 177 **"There must be some diligence on the respondent's part":** Judge Hackland's decision, Magder v. Ford, 2012 ONSC 5615, November 26, 2012.

pg. 178 **"Rob Ford says 'left-wing politics'":** Marcus Gee, "Rob Ford's Self-Inflicted Downfall," *The Globe and Mail*, November 26, 2012.

pg. 178 **"The judiciary being asked to decide":** Simon Kent, "Rob Ford Case Had No Business Being in the Courts," *Toronto Sun*, November 26, 2012.

pg. 178 **"History will write him up as a hero":** Daniel Dale, "Meet Adam Chaleff-Freudenthaler: The 27-Year-Old Who Triggered Rob Ford's Downfall," *Toronto Star*, November 27, 2012.

pg. 178 **"It's more disappointing than surprising":** David Rider et al., "Rob Ford Out: Mayor's Attack Dog Mammoliti Quits Top Committee," *Toronto Star*, November 26, 2012.

pg. 178 **"I know the stress":** Interview with Doug Holyday, August 14, 2013.

pg. 179 **"It is critical, in my submission":** Robyn Doolittle, "Rob Ford Libel Trial: Faced with Corruption Allegation, Pub Owner Had to Sue, Lawyer Says," *Toronto Star*, November 15, 2012.

pg. 179 **"My wife was distraught over it":** Robyn Doolittle, "Rediscovered Audiotape Throws a 'Curveball' into Ford Libel Trial," *Toronto Star*, November 14, 2012.

pg. 180 **It was a "curveball," Tighe admitted:** Robyn Doolittle, "Rediscovered Audiotape Throws a 'Curveball' into Ford Libel Trial," *Toronto Star*, November 14, 2012.

pg. 180 **"money was being exchanged" … "Not following the process":** Natalie Alcoba, "'When They Don't Follow the Process … I Call That Skullduggery': Rob Ford Redefines Corruption in Defence of 2010 Comments," *National Post*, November 16, 2012.

pg. 180 **"They [councillors] don't follow the process":** Remaining dialogue between Ford and Shiller in Rosie DiManno, "Rob Ford Runs Afoul of One Dangerous Little Word: Corruption," *Toronto Star*, November 17, 2012.

pg. 182 **"ultra vires" … "a nullity":** Rob Ford appeal factum, by Alan J. Lenczner, of Lenczner Slaght Royce Smith Griffin LLP, p. 2, December 12, 2012.

pg. 182 **One municipal lawyer watching the case:** This was lawyer John Mascarin. Robyn Doolittle, "How Toronto Mayor Rob Ford Won His

Appeal: An Argument About 'Technical Jurisdiction,'" *Toronto Star*, January 25, 2013.

pg. 182 **"collateral attack"**: Daniel Dale, "Rob Ford Appeal Hearing Presents Two Visions of the Mayor: Honest Man—or Stubborn Lawbreaker?," *Toronto Star*, January 7, 2013.

pg. 183 **"We won," he said**: Robyn Doolittle, "How Toronto Mayor Rob Ford Won His Appeal: An Argument About 'Technical Jurisdiction,'" *Toronto Star*, January 25, 2013.

pg. 183 **"very, very humbling"**: Lesley Ciarula Taylor, "What Mayor Rob Ford Said," *Toronto Star*, January 25, 2013.

CHAPTER 9: THE GARRISON BALL

pg. 185 **"We put our foot on their throat"**: Phil Rosenthal, "Cooke Returns Shots in New Bravo Series," *Chicago Tribune*, July 14, 2006.

pg. 187 **"He told me he was in Florida"**: David Rider, Jeff Green, and Rachel Mendleson, "Rob Ford: Sarah Thomson Wants Apology After Accusing Toronto Mayor of Inappropriate Touch," *Toronto Star*, March 8, 2013.

pg. 188 **Thomson said Ford had been "completely wasted"**: "Sarah Thomson Alleges Rob Ford Was High When He Allegedly Grabbed Her from Behind," Sarah Thomson interview on *The Roz & Mocha Show*, KiSS 92.5 radio, March 11, 2013. See www.kiss925.com/2013/03/11/roz-mocha-exclusive-interview-sarah-thomson-alleges-rob-ford-was-high-when-he-allegedly-grabbed-her-from-behind.

pg. 190 **"We've got a problem"**: Interview with Paul Ainslie, July 2013.

pg. 190 **Towhey was suspicious of Lisi:** We didn't know this at the time. This came out in Project Brazen 2's "Information to Obtain Search Warrant" court documents.

pg. 190 **Ford tripped on the stairs:** This is according to two members of the organizing committee, who were told by the impacted staff members.

pg. 191 **"We know each other, and he stopped me to say hello":** This is according to a third member of the organizing committee interviewed August 20, 2013.

pg. 193 **In a front-page story on March 26, 2013:** Robyn Doolittle and Kevin Donovan, "'Intoxicated' Ford Asked to Leave Gala," *Toronto Star*, March 26, 2013.

CHAPTER 10: PATHOLOGICAL LIARS

pg. 196 **a named woman who saw the mayor "inebriated":** Interview with Jennifer Gordon, March 26, 2012, and March 25, 2013.

pg. 196 **"Do you plan to sue, Doug?":** "Doug Ford Responds to Star Story About Mayor Rob Ford's Behaviour," *Toronto Star*, March 26, 2013.

pg. 198 **"Mayor!":** "Toronto Mayor Rob Ford Calls Allegations of Intoxication 'Nonsense,'" CityNews, March 26, 2013. Video at www.citynews.ca/2013/03/26/video-toronto-mayor-rob-ford-calls-allegations-of-intoxication-nonsense.

pg. 198 **"For the record, the mayor was not asked to leave the gala":** David Rider, "Mayor Rob Ford Calls Alcohol Abuse Report 'An Outright Lie,'" *Toronto Star*, March 26, 2013.

pg. 199 **"George, I want to thank you for being a friend to our family":** "Mayor Rob Ford presents George Chuvalo with Key to the City," CityNews, March 26, 2013.

pg. 199 **"Mayor Ford, can you address":** Video at "Three Councillors Now Claim Rob Ford Has a Drinking Problem as Toronto Mayor Is Encouraged to Seek Treatment," *National Post*, March 27, 2013.

pg. 200 **"I think many of us have witnessed things":** Joe Mihevc interview with 680News, March 27, 2013. See www.680news.com/2013/03/27/ford-not-asked-to-leave-military-event-some-organizers-say.

pg. 200 **"It has been known at City Hall for quite a while":** Daniel Dale, "Rob Ford: Mayor Has Appeared Intoxicated, Says Councillor Sarah Doucette," *Toronto Star*, March 26, 2013.

pg. 200 **"Ms. Doucette confirmed making the statement":** Natalie Alcoba and Josh Visser, "'Pathological Liars': Mayor Rob Ford Has Furious Outburst as He Denies 'Intoxicated' Report, Staff Wants Him in Rehab," *National Post*, March 26, 2013.

pg. 201   **Councillor Mike Del Grande called it "sour grapes":** Sunny Dhillon and Elizabeth Church, "Ford's Chief of Staff Denies Being Asked to Have Mayor Leave Gala," *The Globe and Mail,* March 26, 2013.

pg. 201   **"No one asked the mayor to leave":** Sunny Dhillon and Elizabeth Church, "Ford's Chief of Staff Denies Being Asked to Have Mayor Leave Gala," *The Globe and Mail,* March 26, 2013.

CHAPTER 11: FOR SALE

pg. 205   **Four days later, my cell phone rang just after 9 A.M.:** During the six-week period between the time Mohamed Farah phoned me and the story of the video ran on May 16, I kept a diary of the daily updates and events. The following, including the dialogue, is based on my notes taken at the time.

pg. 206   **One of them, he said, worked in New York:** To this day, I don't know who Farah was referring to or if this person actually exists. Before the video scandal, Farah did not know Gawker editor John Cook, who works out of New York.

pg. 207   **a crack house, he said:** Numerous neighbours have told me and my colleagues at the *Toronto Star* that the brick bungalow at 15 Windsor Road is a drug haven. Internal police documents also describe the home as a "crack house/stash house." Wiretap conversations connected to Project Traveller capture alleged drug dealers in the area discussing selling crack at the location.

pg. 209   **It is explicitly stated in the newspaper's code of conduct:** "*Toronto Star* Newsroom Policy and Journalistic Standards Guide." See www.thestar.com/opinion/public_editor/2011/12/07/toronto_star_newsroom_policy_and_journalistic_standards_guide.html.

pg. 210   **"politically kill Rob Ford":** Doug Ford on *The City*, Newstalk 1010, March 31, 2013.

CHAPTER 12: ANYTHING ELSE?

pg. 225   **"information that is reliable and in the public's interest":** Grant v. Torstar Corp., Docket 32932, December 22, 2009. See http://scc.lexum.org/decisia-scc-csc/scc-csc/scc-csc/en/item/7837/index.do.

pg. 227 **"Okay," Nair began:** Reshmi Nair, CBC News, May 17, 2013. Video at www.youtube.com/watch?v=NqyaldTVK5E.

pg. 228 **"Absolutely not true":** Video by Bernard Weil, "Mayor Rob Ford Crack Cocaine Scandal," May 17, 2013.

pg. 228 **"I have bad news for you, Canada":** Josh Barro, "The Almost-Good Reasons Toronto Elected Rob Ford," Bloomberg, May 17, 2013. See www.bloomberg.com/news/2013-05-17/the-almost-good-reasons-toronto-elected-rob-ford.html.

pg. 229 **"Unless he was entrapped by the government":** Will Sommer, "Crack-Smoking Mayors: Not Just for D.C. Anymore," *Washington City Paper*, May 17, 2013.

pg. 229 **"Anyways, like I said this morning":** Daniel Dale and David Rider, "Rob Ford Crack Scandal: Toronto Mayor Refuses to Discuss Specifics of Video," *Toronto Star*, May 17, 2013.

pg. 229 **"monitoring the situation closely":** Rachel Mendleson and Amy Dempsey, "Mayor Rob Ford: Police Monitoring Situation Surrounding Video," *Toronto Star*, May 17, 2013.

pg. 231 **"Reporters have asked him directly":** Christie Blatchford, "If the Rob Ford Video Is a Fake, Why Hasn't He Said So?," *National Post*, May 21, 2013.

pg. 232 **"It seems like a form of extortion":** Joe Warmington, "Ford to Make Statement About Alleged Crack Video Tuesday," *Toronto Sun*, May 20, 2013.

pg. 232 **"I'm not speaking for the mayor":** "Doug Ford Calls Allegations Against Toronto Mayor Rob Ford Untrue," Global News, May 22, 2013. See http://globalnews.ca/news/581833/doug-ford-calls-allegations-against-toronto-mayor-rob-ford-untrue.

pg. 234 **"I'd like to take this opportunity":** Video at "Rob Ford Crack Scandal: 'I Do Not Use Crack Cocaine,' Mayor Says," *Toronto Star,* May 24, 2013.

pg. 236 **"Have you done any illegal drugs":** Video at "Rob Ford Crack Video Scandal: More Staff Quit Mayor's Office," *Toronto Star,* May 30, 2013.

CHAPTER 13: VIDEO, SCHMIDEO

pg. 238 **On June 1, Ipsos Reid released a poll:** This poll surveyed 530 Toronto residents through an online panel between May 29 and 31. It was done on behalf of CTV News and CP24 and is considered accurate within plus or minus 5 percentage points.

pg. 239 **"When did the accepted standard for reporters' verification":** Ivor Shapiro, "Video, Shmideo: Reporting Is About Telling What You See and Hear," J-Source.ca, May 25, 2013.

pg. 240 **"People have more sources of information":** Interview with Tom Rosenstiel, executive director of the American Press Institute, September 26, 2013.

pg. 243 **"There was a growing sense in that period":** Interview with Carroll Doherty, associate director of Pew Research, September 20, 2013.

pg. 244 **"We are awash in American coverage":** Interview with politics professor Nelson Wiseman, University of Toronto, September 21, 2013.

pg. 246 **"I'm not a journalist":** Interview with Newstalk 1010 radio host Jerry Agar, October 2012.

pg. 247 **"I would be curious to know just how far":** Complaint letter from Darylle Donley to the Ontario Press Council, 2013. See http://ontpress.com/files/2013/10/Toronto-Star-Donley-complaint.pdf.

pg. 248 **"appeared to suggest every person living in Germany":** Carl H. Ladek v. Globe and Mail 2000/2001. See http://ontpress.com/past-decisions.

pg. 250 **"The *Toronto Star* is glad to be sitting in front of you today":** Michael Cooke's speech to the Ontario Press Council, September 9, 2013. Video at www.thestar.com/news/gta/2013/09/09/rob_ford_offered_14_chances_to_comment_on_crack_story_toronto_star_tells_press_council.html.

pg. 251 **"Council does not agree":** Marco Chown Oved, "Press Council: Ford 'Crack Video' Story Passed Three-Part Test for 'Responsible' Reporting," *Toronto Star*, October 16, 2013.

pg. 251 **"Who is the press council?":** Steve Ladurantaye, "Press Council Dismisses Complaints Against the *Globe*'s Doug Ford Investigation: He Dismisses the Findings," *The Globe and Mail*, October 16, 2013.

CHAPTER 14: PROJECT TRAVELLER

pg. 252 **Thirteen-year-old Connor Stevenson:** Lisa LaFlamme, "The Inside Story: How a Trip to the Toronto Eaton Centre Turned into Horror," *W5*, CTV, February 1, 2013. See www.ctvnews.ca/w5/the-inside-story-how-a-trip-to-the-toronto-eaton-centre-turned-into-horror-1.1139769.

pg. 254 **a 133 percent increase in gun violence:** Curtis Rush, "Toronto Shootings up in 2012, but Deaths Are Down," *Toronto Star*, May 28, 2012.

pg. 254 **a statement declaring "war on these violent gangs":** Statement posted to Mayor Rob Ford's Facebook page, "It's Time for Us to Work Together to Keep Our City Safe," July 17, 2012. See https://www.facebook.com/notes/rob-ford/its-time-for-us-to-work-together-to-keep-our-city-safe/438048056218258.

pg. 254 **"I want something to be done":** Daniel Dale, "Toronto Shooting: Mayor Rob Ford Says Gang Members Should Leave the City," *Toronto Star*, July 18, 2012.

pg. 256 **There it was … Or at least, there it might be, Tim Alamenciak thought:** Interview with Tim Alamenciak, September 23, 2013.

pg. 260 **A woman answered who identified herself as Zen:** Interview with Zen Khattak, May 27, 2013.

pg. 260 **Smith and Khattak had been friends:** Interview with Khattak's mother, Zen Khattak, at her Etobicoke home, May 27, 2013.

pg. 261 **Poisson, along with reporter David Bruser, had recently finished an investigative series:** Jayme Poisson and David Bruser, "The Gun Pipeline" series, *Toronto Star*, April–May, 2013. See www.thestar.com/news/investigations/guns.html.

pg. 262 **"Our confidence that we can consummate this transaction":** "Rob Ford Crackstarter" campaign created by John Cook, May 2013. See www.indiegogo.com/projects/rob-ford-crackstarter.

pg. 267 **Poisson, Donovan, and I published our story about the house on June 5:** Kevin Donovan, Robyn Doolittle, and Jayme Poisson, "Rob Ford Crack Video Scandal: Here's the House Where the Photo Was Taken," *Toronto Star*, June 5, 2013.

pg. 267 **we were able to shed more light:** Jayme Poisson and Robyn Doolittle, "Rob Ford Crack Video Scandal: Resident of Home in Photo Trafficked Cocaine," *Toronto Star*, June 7, 2013.

pg. 267 **Elena Basso Johnson … her brother Fabio:** Details about both the Bassos' criminal history were obtained through court documents.

pg. 268 **Most damningly, the *Star*'s Queen's Park bureau chief:** Robert Benzie and Kevin Donovan, "Rob Ford Video Scandal: Mayor Ford Said He Knew Where Video Was, Sources Say," *Toronto Star*, May 30, 2013.

pg. 268 **"I'm embarrassed, but actually":** Interview with Jaye Robinson, August 12, 2013.

pg. 271 **"ground zero for the alleged Rob Ford crack cociane":** "Massive Police Raid," live blog, *Toronto Star*, June 13, 2013. See http://livenews.thestar.com/Event/Live_Massive_police_raid_in_Toronto ?Page=0.

pg. 271 **"highly placed source":** "Toronto Police Probing Alleged Crack Video Linked to Ford Weeks Before Story Broke," CTV News, June 13, 2013. See www.ctvnews.ca/canada/toronto-police-probing-alleged-crack-video-linked-to-ford-weeks-before-story-broke-1.1323657.

pg. 271–272 **"This gang has been networking":** Deputy Chief Mark Saunders and **"I think we've cut off that pipeline … all of the evidence":** Chief Bill Blair, Toronto police news release, "Project Pinpoints Gang with Video," June 13, 2013. Video at www.torontopolice.on.ca/modules.php?op=modload&name=News&file=article&sid=6878.

pg. 272 **"I'm not in a position to disclose that":** Rosie DiManno, "What Blair Didn't Say Speaks Loudest," *Toronto Star*, June 14, 2013.

pg. 272 **"Given the intense speculation since Crackgate exploded":** Rosie DiManno, "What Blair Didn't Say Speaks Loudest," *Toronto Star*, June 14, 2013.

pg. 272 **"I understand there were some raids":** Don Peat, "'I Have Nothing to Hide': Mayor Rob Ford," *Toronto Sun*, June 13, 2013. Also, video at "Ford Brushes off Journalists with 'Thick Skulls,'" *Toronto Star*, June 13, 2013.

CHAPTER 15: OUTRIGHT WAR

pg. 274   **When Alexander "Sandro" Lisi left his Etobicoke home:** Information relating to police surveillance of Lisi and Rob Ford was sourced from Project Brazen 2's "Information to Obtain Search Warrant" court documents.

pg. 274   **Ford's approval rating had climbed 5 points:** Forum Research, "Mayor Ford's Approval Up Sharply," June 26, 2013.

pg. 276   **Bellissimo, an admitted crack user:** From Project Brazen 2's "Information to Obtain Search Warrant" court documents.

pg. 277   **Ford had gone to visit Bellissimo at the Toronto West Detention Centre:** Some of this information is included in the Project Brazen 2 search warrant documents. Additionally, I have confirmed the account with two sources within the facility, one of them a guard working that night. *The Globe and Mail* broke the story about this visit: Greg McArthur, Shannon Kari, Patrick White, and Elizabeth Church, "Rob Ford Sought Meeting with Inmate in After-Hours Jail Visit," *The Globe and Mail*, August 12, 2013.

pg. 277   **telling people on the street he wanted to go "party":** For video, see www.youtube.com/watch?v=XR_TQlmPDVM.

pg. 277   **In the middle of August, the *Toronto Star* published a front-page story:** Kevin Donovan and Jayme Poisson, "Police Probe Mayor Rob Ford Friends Who Sought Crack Video," *Toronto Star*, August 16, 2013.

pg. 277   **On August 27, police were yet again called:** From Project Brazen 2's "Information to Obtain Search Warrant" court documents.

pg. 278   **Even the Fords knew they were being watched:** Joe Warmington, "Cops Using Cessna to Spy on Mayor's Family: Doug Ford," *Toronto Sun*, October 4, 2013.

pg. 278   **"He's a good guy":** Kenyon Wallace, Dale Brazao, and Kevin Donovan, "Rob Ford Frequently Visited Alexander Lisi, Now Charged with Drug Offences," *Toronto Star*, October 2, 2013.

pg. 281   **"Are you a focus of the police probe?":** "Rob Ford: Shaken Toronto Mayor Clashes with Reporters," *Toronto Star*, October 31, 2013. See

www.thestar.com/news/gta/2013/10/31/rob_ford_shaken_toronto_
mayor_clashes_with_reporters.html.

pg. 281 **"In November, December 2012 and into January 2013":** From Project Brazen 2's "Information to Obtain Search Warrant" court documents.

pg. 282 **The July 8 flood was the most costly natural disaster:** Carys Mills, "Toronto's July Flood Listed as Ontario's Most Costly Natural Disaster," *Toronto Star*, August 14, 2013.

pg. 282 **Ford may have been paying the Bassos' water bills:** The Project Brazen 2 search warrant documents include references to the fact that Ford seemed to be contacting the city water department on behalf of 15 Windsor Road and that he kept a list of outstanding bills for the property. The investigator writes, "One possible explanation for these entries could be that the Mayor is dealing with house maintenance and bill payment at 15 Windsor Rd."

pg. 283 **"Good morning, ladies and gentlemen":** Chief Bill Blair press conference, October 31, 2013. See www.youtube.com/watch?v=Gne ADuHDJBA.

pg. 285 **"This was a victory for journalism":** Kathy English, "Rob Ford and 'Crack Cocaine' Video: Now, Do You Believe the *Star*?: Public Editor," *Toronto Star*, October 31, 2013.

pg. 286 **"I think everybody has seen the allegations against me":** "Rob Ford Investigation: Live Updates on the Police Probe into the Alleged Video," *National Post*, October 31, 2013.

pg. 288 **"Chief, I'm asking you to release this video":** Daniel Dale, "Rob Ford Says He Made 'Mistakes' but Plans to Stay," *Toronto Star*, November 3, 2013. Audio file at www.thestar.com/news/city_hall/2013/11/03/ rob_ford_says_he_made_mistakes_but_plans_to_stay.html.

pg. 289 **"You're going to curb your drinking":** Natalie Alcoba, "Rob Ford Says 'If I Did Something Illegal, Then Arrest Me,' Admits Needs to 'Slow Down' on Drinking," *National Post*, November 3, 2013.

pg. 289 **"[Blair] believes he's the judge":** Daniel Dale, "Doug Ford Calls for Probe into Toronto Police Chief Bill Blair," *Toronto Star*, November 5, 2013.

pg. 290 **"You guys have asked me a question":** Rob Ford press conference, November 5, 2013. Video at www.youtube.com/watch?v=VsjlNNsChZ4.

pg. 292 **the *Star* revealed it had obtained another video of the mayor:** The *Star* purchased this footage for five thousand dollars. The *Star* decided to pay for the video, editor-in-chief Michael Cooke explained, "because of the huge public interest both in Toronto and worldwide. We weren't paying a source for information; we were purchasing a video, something newspapers and TV stations do every day. I've paid more for a book excerpt." Kevin Donovan, David Bruser, and Jesse McLean, "Rob Ford Caught on Video in Violent Rant," *Toronto Star*, November 7, 2013.

pg. 292 **"I just wanted to come out":** "Rob Ford Admits Being 'Extremely Inebriated' in New Video," CBC News, November 7, 2013.

pg. 297 **"I'm going to eat you out" ... "I banged your pussy":** From Project Brazen 2's "Information to Obtain Search Warrant" court documents.

pg. 299 **"I have no other choice" ... "eat at home":** Video at "Rob Ford's Shocking Statement," *Toronto Star*, November 14, 2013.

pg. 299 **"I might have had some drinks and ... driven":** Robyn Doolittle, "Rob Ford's Vulgar Retort Proves the Last Straw as Council Plots to Strip His Powers," *Toronto Star*, November 15, 2013.

pg. 300 **"unforgivable language":** Robyn Doolittle, "Rob Ford's Vulgar Retort Proves the Last Straw as Council Plots to Strip His Powers," *Toronto Star*, November 15, 2013.

pg. 300 **"The things we are seeing and hearing":** Robert Benzie, "Rob Ford Crisis: Wynne Lays Out Conditions for Intervening," *Toronto Star*, November 14, 2013.

pg. 301 **"I'm not an addict!" he said. "You guys can spin it":** Bill Weir, "Rob Ford: 'I'm the Best Father Around': Blames 'Rich, Elitist People,'" CNN, November 18, 2013. Video at http://cnnpressroom.blogs.cnn.com/2013/11/18/rob-ford-im-the-best-father-around-blames-rich-elitist-people-video/.

pg. 301 **"barely even remember":** Matt Lauer, "'I'm Not Perfect': Defiant Toronto Mayor Rob Ford Insists He Can Lead," *Today*, November 19, 2013.

pg. 302 **"This is nothing more than a coup d'état"**: Rob Ford speech in council November 18, 2103. See http://globalnews.ca/news/974912/ council-strips-mayor-rob-ford-of-budget-powers.

CHAPTER 16: FORD MORE YEARS

pg. 305 **Another survey by Forum Research …:** Some people have discounted this survey because it was taken on Halloween night. I think it is useful to consider given that Forum has been the most consistent in tracking Ford's approval rating, using the same methodology each time. The automated phone survey of 1032 Toronto residents on October 31 is considered accurate plus or minus 3 percentage points, 19 times out of 20. See www.forumresearch.com/forms/News%20Archives/News%20 Releases/56871_TO_Mayoral_Approval_%282013.10.31%29_Forum_ Research.pdf.

pg. 306 **"come-to-Jesus moment":** Peter Mansbridge interview, "Rob Ford Says He's Quit Drinking, Has Had 'Come-to-Jesus' Moment," CBC, November 18, 2013.

pg. 308 **"He's run the city well despite his private life" … "fancy people":** *Ford Nation* show on Sun News Network, November 18, 2013. See www.sunnewsnetwork.ca/sunnews/politics/archives/2013/11/20131118 -205516.html.

pg. 309 **Barbara Hall had done "well in the older cities of Toronto":** John Sewell, "The Mourning After," *NOW* magazine, November 13–19, 1997.

pg. 309 **"The air went out of Toronto's balloon last Monday night":** Royson James, "Let's Give Lastman What He Deserves: A Chance," *Toronto Star*, November 14, 1997.

pg. 309 **In their book *The Big Shift*:** Darrell Bricker and John Ibbitson, *The Big Shift* (Toronto: HarperCollins, 2013).

pg. 310 **"The way that I think the elites in Toronto":** Interview with Darrell Bricker, July 15, 2013.

pg. 311 **"Yes, one day I do want to run for prime minister":** John Roberts, "Rob Ford: 'Yes, One Day I Do Want to Run for Prime Minister,'" Fox News, November 18, 2013. See http://video.foxnews.

com/v/2848908070001/rob-ford-yes-one-day-i-do-want-to-run-for-prime-minister/?playlist_id=86857.

pg. 311   **"will be premier [of Ontario] one day":** Daniel Dale, "Hear What Mayor Rob Ford Said in Surprise Interview on Oakley's AM640 Morning Show," *Toronto Star*, November 4, 2013.

ACKNOWLEDGMENTS

The morning of May 27, 2013, I was sitting at my desk at City Hall, minding my own business, when a very scary email landed in my inbox, subject line: "query from a literary agent."

It was from Martha Magor Webb, the person to whom I owe the most thanks as I sit down and consider all the people who helped make *Crazy Town* happen. Martha, without you, and Chris Bucci and everyone at Anne McDermid & Associates, I would never have thought of turning my reporting into a book. I will be eternally grateful. Thank you.

To the wonderful people at Penguin Canada, and especially my editor, Diane Turbide. You took a chance on me—a young news reporter with zero experience writing anything longer than a few thousand words—and gave me the confidence I needed to get this thing done. Diane, you have been so lovely and encouraging (and just the right degree of ruthless) throughout this process. I have become a much better writer having worked with you. Also to Alex Schultz, David Ross, and Ashley Audrain, thank you.

Every day, I feel proud and grateful to work at the *Toronto Star*. There are so many people to thank there, not just for supporting this book, but for encouraging the kind of reporting that made it possible in the first place. To all of the leadership at the paper and the editors involved in this story—editor-in-chief Michael Cooke, managing editor Jane Davenport, publisher John Cruickshank, chairman John Honderich, city editor Irene Gentle, lawyer extraordinaire Bert Bruser, among others—thank you for your vision and passion, thank you for backing the entire team throughout this saga, thank you for continuing to champion this (expensive) kind of journalism, and, of course, thank you for all your good wishes and support while I wrote this book.

When I mention the "entire team" working on the story, that's because the investigation into Rob Ford involved dozens of people, from reporters and photographers to editors and designers. If I tried to thank everyone, I'd definitely miss some, but I do want to single out a few, especially my colleague Jayme Poisson, who has completely owned the Project Traveller and Dixon City Bloods angle of this story. Of course, I need to thank the incredible Kevin Donovan, the *Star*'s head of investigations, as well as Jesse McLean, Robert Benzie, Kenyon Wallace, David Bruser, Dale Brazao, Emily Mathieu, Mary Ormsby, Jennifer Pagliaro, Daniel Dale, David Rider, Paul Moloney, Royson James, my two journalism idols, Rosie DiManno and Michelle Shephard, and all of my predecessors in the City Hall bureau. And special thanks to the amazing Steve Russell for his help with the photos for this book.

If you look at the Notes section of this book, you'll see the names of dozens and dozens of reporters, radio hosts, and columnists whose work I have relied upon. I do need to single out the very talented Greg McArthur and Shannon Kari for their investigation into the Ford family's history with drug dealing published in *The Globe and Mail,* as well as their (and their colleague Patrick White's) reporting on how those early relationships continued to play a role in Rob Ford's life. I'd also like to acknowledge Jonathan Goldsbie, currently a reporter at *NOW* magazine, who can find anything on the internet and who has helped me so much through the years, and John Cook from Gawker, who came up to Toronto to investigate a tip, dropped a bomb on the city with the video story, and then stayed with it through every twist, drug raid, and pipe attack. And finally, my research assistant, Simon Bredin, who was given the horrible task of calling hundreds of people who went to high school with the Ford brothers. Thank you all so much.

I had three months to write this book, start to finish, including research. If I listed everyone who took me out for a meal during that time because I had no food in the house, or came over to walk the dogs, or offered to clean my condo, or helped me work through writer's block, I'd need a whole other chapter. But to a handful of people—my mom and dad, sister Jamie, and soon-to-be-brother-in-law Peter, to Emma, Daniel, Emily, Janean, Matt, Cliff, and my writing buddy Lauren—I need to say quite sincerely, I could not have gotten through this without you. Thank you.

Finally, to Graham Parley, my (now retired) former city editor at the *Star,* who gave a first-round edit to every chapter before I sent it along to Penguin. There's a reason you were my first call after I got this book deal. Graham, you are one of my favourite people in the world. "Mentor" sounds entirely too cheesy, but something like that. Thank you.

INDEX